## STRAIGHT FROM THE BENCH

No serving judge has ever written a book like this. It
is a courageous book, by an outspoken man, who
breaks down the conventions of judicial silence
to say directly what must be said: that there is
much that is wrong with the way our justice is
administered by those in authority and, indeed,
often with the system itself. Relying heavily on his
experience gleaned from over twenty years serving
as a judge, he argues strongly for fundamental
reform in major areas of law.

On a wider level, Judge Pickles examines critically
the higher echelons of the judicial system,
explaining among other things the unique position
of the Lord Chancellor's Office in the appointment
and sacking of judges, and the role that judges
should play in society and what society should
expect from them.

Some might argue that the judiciary should not
contribute to the public debate on such vital issues.
STRAIGHT FROM THE BENCH proves cogently why
those who sit in judgment should lead the way to
reform.

'Pickles is at his best when putting the case for modernizing the judicial system. Here reformer and raconteur come together . . . What he *does* say is dramatic and unpredictable'
*New Society*

'Tells of his controversial career and presents the Pickles philosophy of justice . . . No sensible person can but agree with him when he exposes the questionable practice in which the Lord Chancellor and the Lord Chief Justice participate in the interests of the controlling of our judiciary'
*Daily Telegraph*

'On whatever aspect of the law he is summing up, Judge Pickles is never less than hugely entertaining and refreshingly informative'
*Manchester Evening News*

# Straight From the Bench

---

## Judge James Pickles

**CORONET BOOKS**
Hodder and Stoughton

**To my wife, Sheila**

Copyright © 1987 James
Pickles, new material © 1988
James Pickles

First published in Great
Britain in 1987 by Phoenix
House, an imprint of
J. M. Dent & Sons Limited

*Coronet edition 1988*

**British Library C.I.P.**

Pickles, James
   Straight from the bench.
   1. England     2. Justice,
   Administration of –
      England
   I. Title
   344.207      KD660

   ISBN 0-340-42271-8

Printed and bound in Great
Britain for Hodder and
Stoughton Paperbacks, a
division of Hodder and
Stoughton Limited, Mill Road,
Dunton Green, Sevenoaks,
Kent. TN13 2YA. (Editorial
Office: 47 Bedford Square,
London WC1B 3DP) by
Richard Clay Limited,
Bungay, Suffolk.

# Contents

# Foreword and Acknowledgments

This book is intended for members of the public, whom the law ought to serve. It comes out of my work in the courts. I was born in 1925, called to the Bar in 1948, and first sat as a part-time judge in 1963. Since 1976 I have been a circuit judge, sitting in crown and county courts, mainly in Yorkshire. Most of my work in the law has been done in that great county, where I was born and brought up.

The views I express are mine only. I happen to be a radical, and this causes clashes with some of the conservatives who dominate the legal profession. I believe that complacency, conservatism and conformity hinder progress in legal and other fields. Whether I am right or not, the reader must judge. Certainly I do not claim always to have been right in what I have said and done.

Some of the material in this book has been published before: as in evidence I sent to two Royal Commissions, speeches to magistrates and articles in the press. But much is new. I hope the book may be of some interest: the law and the way it works affect us all.

I am grateful to my wife, Sheila, for all her help with advice and typing; to my children Roger, Carolyn and Simon for reading and commenting on early drafts; to my daughter-in-law, Christine, for doing the index, and to Alan Rusbridger for allowing me to reproduce his notes taken from the meeting between Lord Hailsham and Manus Nunan (see pp. 35–40). I thank, too, the *Daily Telegraph* for permission to reproduce my article 'A Place for Punishment', which appeared on 22 March 1985. Also to some judges, counsel, solicitors and administrative staff on the North-Eastern circuit for their help and advice on technical and other points. None of the above persons is, of course, in any way responsible for the contents of this book or any of the opinions I express. Some of them probably disapprove of the whole venture. Their forbearance when dealing with an author who at times can be tedious and difficult, is also appreciated.

# Chapter 1

# How Judges are Appointed

## The Office and Role of Lord Chancellor

Parliament is an antique place, encrusted with tradition, and no part is more so than the office of Lord High Chancellor. Television has let us see him sitting on the ancient Woolsack, a large square bag of wool covered by red cloth and lacking a back or sides. The Woolsack symbolises something from our misty past, but it is not clear what. It may have been the place wool had in medieval trade, but it does not matter; it is there because it has always been there and lord chancellors will go on sitting on it because that is what their predecessors have always done. This is how our country works. The Woolsack is technically outside the House of Lords, which is odd as the Chancellor presides over the assembled peers as their Speaker. He has no disciplinary powers and their lordships do not even address him but each other ('My Lords'), and the only way to cut a speech short is to move 'that the noble lord be no longer heard', but they are too polite to do that, except rarely.

Americans – and I confess I ally myself to them in this – are said to be flabbergasted to see the Lord Chancellor sitting on his Woolsack, his full-bottomed wig bandaging his face, as the wig rests on the black silk gown covering the eighteenth-century court suit of black cloth. Knee breeches reveal black silk stockings, the feet of which are elegantly encased in black buckled shoes. On top of all is placed a black tricorn hat, but only fleetingly when signifying the Royal Assent to a bill or swearing-in a new peer.

Those are only the Lord Chancellor's everyday working clothes. On state occasions he wears his black and gold state robe of flowered damask, lace cuffs and white gloves. On formal occasions, as when parliament is opened, thus caparisoned the noble lord has five attendants about him. First goes the tipstaff. I do not know what his function is and he may not know himself; if asked he might say, 'To march ahead in a slow and dignified way.' He does what others have done before him. Then comes the permanent secretary, the head of the Lord Chancellor's department. Next walks the mace-bearer; his office is self-explanatory, as are those of the other two, the purse-bearer and the train-bearer. Whether there is anything in the purse, I am not privy to; perhaps no one has opened it for centuries. The train-bearer presumably holds the damask robe and, like a bridesmaid, prevents it from sweeping the ancient floor of that ancient place.

Some say the office of Lord Chancellor dates from 615 AD, but the more meticulous scholars do not. Some think the office began in the reign of Edward the Confessor (1042–1066), the first English king to have a Great Seal.

After the Conquest the Lord Chancellor, then a cleric, was in charge of the secretarial business of the royal court. He still signs official documents 'Hailsham, C'. He is high in the order of precedence, following the Archbishop of Canterbury. The Chancellor comes before the Prime Minister whose office – and certainly whose title – is relatively new. But the PM may come first as First Lord of the Treasury, so it is all a bit confusing to commoners like me. One thing is certain: the other chancellor – he of the exchequer – is inferior in that his office came about much later. He is an upstart, relatively.

The office of Lord Chancellor is odd. It refutes in one man the idea that we have 'separation of powers'. The American Constitution was based on that idea – that no one may at one time serve in more than one branch of government. Those are the legislature (congress or parliament), the executive (the cabinet) and the courts. The men who drafted the constitution were influenced by Montesquieu's book *L'Esprit des lois* ('The Spirit of Laws') which was published in 1748 and purported to show that government in Britain rested on the separation of powers. But Montesquieu wrote before the full development of cabinet government, so his analysis is incorrect today.

The Lord Chancellor is in all three branches of government. He sits in the House of Lords as a legislator and also as a judge, and he is in the cabinet. This makes difficulties for any lord chancellor in two respects. First, he is extremely busy and cannot give all his time to manning and running the courts. He has no junior minister in the Commons, where the Home Secretary and Attorney-General help him out. This gives wide power and influence to his civil servants. Secondly, the Chancellor has to be careful which hat or wig he is supposedly wearing at any one time. When dealing with a judge for stepping out of line, out of court, he must try not to silence the judge merely for words that embarrass the government. That would confuse his headship of the judiciary with his position as a minister.

The Lord Chancellor speaks in the House of Lords for the government on non-legal subjects. He attends cabinet meetings. As president of the supreme court of judicature he appoints high court and circuit judges. The Prime Minister is consulted when the Lord Chief Justice or Master of the Rolls is appointed: they have charge of the criminal law and the civil law respectively. The Prime Minister has, or sometimes has, influence on the selection of lords justices of appeal and law lords, but the strongest influence in all those selections must be that of the Chancellor and his top men. Lower down the scale – with circuit judges, recorders and magistrates – he can know little about candidates but what is told him by his advisers. (He appoints JPs, even in Scotland, but not in the Duchy of Lancaster: quaint.) Members of tribunals which decide whether unemployment benefit has been wrongly withheld and the like are also chosen in the Chancellor's name. Further, he has wide ecclesiastical patronage, which means he appoints many vicars.

In 1895 Lord Chancellor Herschell said the strain was too great for any man to hold the office for more than three years, yet Lord Kilmuir held it from 1954 to 1962, and Lord Hailsham from 1970 to 1974 and from 1979. As I write in 1986 he is seventy-nine.

The holder of the Great Seal has power and patronage which would have made Henry VIII envious, though the Chancellor cannot chop off heads: what deprivation! He also has a luxury flat over his office. We might expect aspirants to queue all round Downing Street when a new name is awaited, but the choice is very limited. A lord chancellor is usually a QC and a leading politician of the governing party. He must abandon all hope of getting to Number Ten. The chancellorship lies on an elegant, distinguished road, but it is the end of the road. John Simon and Quintin Hogg (now Lord Hailsham), both clever classicists, leading lawyers and MPs, coveted the premiership but missed it. Another limiting factor is that the Prime Minister's first choice may be an MP with an unsafe seat, and elevation to the Lords would mean a by-election. These may be some of the reasons why Lord Hailsham still serves when, were he a judge, age would have debarred him.


## How Judges are Appointed


One of the problems under our system is that barristers become judges by accident, in the sense that they start by wanting to be advocates and then find at about the age of fifty that the only sensible course is to sit for fifteen years on the bench: status, a relaxed life – and a good pension based on half-pay, which civil servants have to work for forty years to earn. The alternative for most barristers is a gradual winding down into poverty and degradation as younger barristers pass them by. There are some QCs who earn too much to afford a judge's salary and who can buy an adequate pension, but they are rare. So barristers become judges, although they did not initially set out to do so and may not be fitted for it. The qualities required for the two jobs are not the same. A good advocate may be a bad judge; an eloquent, forceful, thrusting counsel may talk and interfere too much when promoted to the bench. Many a mediocre, shy, taciturn barrister has made an excellent tribunal. I tend to be in the former category.

Some lads want to be engine-drivers, but I always wanted to be a barrister. Perhaps I was lured by the smoke and flame of conflict, fascinated by the slow, piston-like clanking of that ancient engine, the English legal system. In my early halting, fitful days at the bar, I never dreamed I might become a judge. Such heights were not for the likes of me; I was modest then. Judges were austere, remote beings. At a signal his lordship or his honour floated in from the wings, dolled in his eighteenth-century costume – symbolic of so much that is antique about the law. He presided magisterially, then floated out of sight again. I rarely saw a judge outside court, off duty.

One day I got a shock as I sat on top of a Bradford-Keighley bus – I could not afford a car for several years, and then only because my parents gave me the money for one. The face of the ageing man next to me rang a remote bell; he grasped an old suitcase on his knee and puffed nervously at a cigarette. I looked again. Yes, it was, it really was Judge Rice-Jones, the first county court judge I had appeared before. I was due to be before him again that day. To see him like this: it was like wandering into a room in a theatre and finding an actor in his underpants. (Judge Rice-Jones was a kind man, too kind. In court he puffed his cheeks in anxious indecision, and afterwards paced his room wondering if he had done right. A judge should worry before making a decision, but not afterwards.)

My first appearance on the bench came unexpectedly. It was in 1963 when I was thirty-eight and had been at the bar for fifteen years. In those days most cities and large towns had a court of quarter sessions, which originally had sat four times a year. They tried mostly criminal cases and were presided over by 'recorders' – barristers who are part-time judges. At a busy place the recorder could appoint one or more assistant recorders, who had to be approved by the Lord Chancellor's office in London. The Recorder of Middlesbrough was Henry Suddards, a member of our chambers in Bradford, who became a county court judge. His previous assistant Geoffrey Baker – also in our chambers and now a circuit judge – was asked to sit as deputy pending the selection of another recorder, and he asked me to sit as his assistant. I had had no experience or training for the bench; in those days one learned to be a judge by watching others do it and doing it oneself, much as labourers and bricklayers do. It seemed to work, but now there is brief training and I welcome it, especially for those barristers who do no criminal cases. The only vetting I had, so far as I know, was a phoned question from an official in the Lord Chancellor's office – Brigadier somebody, I think – to Suddards: 'Is Pickles all right?' I don't know precisely what the reply was, but Suddards said about me to our clerk, 'I hope he doesn't put them all on probation.' Well, I have not.

Middlesbrough Quarter Sessions were held in the town hall, which had only one courtroom: that was before Teesside and its modern crown court building came about. I sat in the council chamber and the town clerk let me use his room for robing, if there was no one else there. One day I asked him what would happen about court accommodation when Teesside was set up. 'I couldn't care less,' he said. He had far more important problems to think about than courts: a fairly typical local government attitude. To get into what was usually the mayor's chair, I had to climb over some obstacle – a sort of gate, I think. Presumably the mayor had to do the same; mayoral dignity may be easier to achieve than judicial dignity, though I never actually fell on my face – not literally. One day a lump of ceiling decoration did fall and just miss me during a trial. 'Divine intervention,' the defendant must have thought as he sat on the councillors' bench with prison officers. If it was, He missed. It may have been only a warning.

Facilities for the bench, bar, solicitors, litigants and the public are still poor at some court buildings on the north-eastern circuit. England must have some of the worst court accommodation in Europe. I once appeared at a county court which then sat in a Sunday school building; there was no robing-room and we put on our wigs and gowns in full view of everybody. Conferences with clients were held standing up in a draughty yard. Things are gradually improving as modern courts are built.

Sitting on the bench for the first time was like driving on the Continent: everything seemed the wrong way round. I found myself saying, 'May it please you,' which is what barristers say to judges – presumably because they always have. The first case was about two men doing wrong things to two girls. When I nervously took my place in the mayoral chair, having sworn to do right to all, the defending barrister – who had come from London for the case but had been born abroad – rose and asked to see me in my room. I hardly ever agree to that now, as I explain in Chapter 8, but on that occasion the barristers did come to see me in private. Defending counsel said his clients would plead guilty if I could say they would not go to prison. Plea-bargaining already, and in its crudest form! I soon sent him packing, the trial went on and the men did go to prison. My judicial career had begun. The new Recorder of Middlesbrough, Douglas Forrester-Paton – now a circuit judge – asked me to continue as assistant recorder. He is a tall, kind, modest, lovable lowland Scot and a profound lawyer, with a distinguished record in the wartime RAF and at Oxford afterwards: one of the colleagues who make life in the law worth while, despite its frustrations.

After sitting at Middlesbrough for several years I became an assistant recorder at Leeds. Several barristers junior to me were made recorders, but I did not know why. I did not ask and, anyway, no one would have told me. Recorderships varied in importance according to the size of the town, Leeds being the senior post. When a recordership became vacant, there was a shuffling-up of the recorders in smaller towns and a new barrister got in at the bottom. Applications had to be made to the Lord Chancellor; a top civil servant in his office called 'the deputy clerk to the Crown' dealt with them. We did not know whose word was decisive. The process was befogged in secrecy, as is so much in British public life. The Lord Chancellor and his advisers did not know me or most of my colleagues on the north-eastern circuit; we were only names to them. It was assumed that they relied on the high court judges who had been on our circuit and did know us, but nothing was certain.

All judicial appointments were and are in the name of the Lord Chancellor. He gives no reasons for saying yes or no, and there is no appeal. Some said that his office kept files on barristers, but we did not know what went into them if they existed, and no one would have dared to inquire. It is a misty world in which a remote being seems like a brooding, quixotic dictator with despotic power, advised by shadowy figures who are mostly 'top-drawer'. (The women who work in the Lord Chancellor's department sound on the telephone as if they had been to Roedean.) All this may seem more sinister than it is, because of the remoteness, the secrecy and the power. On the rare occasions when I meet the top civil servants, they are pleasant, cultured and polite; they do their best to work a system they did not devise and cannot change. They are stereotypes, embodying all that makes the products of public schools and Oxbridge both good and bad. Good for politeness and erudition; bad for over-attachment to tradition, lack of imagination, and hostility to change or reform.

How does the system of selecting judges and recorders work in practice? I must now tell of my experience with the late Mr Justice Hinchcliffe. I do so because it shows what can happen under our system (which has, however, been in part improved since those days, as I discuss later). It illustrates the working of the legal establishment. Raymond Hinchcliffe practised on the north-eastern circuit and took silk not long before I joined it. It is said that he did so when he learned that Ralph Cleworth was applying. Both men were made QCs. Cleworth sank like a stone and became stipendiary magistrate of Leeds. Hinchcliffe rose like an uncertain, slowly deflating balloon, and became a high court judge. In ability there was little to choose between them.

Hinchcliffe was born in 1900; his father, a Huddersfield solicitor, sent him to the Leys school, Cambridge, and then to that town's university: money mattered more in those days. Hinchcliffe took a pass degree at Cambridge, not I assume from lack of effort but from lack of intellect: he could not follow points of law of any complexity. How did he become a judge? By carefully husbanding such talent as he had, saying the right things to the right people – and luck. He was thick-set, of medium height and had a resonant, carefully modulated voice. He was dignified in manner and attached a lot of importance to that: a barrister's unpressed trousers aroused in him more hostility than did incompetence. Like many people in public life, Ray Hinchcliffe was concerned about manner rather than matter, form rather than substance. He was careful in all that he did, and this can take the untalented a long way. He was a good judge in criminal cases: he kept quiet most of the time, took detailed notes and summed-up with the help of notes he had prepared on various types of offence. In civil cases, where more mental equipment is needed, he was at sea. But again, he took careful notes – of the plaintiff's counsel's 'opening' for example, and back it would come when he recited the facts in his judgment. When he did civil cases at the bar, he was notorious for turning round to his junior and asking, 'What do we say to that?' When he sat with other judges in the divisional court or court of appeal, he kept his mouth shut lest he put his foot in it.

Hinchcliffe made well-prepared, amusing speeches at the barristers' dinners when he was leader of the circuit – which he attained by seniority – and later when he came as a guest to judges' nights. He knew he was a bit of a buffoon, and on the surface he affected bonhomie. He used to hold court at Carr Manor, the 'judges lodgings' for the high court judges at Leeds, inviting his favourite counsel to dine there. Oh the fawning and the flattery that went on! Under the surface Raymond Hinchcliffe envied abler people – most people – and he could be malicious, though he was too wise and too devious to show it. He did not like barristers who stood up to him in court. What led to his elevation to the High Court? It was said he had been promised the recordership of either Manchester or Liverpool – full-time posts – but the northern circuit objected. It was rumoured that when the Lord Chancellor sent for him Hinchcliffe did not know whether he was to be offered a high court or a county court judgeship, but would have taken either. (A county court judge was similar to a circuit judge, but tried only civil cases.)

In about 1968 at Leeds Assizes I defended a man who was on two series of charges: for company fraud and for receiving stolen goods. He had signed a confession to all the offences. The fraud charges were tried by Mr Justice Crichton (Sedbergh and Oxford), a kind and fair judge who, it was said, sometimes fell asleep on the bench in the afternoon. He kept awake during that case, in which I cross-examined the police about the way in which the confession had been obtained: improper pressure, a cold cell, no blankets, and so on. There was no trouble between the judge and me, and the defendant got off.

Then came the trial before Mr Justice Hinchcliffe for the receiving offences. I cross-examined in the same way, but this irritated him. 'Mr Pickles, the officers were only doing their duty.' 'And I am only trying to do mine, my lord.' A little later the judge said, 'It's the way you do it, Mr

Pickles. You do it in a *sneering* sort of way.' I blame myself in part for what happened next. I could have been more tactful, but I had to reply there and then, and I said, 'I find that remark highly offensive.' 'Oh, you do, do you?' 'Yes, my lord, I do.' 'Oh. Go on then.' I continued to cross-examine, but about ten minutes before the normal time for the luncheon adjournment Hinchcliffe jumped to his feet saying, 'I can't stand any more of this,' and walked off the bench. The jurors must have been on the edges of their seats after lunch, but there were no further fireworks. In dealing with the episode in my final speech I said, 'You will recall, members of the jury, that at this stage I incurred his lordship's wrath. It is one of the hazards of my profession to incur judicial wrath from time to time, but I am here to present my client's case and I have tried to do just that.'

In his summing-up Hinchcliffe said, 'Members of the jury, in the course of what I am sure you will agree was a splendid address, Mr Pickles said that he has incurred my wrath. Of course he hasn't. Mr Pickles was only doing his duty . . .' The defendant was understandably convicted and imprisoned. After that I sensed Mr Justice Hinchcliffe's dislike for me. In court he was cool; at judges' nights he ignored me. He had never been a fan of mine: I was too outspoken, abrasive even.

In December 1971 preparations were being made for the new crown court system to start on 1 January. This abolished the old courts of assize and quarter sessions. Recorders were no longer to be attached to any one town. I applied for one of the new recorderships, but then I learned that other applicants had been told they would be appointed and I had heard nothing. Some of the new recorders had sat for a much shorter period than I had. Under the new system there were to be two high court judges to act as 'presiding judges' of each circuit. The senior one for the north-eastern circuit was Mr Justice Hinchcliffe. The junior one was Mr Justice Cumming-Bruce, a very different type: astringent, able, scholarly, fair. I went to see the new circuit administrator, Peter Robinson, who had been the clerk of assize and whom I knew well. We were at the bar together for several years. He said there were some strange omissions from the list of recorders and I was one of them. There was nothing he could do about it.

I rang John Cobb QC, the leader of the circuit bar – elected by the rest of us to be our chairman and spokesman – and I went to see him on Saturday 11 December 1971; the list of recorders was to be published on the following Monday. Cobb was an interesting man, one whom I was fascinated to know and analyse and whom I now remember with affection. I put him in a difficult position. He had a duty to me as my shop steward (how he would have flinched and frowned at the description!) and so had to stand up for me against Hinchcliffe. But Cobb was a very ambitious man; he had long had his heart and mind on becoming a high court judge, and one of those whose say on that would count was Hinchcliffe. Cobb said Hinchcliffe did not like him, because when Cobb applied for silk he did not ask Hinchcliffe to sponsor him. The judge was small enough for that, though I suspect a stronger reason for his dislike: Cobb's ability.

John Cobb was born in 1922, the son of a Sheffield surgeon, and he went to Winchester and Oxford. He was not an outstanding scholar at either place, but an extremely hard worker. His capacity for work was staggering; one might say his *gluttony* for work. I have never known a person who had such application, who worked so hard and so conscientiously — within the limits of the ingrained conservatism and narrow outlook that his background and education made almost inevitable. He was tall with a small head, a receding chin and poor eyesight. He had no eloquence or feeling for words and used such expressions as 'in the fullness of time', but he mastered details and that is one of the keys to success in so much in life. His was the skill of the house-painter rather than the artist. Every bit of wall and window-frame would be beautifully decorated, with no paint-splashes, but ask him to paint a picture and he would not know how. He cross-examined Poulson in the famous corruption case on our circuit, and his junior, Peter Taylor QC — now a high court judge — cross-examined Pottinger. It was said that Cobb's performance was saturation-bombing: every part of the target was methodically attacked bit by bit, leaving nothing untouched. Taylor's cross-examination was selective-bombing: the key bits of the targets were picked out, the whole attack having shape, style and panache.

John Cobb once led me in an accident claim for a plaintiff, and he discussed the case with the client in conference — or 'consultation' as it is for some reason called when a QC is involved — without taking the tape off his brief: the measurements and other details were in his head.

Cobb lived at Follifoot near Harrogate where he had a study over the garage across a courtyard. He had a complete set of law reports and other books of reference. When not in court he worked there for hour after hour, including weekends; he did all his own typing. His handwriting was beautiful. He was a perfectionist journeyman in all that he did. An unkind QC said it was the way he was potty-trained as a child that made Cobb so. He did not like to go away on holiday; after a few days his desk and all those sets of instructions tugged him back. At Oxford he won a half-blue at golf, but he even gave up golf. He was called to the bar a few months after me, but he soon had a flourishing practice, deservedly. His qualities were sure to take him high: ambition, conscientiousness, capacity for effort — and the way he flattered solicitors and others on whose support he relied. John Cobb had other faults — I say 'other' because I do regard excessive flattery as a fault, though to him it probably came naturally, and if one had raised it with him he would have said he was merely polite and tactful.

Cobb lacked vision, imagination. I recall two instances from the same meeting of the circuit committee which I attended because seniority had taken me to the office of 'attorney-general' of the circuit: a largely ceremonial office, the chief duty being to try to make a witty speech at a dinner. There was and is a shortage of places in barristers' chambers for beginners, and the Bar Council in London was rightly concerned. Cobb remarked that they had threatened to have an inquiry into our circuit, which was said to have fewer barristers per head of population than most others. 'We must avoid an inquiry, at all costs.' I said, 'If we don't put our house in order, we *deserve* an inquiry.' Cobb had not looked at it like that. Soon afterwards I circulated my detailed views on places in chambers, and it is fair to say that Cobb adopted them. The other item at the meeting concerned a member of the circuit, whom I had never met but who was on the verge of bankruptcy, the chief creditor being his wine merchant. Cobb said the bar ought to lend him money, as he was 'one of us' and if he went bankrupt he would be disbarred. I said we ought not to help him. Cobb's instincts were typical: not to help would-be barristers, but to help 'one of us', however unmeritorious. This is the 'old boy' reaction: pure public-school.

When I rang John Cobb and asked to see him on the Saturday about my omission from the list of recorders, his first reaction, sighing, was that he was very busy and I was not the only one involved, but he would see me at any time on the Saturday between 9 a.m. and 6 p.m.: he would be in his study, working. When I went I said I thought Hinchcliffe was behind my exclusion, because of the row in court. Cobb was sceptical and asked what other reasons there could be, making notes as I cast around for possibilities. He said I must leave it all to him and he would see what could be done. The more I thought about it as I drove home, the less I was ready to leave it to Cobb. Peering through the mists I could see the shadowy establishment at work. Whose side was Cobb on? What would he say about me to Hinchcliffe and the Lord Chancellor's office? Those at the bar to whom I spoke said there was nothing I could do. My wife and parents urged caution: high court judges were powerful. I sat through one night writing a long memorandum on the appointments system and its shortcomings. I got worked up, becoming more than usually absent-minded.

The more I pondered everything the more determined I was to take it in my own hands and act. I could not let things slide and be smudged over. The list of recorders was to come out on Monday 13 December; I decided that was the day to act, and I must confront Hinchcliffe. I wrote to Cobb telling him of my intention and saying he could come if he wished. Later he said he did not get the letter in time, and that may have been so. My clerk saw the judge's clerk and got me an appointment to see Raymond Hinchcliffe at 4.30 p.m. That day I was prosecuting a forger for the Director of Public Prosecutions, and yet I had to work out in my mind what to say to this man of power and be sure to get it right. If the interview went wrong, all could be lost, my career blighted. Looking back, my decision to see Hinchcliffe was daring to the point of suicidal.

As I entered the judge's room dressed in my drab barrister's gown, Hinchcliffe stood there in his scarlet and ermine. Afterwards he said to a toadying QC, 'Pickles came in, his eyes blazing. I thought he was going to strike me.' He would have liked that – apart from his initial discomfort, it would have proved he was right about me. In fact I said, 'Are you going to ask me to sit down?' 'Oh yes, yes, certainly.' I told Hinchcliffe that my omission from the list of recorders was bound to reflect against me, as if I'd done something wrong. 'Someone has put the poison in, and I think it's you.' 'Me? But why? Why should I?' 'Because we had a row in court.' 'Oh, no, no, no, never. I was astonished when I saw your name wasn't on the list this morning.' The rest of the interview is summarised in my note to the judge which is printed below. I ended by saying I was sorry I had had to be so frank. 'Oh, but I'm a Yorkshireman,' replied the senior presiding judge. Afterwards he said no one had ever spoken to him as I had. Next day he cancelled his sitting and went to London, having written me this note:

Dear Pickles, I had a word with Mr Justice Cumming-Bruce about what you said to me yesterday evening and we both feel that you should take up the matter with the Lord Chancellor's department as you suggested. We feel that you should point out to them as you did to me how long you have sat as assistant recorder and in particular how you have been sitting regularly at Leeds. As I told you, I think sponsors are expected when one is making application for a permanent appointment.

My reply was:

Dear Judge, Thank you for your courtesy in seeing me yesterday and in writing to me today. I am afraid that there has been a misunderstanding as to my reason for seeing you yesterday. I did not come in pursuit of a recordership. In order to clarify matters I have made notes of our conversation and a copy is enclosed. Should I have got anything wrong I will be very much obliged if you will please put me right. I do apologise for troubling you further in this matter.

[*My note*]

1 Pickles stated that:

(a) He came diffidently and with respect. He had not come to ask any favour. He was not there merely to put his own case; there were others in a similar position to himself. He did not wish it to be thought later that he had gone behind the back or over the head of the circuit's senior presiding judge.

(b) He had sat as assistant or deputy recorder for eight years. This had been his own choice, but he had done it in part because people of his seniority were expected to. It had adversely affected his practice (inevitably). The remuneration had been modest. He had never been told that he was considered by the Lord Chancellor to be unfit to sit. By implication, however, the Lord Chancellor now considered him to be so unfit.

(c) It was known to many that he had been sitting at Leeds for several years and had applied for a new recordership. His omission from the list might indicate to (among others) his clients and his colleagues that (presumably for reasons discreditable to himself) he had been 'sacked'. He was anxious to preserve his reputation.

(d) He felt entitled to know

(i) Why he had never been told that he was considered unfit to sit;

(ii) Why he was considered unfit, i.e. the source and content of the adverse report or reports which someone must have made to the Lord Chancellor.

(e) If necessary, he was prepared to approach the Lord Chancellor personally.

(f) He would not accept a recordership at the present time, even if it were offered to him.

(g) He regarded all those in the list of recorders as able.

(h) Many members of the circuit were currently unhappy at the way in which appointments were apparently being made. He declined to give any names.

(i) In answer to the judge, he said that he had not given the names of sponsors because he had not been asked by the Lord Chancellor to do so.

2 Mr Justice Hinchcliffe stated that:

(a) He had only learned the names of the new list of recorders that morning [Monday].

(b) He had been surprised by the omission of Pickles' name. He regarded Pickles as fit to be a recorder.

(c) He had no say in the appointment of recorders.

(d) He did not know who had reported adversely upon Pickles, but certainly he himself had not done so.

(e) He did not know what had weighed against Pickles with the Lord Chancellor. He would, however, find out and let Pickles know, either in person before Friday 17 December or by letter thereafter.

My letter and note were handed to Hinchcliffe as he arrived at Leeds Club on the Tuesday evening for judges' night at the bar mess. When he was told the missive was from me, he said, 'Oh dear, it'll be rude.' 'Pickles is rude to everybody,' said some sycophant. 'I'm not going to read it; it'll spoil my dinner,' remarked the judge, putting the envelope in his dinner-jacket pocket. His speech that evening was restrained; he said they had tried so hard to get the new crown court system right, but no doubt they'd got some things wrong. I sat at the angle where one of the tables met the top table, so I was near to Hinchcliffe, and during the evening he went out of his way to make bantering conversation instead of ignoring me. I handed Hinchcliffe a note; this must have terrified Cobb, who sat next to the judge and must have wondered what on earth I was up to now. The note had been written to me by Hinchcliffe twenty years previously after I had defended someone before him; it congratulated me on the tactful way I had handled the case. Hinchcliffe gestured as if to say, 'Shall I tear it up?' but I gestured that I wanted it back. During the interval he spoke to a QC in the loo, asking who were the people I said were dissatisfied about appointments. When he was told, Hinchcliffe began in effect to buy them off by saying, 'Oh, he's all right, he's going to get a stipendiary magistrate's job' (he did) and so on.

Three days later Hinchcliffe wrote to me:

Dear Pickles, The request in your letter of 14 December last that I should check and put right your notes of a private and confidential interview is one that astonishes me and I am not prepared to do as you ask. You are quite right in saying that I have misunderstood your reason for asking to see me. I thought it was so that I might help and advise a member of the circuit who was upset by his omission from the list of recorders. This is what I tried to do. I seem to have been singularly unsuccessful. You really must appreciate that there have been several hundred members of the bar who have been approved over the years by lord chancellors as eligible to sit in the temporary office of assistant or deputy recorder. Only a fraction of them could be appointed to permanent office under the new regime. If you still feel a grievance, you should take it first to the leader of the circuit and then, if necessary, to the Lord Chancellor. As you now write that you do not wish to be a recorder, I am at a loss to understand for what reason you wish to preserve your notes which I regard as having but a slender relation to the interview.

The bluster of a weak man.

I had another meeting with Cobb, and several phone calls. In one of them Cobb said that Hinchcliffe had rung him about something else but had happened to ask if I had taken the matter further. Despite the tone of his letter, the judge was worried lest I might go to the Lord Chancellor. I told Cobb I had done nothing further. I knew I had gone far enough. Cobb said the best way to clear my name would be for me to accept a recordership. He was going to the Lord Chancellor's office to see Hume Boggis-Rolfe (Westminster, Freiburg University and Cambridge) and would I like to come? I said I would leave it to Cobb as the leader of the circuit. Boggis-Rolfe was deputy clerk of the crown. I had never met him and I never heard of his visiting the north-eastern circuit. I assume that he did his job in the way that it had always been done; it was not for him to change procedures. I do not suggest he did anything he knew to be wrong. After seeing him, Cobb told me there was no mark against my name, and that 'things will come right, in the fullness of time', but there was no way in which I could ever find out why I had not been in the list of recorders. Appointments were a matter of 'prerogative grant' in the name of the Queen. In fact, by chance years later I did find out: a high court judge told me that Hinchcliffe *had* had it in for me. What I believe must have happened was this: Boggis-Rolfe asked Hinchcliffe for a list of suitable recorders, and Hinchcliffe selected those he liked, omitting those he disliked, never thinking that the latter would have any remedy. Boggis-Rolfe accepted the list in good faith, having no means of verifying it and perhaps no time to query it – he had the whole of England and Wales to deal with: six circuits.

On 2 February 1972 Boggis-Rolfe wrote to me offering a recordership on the northern circuit, where he said there was a shortage. I accepted, and sat happily in Manchester until I became a judge in 1976. I never knew whether I had in some way been 'exiled'. Nor did I know whether the Lord Chancellor, Lord Hailsham, himself had a hand in any of those events. I doubt whether he did; he is too busy, and has to leave such details to others. When my appointment as recorder was announced, Raymond Hinchcliffe wrote me this note:

Dear Pickles, All is well that ends well. I send you my warm congratulations and good wishes. I hope you will have many happy days sitting in a court of your choice – but do not let it unduly interfere with your practice. All good wishes.

If I had not been rash enough to stand up to Hinchcliffe, things would, I suspect, have turned out differently. My file would have been noted: 'There is something wrong with this man: Mr Justice Hinchcliffe did not approve him for a recordership.' I would never have known what was blocking my progress, and no one would have told me. As it was, Mr Justice Cumming-Bruce (later a lord justice of appeal) became a supporter of mine, and this was one of the factors that led to my appointment as a judge. In my written evidence to the Royal Commission on Legal Services in 1977, I dealt with the system of judicial appointments, pointing out the shortcomings and alluding briefly to my own experience.

It is fair to concede – indeed it is obvious – that whatever I may criticise about the system, it was liberal enough to appoint me although 'they' knew all about me. They knew I could stand up to authority and was abrasive at times. It is also fair to concede that now they almost certainly regret that they let me in.

John Cobb did become a high court judge, deservedly, in 1975, but within two years he was dead. All that work and effort and self-denial over the years, to end like that! Did he enjoy life? It is a pointless question. He was programmed by early influences and could not re-programme himself. He had some fine qualities and I am glad I knew him. Mr Justice Hinchcliffe died in 1973 and was acclaimed in public for his greatness. In a different way I am glad I knew him too: I learned a lot about people in top positions, how some of them get there and how they work. Both men are firmly embroidered into the tapestry of my life, and will be until I follow them to the same oblivion – though from greater obscurity.

How are high court judges and those above appointed or promoted? You do not apply; the Lord Chancellor asks you, if you are fortunate. Some leading QCs wait year after year and the call to the high court never comes. Nowadays they can usually get on to the circuit bench, where there is a shortage of suitable applicants; there is no certainty even about that, however. I remember one man who had been chairman of the Bar Council – usually a step to the high court – but the call never came, though he did get a consoling knighthood. I do not know what 'they' told him, if anything, but the bar assumed that the QC concerned was too outspoken. He may have upset the then Lord Chancellor by a chance remark – who knows? Should his future have possibly depended on one man's opinion, based on pique? Such a system cannot be in the public interest, to say nothing of fairness to able aspirants.

There are fewer posts on the high court than on the circuit bench. High court judges and above only number about a hundred, whereas there are about 400 of us lesser mortals. So the Lord Chancellor is more likely to know candidates for the high court personally. His adviser in this area, and also in selecting applicants for 'silk' (to become QCs) is his permanent secretary, at present Sir Derek Oulton KCB, QC.

The Permanent Secretary and his fellow-top-advisers to the Lord Chancellor – most of them barristers – are a sort of 'praetorian guard', a small elite corps dedicated to applying the Lord Chancellor's precepts and preventing breach or change. As we shall see, when the Permanent Secretary writes to a judge he does so with self-assurance and authority, reflecting those of his master, whom he serves doggedly, as is his duty. On the rare occasions when I met Oulton or spoke to him by telephone he was courteous and well-mannered. He used to employ such deferential phrases as 'speaking as a mere civil servant', but that is no apt job-description. He has enormous power and influence, especially over those who hold, or would hold, judicial positions. The Lord Chancellor is out of the office much of the time, but the Permanent Secretary is there all the time, making decisions or recommendations. He will be scrupulous in obtaining his master's signature or initials whenever a decision is formally that of the Lord Chancellor. I have to say that I am not happy about Oulton's influence. The dealings I have had with him, and those I have heard he has had with the media, make me think he is anything but progressive under his smooth, polite exterior. To be fair, however, he is only doing his job as his predecessors have done, and his conservatism comes naturally; he was chosen for it. But there is no malice in him. His motives, as he sees them, are good.

The system is better than it was in Hinchcliffe's day. Under the Permanent Secretary are two men – they could be women, but somehow the idea is unthinkable, though it should not be. They are of equal rank. One deals with all matters except judicial appointments. The other is 'head of the judicial appointments division', the successor to the deputy clerk of the crown. Tom Legg (Frensham Heights School and Cambridge) is the present holder. Able, sensitive, conscientious, hard-working, he deals with the appointment of circuit judges, recorders and assistant recorders. He regularly goes round the six circuits, having long interviews with circuit judges and others about candidates and their suitability. He knows a lot about people; he has to. He builds up a picture about applicants. He knows what they are like as advocates, something of their performance on the bench – if they have yet sat – and a lot about their drinking and sexual habits. He looks for solid, reliable, middle-of-the-road judges who will get the right answer without appearing in the press too often for what they do or say on or off the bench. I know that Legg does a good job. Given the system, no one could do it better.

But the system has drawbacks. Legg has tremendous power, and despite his qualities he remains a 'faceless' civil servant, responsible only to the Lord Chancellor. Further, candidates have no means of knowing what goes into their files. Information comes from so many sources now, however, that any one person's malice or mistake should be detectable. And it would be embarrassing to have to tell an unsuccessful candidate, 'We think you drink too much,' or, 'The consensus is that you've been married too often,' or, 'They say you're too rigid in your attitude to sentencing.' In fairness, Legg would probably give some indication to anyone courageous enough to ask why he had been passed over; he is himself courageous enough to say.

Applicants for a circuit judgeship are interviewed in the House of Lords. I was interviewed in January 1976 by Wilfrid Bourne, then number two in the Lord Chancellor's office, and Derek Oulton, then number three. It was an odd experience, going to St Stephen's entrance and being shown up in the lift, dressed in my Sunday best. I had never gone for a job before – jobs had come to me when they did come. I did not know what was in my file and I did not ask. The interview lasted about half an hour and ranged over several subjects, including Bourne's and my having been at

Oxford at the same time, though we did not know each other then. I was asked if I encountered barristers who drag out cases. Then I found myself saying things I knew I should not such as, 'I prefer advocacy to the bench, which can be boring.' Perhaps my frankness appealed. When I was asked if I would take a judgeship in Birmingham I said, 'Oh no. I'm a Halifax chap and it's too late to move now.' It may have been a trap question, to find out how desperate I was for elevation. About six months later Bourne wrote offering me a job in the Sheffield area and I accepted.

Who decided to appoint me? The Lord Chancellor, Lord Elwyn-Jones, did not know me. The answer must be that Bourne made a recommendation, based on meeting me and collating what others thought of me.

Being sworn-in before Lord Elwyn-Jones was a great day. My parents, my three children and my kind, dear clerk, the late Peggy Maud, were there in the Lord Chancellor's oak-panelled room looking on to the Thames. Before we went in Bourne gave me the card with the words of affirmation on, and I studied it. 'We don't expect you to learn it,' he said lightly.

There was a brief ceremony when his lordship entered. I had to move two paces forward, place my white gloves on a table, then read from the card. It took about two minutes. Then Lord Elwyn-Jones chatted amiably to us for a few minutes: a pleasant man, not pompous, and his Welsh lilt delights. My father remembered going to the same building to see some official – a brigadier, I think – when my father was chairman of Halifax magistrates. I was glad he lived long enough to see his wayward son achieve apparent respectability.

When I joined the north-eastern circuit virtually all the QCs and judges from there were public school and Oxbridge products. The position has obviously changed to some extent since those days, but the ethos of the bar and so the bench is still essentially public-school: the insistence on seniority – if two barristers go through a door, the junior one waits; 'don't let the side down'; the 'old-boy' attitude. Why does the tiny proportion of people who go to so-called public schools and Oxbridge dominate the bar and bench – and indeed so many top jobs in other areas including the Church of England, the City and parliament? There are various explanations for this dominance of the few over the rest. The simple one is that education in those educational places is good; but it is not so much better than at some day-schools and provincial universities. A stronger reason is that those who appoint to positions prefer their own kind. Recently the Lord Chancellor and his then permanent secretary had both read 'classics' at Eton and Oxford.

A stronger reason still is that public schools can give to the mediocre an appearance of ability. At the bar self-confidence is vital; we are as able as we feel. An Etonian *knows* that he has been to the best school in the world; they trained him to be a leader; he has the assurance and feeling of superiority which help in achieving success at the bar and on the bench. I have seen many colleagues rise high on very little real ability, but which laymen can assess that? Manner can be more important than matter. Impeccable 'manners' – to which I do not object – an upper-class accent, fastidious dress and self-confidence, the *bearing* of an important person, can bring success. The same man born in a humbler bed and given state education would not get as far. Our nation has paid and is paying a high price for this mediocrity in high places. Many of our leaders in politics and industry cannot compete with the state-educated products of Germany and Japan. In West Germany only the failures go to boarding schools; the bright pupils are educated at the same excellent state day-schools.

I am not wholly decrying the education at public schools (I sent my son to one) and they should not be abolished by law – parents should have free choice – but I would like to see them gradually wither away. This is no more likely than the withering away of the state under Marxism, which Lenin predicted. Snobbery and class divisions are not desirable. They can never be got rid of altogether, but public schools and the fancy 'upper-class' accent and attitude which they perpetuate, feed and foster them. We are two nations, from childhood on. In my own town public-school products congregate together as children; they do not know or want to know those at state schools. Their parents – and they later – get together and keep together socially, at coffee-mornings, cocktail parties and shooting-parties, where stilted conversation dominates. False values: how I abominate them. Yet money can buy one's children into that world and does. Lesser breeds ape their 'betters' in voice and manner. Waterloo may have been won on the playing-fields of Eton, but the battle to modernise Britain has been lost there. We are being overtaken and laughed at by other nations, and complacently we do not care.

To return to the law, I would like to see more 'working-class' people coming to the bar. This would mean that eventually more of them would get on the bench. Some judges know a lot about life in ancient Greece and Rome, but not enough about life at any level but their own in modern Britain. Some of them have much learning and little common-sense. There is a big problem: the bar operates a closed-shop, and there is a bias in favour of those from public schools and Oxbridge. It is far harder for the state-educated to get into busy chambers, which is the key to success at the bar. (I dealt with this in my evidence to the Royal Commission on Legal Services: see Appendix V.)

A word about the chambers system. A man who has been called to the bar has to find a barrister who will take him as a pupil. Barristers operate in sets of chambers. They are not partners, as they do not share profits. They do share the expenses of running the chambers: rent, rates, staff wages, etc. They have a clerk, who is a powerful person: he negotiates with solicitors, from whom the briefs come. If his Mr A. has two briefs on one day and cannot do both, the clerk tries to arrange with the solicitor for another man in the chambers to do one of the briefs. Some briefs come in with no name on and the clerk decides which barristers shall do them. After twelve months' pupillage a young barrister has to get a permanent seat in chambers, hopefully in the set where he has been a pupil and has already made contacts with solicitors. But there may be five pupils and only room for one or two of them as permanent members. The others have a desperate struggle to find a place elsewhere, but many cannot and drift off into other jobs, never having had the chance to show what they can do at the bar. They have been kept out by their potential competitors.

It will surprise no one to be told that judges in England and Wales – I know little of those in Scotland, though they are probably similar – are on the whole deeply conservative in outlook. Indeed, the conservatism, complacency and conformity of the legal profession as a whole have to be experienced to be credited. They extend to a fair proportion of judges, barristers and solicitors. All professions tend to be conservative, being led by those who have been immersed in practices and traditions for so long that they naturally think the established ways must be correct. And professions draw many of their recruits from the middle class, which tends to be conservative in outlook. A youngster soon finds that if he wants to succeed he had better go along with the herd, and that those who straggle and stray get left behind. Certainly that is so with the bar.

We are all conservatives in some respects. Methods that have been hallowed by experience may well be the best. They should not be cast aside without reason. Sadly, however, there is a reluctance to cast anything aside. At the bar and on the bench I have from time to time put forward ideas for improving things. The initial reaction of barristers and judges is usually tepid or apathetic, if not hostile. Let me give detailed examples.

K. was a circuit judge (now dead) I had known ever since I joined the north-eastern circuit. In those early days I used to play him at squash. There was no ill-will in him but he was very right-wing. He did not get that from a public school – he went to a grammar school and Oxford. He became a judge several years before me. Quite recently I was transferred to a group of county courts where he also sat. When I arrived I found there were several improvements which could be made, so I wrote him a note asking for a discussion and listing the points. I did not want to make changes without consulting him, and I hoped he would agree.

I had been approached by the president of the local (solicitors') law society, who knew me. He wanted to meet me to talk about fees and the way appointments were made in divorce matters. The judge has to see the parent who has the care of the children if they are under sixteen, to approve the arrangements. Solicitors appear in about half those children's appointments and they wanted their cases grouping together instead of being scattered about a morning. Applications for injunctions, such as for non-molestation or ejection from the home, were put first and sometimes they held up a lot of people.

In my note to K. I made suggestions for improving the system, aimed at reducing wasted time for parties and their solicitors. I also suggested we set up a committee to meet twice a year, consisting of him, me, the county court registrar (a sort of mini-judge), the chief clerk and two law society representatives. We could thus exchange views and make any necessary changes.

I had found it confusing that on some days the county court sat at 10 a.m. and on others at 10.30. I thought the latter time preferable: to be consistent and to give ample time for lawyers to confer with their clients – not easy if a barrister has to travel twenty miles.

At the meeting with K. I also raised the desirability of sitting with a divorce court welfare officer on children's appointments. With many other circuit judges I have found this enables me to sort out some problems there and then – especially as to access, which is a common irritant for the newly divorced. The parties go out of my room with the welfare officer and usually return with the problem either solved or reduced. This avoids the delay and expense of a written report. A few days before my meeting with K. I had been at a conference of divorce judges in London where this system had been approved. (The cost of each written report was said to have been assessed at over £700.)

When I entered K.'s room ready to discuss those points I was met by a tirade. 'When I read your note I was shocked! The arrogance! You've only been here five minutes, and you want to change everything. I don't believe in change for the sake of change.' He refused to discuss any of the points. He would change nothing. He had only a few years to go before he retired and he was not going to be dictated to by me. He hoped I would soon be moved.

I kept cool. I tried to explain the need for the changes, but to no avail. So there were two systems in the county courts where we sat, K's and mine, which must have confused some. I do not say K. was typical, and I have no wish to defame his memory, but I can only bring my thesis on conservatism to life by giving real instances.

Let us now meet Mr Justice Jupp. I stress that he means well and endeavours to do right. A southerner, he went to Perse School (Cambridge) and Oxford, where he studied with distinction Latin, ancient Greek, ancient history and ancient philosophy. He has since taken up other areas of scholarship including more long dead languages. I admire that: disinterested scholarship, learning how others lived and wrote centuries ago, must be absorbing and certainly could not be called harmful to anybody. Kenneth Jupp is very conservative in his views. He would appear to accept without query that the Church of England, the army – in which he served with distinction in the 1939 war, obtaining the Military Cross – the monarchy and the Tory Party are institutions which have a kite-mark of approval. I doubt he would ever question anything done or said by anyone in authority over him: that would, I expect, go against all he has learnt from his earliest years and certainly from the day he entered prep-school. The word of the Lord Chancellor is to him, probably, only less authoritative than that of the Almighty.

At the bar in London he apparently had a practice in one of the rarefied byways of civil work: there are few specialists, and lots of money is involved for litigants. I had never heard of him before he became a judge, but that should be put at my door, not his. He presumably had a flourishing practice. It is said that his last case at the bar lasted six months. It will not surprise the reader that soon after Mr Justice Jupp's appointment to our circuit as a presiding judge, he and I were at odds. The faults were more mine than his, but what happened spotlights much of what I have to say on conservatism and tradition and the effects they have, and also on the type of people who are appointed as judges and why.

I think my first dealing with him took place before we had even met; certainly before we knew each other well. Soon after I was appointed in 1976 I sat at Hull and Beverley crown courts and found the accommodation at both inadequate. I do not mean the facilities for judges, but for litigants, lawyers and the public. So I wrote to various people including the courts administrator for my group of courts, the then permanent secretary to the Lord Chancellor, and Mr Justice Jupp. At Hull the crown and county courts sat, and sit, in the Guildhall. I told his lordship that there was only one room for conferences with clients and it adjoined a busy, noisy street. Witnesses, jurors and defendants had no separate waiting-rooms and so crowded into the lower corridor, causing a hubbub plainly heard in the county court. If a jury was considering its verdict at lunch-time, only tea and biscuits were available. There was no proper jury-room with its own lavatory. The robing-room for counsel had no easy-chairs and the only telephone for them was a public one. The only refreshments were from a trolley in the corridor in the morning. The judge's telephone was on an outside line; when anyone phoned the crown court, it rang in the judge's and his clerk's room simultaneously. There was no internal phone.

Beverley crown court sits in the old sessions house, an attractive Georgian building that is now much overcrowded. I informed Mr Justice Jupp that the only accommodation for conferences between lawyers and clients was in rooms used for other purposes: the solicitors' room, a general office, the probation officers' room and the probation officers' typists' room. The building had one ladies' lavatory and one gents' for the use of staff, jurors, witnesses and defendants on bail. The one attached to the robing-room was for both sexes. The general office was occupied by three clerks and was congested. The bar robing-room was overcrowded on days when pleas of guilty were taken. No room was set aside for defendants on bail. Court number one acted as a corridor for those wishing to go from the public part of the building to jury-rooms, kitchen, recent files or the copying-machine. When a defendant was taken from the cells to court number two he was taken via the open air in handcuffs. Part of the public gallery was filled with filing-cabinets. Although I did not put it in my list, the two judges shared one room, and if one of them had a hearing in his chambers the other one had to go for a walk or sit outside in his car.

I wrote to Kenneth Jupp because I knew he was going to sit for one day at Hull crown court, calling at Beverley on the way in order to robe. He did not look round the Beverley building when he called. Afterwards he wrote to me saying he could not help; the administrators knew about the difficulties, and nagging complaints would make them take less and less notice of what judges had to say. This points the difference between the conservative and the radical approaches. If I had been in Mr Justice Jupp's position I would have pressed the administrators for solutions and made suggestions. 'Something has to be done. Why can't we get on with it? Can I press the Lord Chancellor's department for more money, or what?' But Kenneth Jupp is not like me. I stand for all he abominates. Ten years later things are much as they were. The phone system at Hull was altered so that an outside caller cannot ring the judge direct. I had some easy-chairs sent to the Hull robing-room from the judges' room at Beverley: this was against the civil service standards, which do not allow for easy-chairs in bar robing-rooms. The site for new courts in Hull has been cleared but no spade has yet bitten the soil. When it does it will taste water eighteen inches down, as the site is near the docks (and not central to the city, as it should be). There will be no scope for a car park in the basement, though there could be for a marina: I would enjoy arriving by boat! In the meantime, everyone going to Hull and Beverley crown courts has to soldier on with a shrug, in the way we British accept.

When sitting out of London, high court judges live in 'lodgings' – palatial houses, usually with extensive grounds. On our circuit, even if lunch is available in the court building, they go several miles to the lodgings by fast Rolls or Mercedes, fully robed and escorted by a police car and police motor-cyclists, who stop other motorists even when the lights are green for them. It is not thought appropriate to lunch with the circuit judges (except perhaps once a week, if the building has a judges' dining-room). Occasionally some circuit judges are invited to go in the official car to the lodgings for lunch. On such an occasion I met Mr Justice Jupp for what I think was the first time. The talk happened to alight on pornography, and I said I didn't know what corruption meant in that context. 'Literally,' he said, 'to break down.' Latin *can* be useful. I said I didn't regard so-called pornography as being harmful to adults – though it might shock – and I saw no reason for the law to interfere to protect people from their own propensities. Mr Justice Jupp must have been appalled to hear that, from a judge.

The next time I met his lordship was at a judges' meeting when the cathedral service devoted to the law was discussed. Once a year, in cities like Sheffield and York, barristers and judges parade in full robes including – for judges and QCs – full-bottomed wigs, to the service and afterwards to sherry provided by the high sheriff. That year the sheriff had asked whether the judges could share the cost of the sherry. I have never gone to any of those services. They are harmless but they symbolise empty ritual. I am an unbeliever. I am prepared to dress up during the week as part of my job, but not on a Sunday. Ceremony and pomp have a place in public life, but they should be kept in proportion. I asked for whose benefit the Church parades and services were held. A judge, who ironically happens to be Jewish, favoured them: the public like to see the scarlet and ermine. I said I was sceptical. Mr Justice Jupp said he believed in the unity of church and state. I asked him why it had to be only one sect of one religion, and he seemed never to have considered that, but perhaps there was something in it.

I next met his lordship on a social occasion. He jocularly referred to a coming church service and remarked that I would not be going. Then I put my foot in it, quite unnecessarily. I said Britain was like the *Titanic*, going steadily to the bottom while the captain calmly distributed titles and medals to the crew. I added hastily, 'I know you've got a title, but—' (all high court judges are knighted). Mr Justice Jupp walked off abruptly and I do not think we have since had a civil word, which is sad because if we had got to know each other better I am sure we would have found areas for deep discussion, though not agreement. I hope that one day we will achieve that.

The next meeting was in thunder. Before I describe it I must tell of an episode which must have been in Kenneth Jupp's mind, though he never referred to it. It must also have coloured Lord Hailsham's attitude to me, though he has never written of it to me. I mean my jury-vetting case.

In October 1979 I was told there was to be an application by the defendant in a case fixed for the following Monday. It was on behalf of two police officers who were charged with assaulting a youth. The defence wanted to vet the jury by getting details of any convictions; they could then challenge such jurors, who might be prejudiced against policemen. There seemed to be virtually no guidance from statute or case law. The Attorney-General had, however, issued guidelines to the police concerning checks on potential jurors in serious cases where strong political motives were involved, such as terrorist or Official Secrets Act cases, or where defendants were believed to belong to a gang of professional criminals. In such cases checks could be made at the criminal record office, on Special Branch records or with local CID officers. The authority of the Director of Public Prosecutions was required and application was made to a judge in private without informing the defence. It seemed to me that if the prosecution could have jurors vetted in cases where there might be bias, the defence should be able to do the same, and I ordered the police to let the defence know of any convictions against the jurors.

The prosecution appealed, but the divisional court upheld me. The case then went to the Court of Appeal (civil division) presided over by Lord Denning, which held that under the Courts Act 1971 there was no right of appeal against my decision; jury-vetting was, however, unconstitutional and the court suggested that the matter be re-opened before me. The appeal decision is reported in 1980 2 All England Reports 444 under *R. v. Sheffield Crown Court ex P. Brownlow*. The point was then re-argued before me. The Court of Appeal's opinion was not binding on me, but was very persuasive. I reserved judgment and pondered and wrestled with the point; no decision has given me more anxiety. How could I, a mere circuit judge, oppose the great Lord Denning? In the end, however, I did, and my judgment can be read in Appendix III. I took time over it and I take modest pride in it.

I got the impression that my refusal to heed the Court of Appeal caused a bit of a stir in judicial and other legal circles. However, the propriety of jury-vetting came up again, this time before the Court of Appeal (criminal division) in *R. v. Mason* 1980 71 Criminal Appeal Reports 157. The appellant complained that the jury in his trial for burglary had been vetted. Three jurors had in consequence been objected to by the prosecution: two appeared to be disqualified by reason of convictions and the third had a finding of guilt for burglary and theft. The court held that vetting was not unconstitutional:

> Since it is a criminal offence for a person to serve on a jury knowing that he is disqualified, for the police to scrutinise the list of potential jurors to see if any are disqualified is to do no more than to perform their normal function of preventing the commission of offences. In the course of looking at criminal records, convictions are likely to be revealed which do not amount to disqualifications. We can see no reason why information about such convictions should not be passed on to prosecuting counsel. He may consider that a juror with a conviction for burglary would be unsuitable to sit on a jury trying a burglar; and if he does so he can exercise the crown's rights. Many persons, but not burglars, would probably think that he should.

(The only convictions which now disqualify a juror are where during the previous ten years he has been sentenced to imprisonment, youth custody, detention, borstal training or community service.) The court said that the

Attorney-General's guidelines were not directions having the force of law, but merely contained advice. Nothing was said by the Court of Appeal about jury-vetting at the request of the defence. I assume there is such a right, though I have not had any further application.

On 16 April 1980 Mr Justice Jupp phoned me at home and asked to see me at the Leeds judges' lodgings on the following Saturday morning. I thought this odd but I did not ask what it was about and he did not say. He was not sitting at Leeds and was to make a special journey to see me; so I learned when we met. This was only sixteen days after my jury-vetting judgment. I did not connect the two events then but I did later. He must have thought I had gone off my head, defying the Court of Appeal: he was not to foresee that another court would later vindicate me.

I had difficulty finding my way into Carr Manor on the Saturday morning: most of the gates were locked and my host had not concerned himself with how I should get in but rather what should happen once I managed it. I did get to the front door of the mansion and pulled on the bell, to be shown in by the butler, and up to the study where his lordship sat at the desk. The butler brought coffee and biscuits and there followed a scene which, looking back now, had its comical side. Jupp was preparing to deliver a furious attack on me. He had decided that this wayward upstart had to be brought back smartly into line. He would deal with me as they did at school and in the army: straight from the shoulder and no bloody nonsense! Yet handing out coffee and biscuits has to be a civilised affair, done politely and with restraint. It does not fit, to bark out, 'Milk and sugar? One lump or two?' So that part was done decorously. I still did not know what was to come. Naïvely I had thought that perhaps my abilities had at last been recognised and I was to be asked to help in something important.

The butler withdrew, and then Mr Justice Jupp uncorked himself explos-ively. 'I am concerned about your conduct as a judge.' He had a pile of documents on the desk and began to go through them. Three of the five complaints about me were from prosecuting barristers which the leader of the circuit, Peter Taylor, then the leading QC and spokesman for the bar (whom we shall meet yet again) had sent to Jupp. I had had no notice of any of these; no one had told me there had been complaints. And some of the cases were about two years old. Those had been sent to a previous presiding judge, Mr Justice Boreham (neither public school nor Oxbridge), who had taken no action, but Jupp had disinterred them and put them with fresher ones.

When he began to go through the first one I intervened to say how old it was. The judge told me not to interrupt. That was my trouble; I could not listen. When he had dealt with that one I asked to reply to it, but at first he said he wanted me to reply to all the cases at the end. Then he gave way on that.

The irony of the procedure was that I was being accused of unjudicial conduct. Yet I had had no notice of the charges the judge was bringing, and he was reluctant to let me give my version to each charge separately. He further made it plain that he was not interested in the *merits* of the complaints; it was the *fact* of them that mattered.

There was undoubtedly substance in some of the complaints. One came from the Court of Appeal – presumably sent by Sir Derek Oulton – which had quashed a conviction because I had asked too many questions of the defendant. I told my presiding judge that I was wholly at fault in that case and had no excuse.

Another complaint was from an MP. 'This is getting worse and worse. The next one is from parliament,' snorted Mr Justice Jupp, as if both houses had solemnly voted to have me disrobed, hanged and drawn. In fact it was from an MP whose constituent had said that I had threatened to keep him in custody if he did not plead guilty. I told the judge that the Court of Appeal would no doubt look into that (they never referred to that aspect when the appeal came up), and Jupp conceded there was probably nothing in it.

There were two cases in which counsel had said that I dealt with the prosecution in a peremptory fashion in shortening the hearings. There was something in that, though the end results were just. In another case prosecuting counsel had complained because I told the jury my critical views about the police taking notes after an interview and not during it. I did that. I sent evidence to the Royal Commission on Criminal Procedure about it. Both South Yorkshire (where that complaint originated) and West Yorkshire now do it 'my' way, as do the Metropolitan Police and some other forces.

The last complaint was interesting in that I had difficulty in getting across to Mr Justice Jupp what had happened. Briefly, several male teenagers had set upon and kicked three young men, one of whom was quite seriously injured. The charge was inflicting *grievous* bodily harm. The defendants were prepared to plead guilty to assaults occasioning *actual* bodily harm. I did not consider that a lengthy and expensive trial on that narrow issue was justified. As the defendants were all under twenty-one, the practical choice was between borstal and detention centre, whichever offence applied. I obtained an estimate of comparative costs as between guilty and not guilty pleas. It was the difference between £700 and £2200: i.e. £1500. I expressed my firm view that the case should not be contested, and that if necessary the prosecution should accept a plea of guilty to the lesser charge. I adjourned the case so that they could have a further think about it. (The complaint about me was my attitude. The prosecution thought I should have let the case go to the jury on the major charge.)

On a second hearing the defendants pleaded guilty to the major charge and all got six months in a detention centre. I told Kenneth Jupp that it would have been a public scandal if the case had been contested: only the lawyers would have benefited.

I kept calm and explained that the difference between him and me was that I was a radical. I also told him I had worked hard as a judge but I knew I had faults. 'Oh you do?' 'Certainly. Do you want me to list them?' He said he did not, which pleased me because it might not have been easy to get it right without giving him unnecessary ammunition.

As I rose to leave, Jupp said that if he had any further complaints he would refer them to the Lord Chancellor, adding, 'I don't suppose you like to hear me say that.' I said I did not, and left.

Although Mr Justice Jupp did it in the wrong way, the experience itself was good for me. We can all benefit from criticism, being made to look at the way we do things. Judges especially need this, as we have so much power and so few critics who are capable of examining what we do and telling us how to improve. I am sure that his lordship will benefit, should he read this book.

Several months later I wrote to him setting out my version of what had happened, pointing out the shortcomings of the procedure and suggesting alterations. Complaints by counsel should be made to the judge concerned in the first instance. If they are then taken up elsewhere the judge has adequate notice of what was alleged. I said I welcomed criticisms, if they were made properly; that it was important to examine their merits; and that it was significant that although some high court judges had a lot said against them there was no procedure for complaints. Finally, I said that complaining counsel were sometimes mainly concerned about wounds to their own pride.

Shortly after that I had a rude letter from a chief constable. I had asked for information as to why an identification parade had not been held; the defendant in a nasty sex assault case had gone free. The Chief Constable went through the roof; it was his own affair how he did his job, he wrote to me. I replied in equally rude terms: I should not have done. He complained to Mr Justice Jupp. So, another venomous interview, after which my senior went to see Lord Hailsham who – without asking for my side of things – wrote me a snotty letter, to which I did not reply.

How does Kenneth Jupp (who is said to lack the common touch) come to be on the high court bench? It is tempting to assume that being a high Tory, C of E, having read classics at the 'right' school and university and got the MC, he must have been an ideal candidate in the eyes of a Conservative Lord Chancellor. But Jupp was appointed in 1975, under the Labour government! Socialist Lord Chancellors have never altered the appointments system. Perhaps they found the Civil Servants too strong, or got seduced by all the power and pomp. Certainly there is a need for a broader based system for selecting judges. A board or committee drawn from a wide section of society would be less influenced by a barrister's 'elite' background.

Most high court judges are of high calibre, intellectually and in other respects, but there have been exceptions caused by political or personal nepotism. The worst example in my experience was Gerald Howard (Harrow and Oxford). He was a Tory MP from 1950–61, and then went on the bench at the age when many judges are about to retire – sixty-four. Lord Chancellor Kilmuir appointed him. Mr Justice Howard looked and behaved like an arrogant eighteenth-century squire. He was idle; he found any excuse for rising early or shortening a case. At 3.30 p.m. he would say, 'Your next witness is bound to take some time, and it is much better not to interrupt him, so we'll rise now and he can be called at 10.30 tomorrow.' If a defendant pleaded guilty to a lesser charge, Howard tried to bully prosecuting counsel into accepting the plea, saying, 'The court has ample powers [of sentence].' He spun out criminal cases so that he would not have to try civil cases, which were too much for his intellect. He was rude to everybody.

In the United States a presidential appointee to the Supreme Court has to be approved by the Senate, and can be interrogated by one of its committees as to his fitness for the job; the President cannot choose anyone he favours. When my late father was chairman of Halifax magistrates, he refused to let my sister's name go forward for the magistracy, as it would look like nepotism. After he retired, she was appointed. I am sure the Lord Chancellor and his men would approve of that attitude.

Remembering my own experience, I have from time to time put in a word for barristers I thought were being unjustly overlooked – not because they had approached me, but because I wanted to see right done. There was one man who should have had a recordership, and I said so repeatedly, receiving nose-enders from Mr Justice Jupp, who took the view that it was for the Lord Chancellor's office to decide. Mr Justice Boreham simply ignored my letters. At least, he never replied. I wrote to him about a dozen times about this and other matters whilst I was a judge and he was my senior presiding judge, and there was never a word of acknowledgment in any form. This is hard to explain, as Leslie Boreham is a good, sound judge and most punctilious in court. I wrote to Oulton, who always replied. Eventually Mr Justice (now Lord Justice) Glidewell (Bromsgrove School and Oxford) arrived as a presiding judge. I spoke to him and – coincidence or not – within a week or so I read in *The Times* of my candidate's appointment as recorder. Ironically, when I wrote him a letter of congratulation he never replied: he had not known and still does not know what I had tried to do for him. Lord Justice Glidewell is one of the 'good guys' amongst the senior judiciary: although no radical, he is approachable and has breadth and common-sense in his outlook. He is not alone in that, though we could do with more high court judges like him. Another similar presiding judge on our circuit was Michael Mustill LJ (Oundle and Cambridge). He is a first-class man with a first-class brain: the two do not always go together. He is surely destined for the House of Lords.

At one stage I was concerned about the number of barristers and solicitors who had for years sat as assistant recorders without being made recorders. They did the same work as recorders, at less pay, but had no tenure: they could be dropped at any time. I felt that if they were able they should be made recorders; if they were not, they should be dropped. I decided to write to the Lord Chancellor's office with details of those concerned, and so I asked the circuit administrator for those details. He referred my request to Mr Justice Jupp, who wrote me a curt letter saying that he had ordered that I should not have the details. So that was that. Since then, some of the assistant recorders I had in mind have been given recorderships and others told that their sitting services are no longer required.


I must now deal with the disturbing case of Manus Nunan: none illustrates more vividly the shortcomings of the system of judicial appointments. After my Kilmuir rules article appeared in the *Guardian* on 14 February 1986, I received a fair number of letters. The most interesting one came from Australia, where Nunan had gone after leaving the English bar to lecture on Oscar Wilde. He wrote that he had been treated worse by Lord Chancellor Hailsham than I had been, and he was not even a radical. He sent me copies of the correspondence he had had with the Lord Chancellor's office about the non-renewal of his recordership, and I have since met him and discussed his case with him and with others in the law.

Manus Nunan is a small, genial, cultivated Irish gentleman whose mother was an actress. He speaks fluent French. He was born in 1926 in Dublin and was educated there, graduating from Trinity College with third-class honours in law: he is no high-flyer intellectually, as he admits, but circuit judges and recorders do not need to be. His Irish Catholic family was one of the few to continue to serve the crown after the partition of Ireland in 1922. His family has a history of service to the crown. One of his uncles, Sir Joseph Nunan, was a colonial judge and his father was twice wounded whilst serving as a British army officer in the First World War.

After call to the Irish bar, Nunan was for ten years in the British colonial legal service, ending as solicitor-general for Northern Nigeria and a QC. He is not a QC at the English bar, to which he was called in 1965, joining chambers in Liverpool. From 1975 he sat as a deputy circuit judge in the crown court and in 1978 he was granted a recordership; this was renewed in 1981 and was due to be renewed again at the end of 1984.

Nunan sat in various crown courts including Manchester, Liverpool, Preston, Bolton, Grimsby, Lincoln and Nottingham; and (in London) at Wood Green, Knightsbridge and Inner London, averaging fifty days a year for nine years. During that time no conviction was quashed for any fault of his and no notice of appeal alleged misconduct by him so far as he knows. He was never warned by anyone in authority about his performance on the bench.

On 10 September 1984, Nunan met Tom Legg, the Lord Chancellor's official who deals with the appointment of circuit judges and recorders. Notes were taken by a clerk in the Lord Chancellor's office. The meeting was at Legg's request. He said that the Lord Chancellor liked to keep an eye on how recorders were doing. To quote from the official note:

> In Nunan's case there were some credits and some debits. He was a popular and much liked member of the circuit, and was regarded as competent, experienced, a man of absolute integrity. However, as a tribunal he was sometimes described as unpredictable, capable of being a little impatient and sometimes a little over-dramatic. Nunan replied that the minor cases in the crown court made an excessive use of a judge's time, and he felt this could be cut down. He said that, in his own defence, he was a lot quicker than most people and wondered if some of the judges might resent this. He went on to say that, as an Irishman, it was possible that he might be over-dramatic at times, but asked Legg to speak to the chief clerks at the various courts where he had sat to get their views on his efficiency. However he told Legg that he would certainly think about what he had been told and would endeavour to correct any of the tendencies mentioned. Nunan told Legg that he had hoped for an appointment to the circuit bench in London. Legg said that the chances were not high, although it could not be absolutely ruled out. In response to a question from Nunan, Legg stressed that his nationality had nothing whatsoever to do with this. Nunan said that his further wish was that he be allowed to do some recorder sittings in London. He had been told that this would not be possible at the moment because of the payment of expenses, but wondered if anything could be done. Legg said that he would look into the matter and let Nunan know.

On 11 October Legg wrote that he had taken advice on the question of expenses and that it would not be possible for Nunan to do some of his sittings as a recorder in London. 'I will be writing to you again in due course about the renewal of your recordership.'

The next day, 12 October 1984, the Brighton bomb, planted by the

IRA and aimed at senior Conservatives including the Prime Minister, went off.

In November letters of renewal were sent to other recorders concerned, but not to Nunan. He was the only Irish citizen amongst them, he believes.

On 7 December Legg wrote, 'The Lord Chancellor has decided not to renew your recordership when your current term runs out on 31st December, 1984.' Not a word of explanation. Nunan felt shattered. His reputation had been destroyed. His position at the bar was now impossible. People would think he had done something wrong, but even he did not know what it was. He asked Legg and Oulton, high court and circuit judges on his circuit, Alex Carlile QC MP, Ben Hytner QC, the leader of the circuit, but no one gave him details as to why he had been dropped after nine years without complaint. He drew the conclusion that his Irish citizenship and the Brighton bomb had led Lord Hailsham – known for his strong Unionist views – to take a hasty decision.

On 18 February 1985 Legg wrote that there had been further extensive inquiries in October and November 1984 about Nunan's performance on the bench. There were substantial adverse reports about his sittings. 'I cannot specify these sources, but they include a substantial number of circuit judges as well as others.' Again, no details.

I know how the system works. The persons best able to assess and report on a recorder's performance, first-hand, are counsel and court-clerks who see him in action. The courts administrators for groups of crown courts get feedback from the chief clerks. One judge virtually never sees another performing in court – unless of course they are sitting on the same case, say in the Court of Appeal. So any complaints a judge passes on about a recorder are necessarily 'hearsay'. If the complaints come from counsel, there is a danger that they may not be based on an entirely objective assessment. Some of the complaints about me by counsel – dealt with in this book – came from those whose feelings I had hurt; the justice or otherwise of the result achieved in a case may not be a complainant's main consideration, and a court clerk's assessment of a recorder may be coloured by the way the latter treats him personally in or out of court.

For months Oulton refused to let Nunan see the notes taken of the 10 September meeting, saying in his letter of 25 March 1985, 'I am afraid there can be no question of releasing such internal papers. You were present and will know what was said.' A fairly typical official attitude.

When Nunan wrote to me I decided to try to help him. On 26 May 1986 a long profile of me appeared in the *Guardian*, written by Alan Rusbridger. When he came to see me to prepare his piece, I told him about Nunan and gave him copies of the correspondence. He interviewed Nunan and on 13 June 1986 the *Guardian* published the result, 'A Recorder who never had a fair hearing', which referred to Nunan's theory about the Brighton bomb.

Rushbridger's article provoked a long and indignant letter from Lord Hailsham which the newspaper published on 14 June. (A reply from Nunan appeared on 16 June.) He stated that if he had not been Lord Chancellor he would have sued for libel. He denied that Nunan's being Irish came into it. A leading article on the same day criticised Hailsham under the heading, 'One unyielding man, many reforms':

Lord Hailsham (whom we welcome in adjacent columns) is eighty next year and shows no signs of relinquishing his office of Lord Chancellor. But the legal system over which he presides is in danger of rotting beneath him for want of reform. From the catastrophic squeeze on legal aid at the bottom of the system to the recent rows over judicial appointments at the top, the evidence mounts of legal services failing disastrously to adapt to the needs of late-twentieth-century life. Lord Hailsham is no reformer. Indeed he has set himself repeatedly against reform − notably in the two fields just cited. The grounds for this opposition may once have vaguely related to a plausible defence of professional independence. But no longer. They now seem increasingly motivated by the plain immobilism of a man apparently determined to leave the legal system as little changed as possible from the system he entered as a young barrister more than half a century ago.

Following representations from the Bar Council, and the matter having been raised vigorously by the Liberal Party in the House of Commons, the Lord Chancellor agreed to reconsider Nunan's case and to hear him personally on Friday 26 September 1986. During the preceding week I put in a lot of work. On Monday I rang a lord justice of appeal, three high court judges connected with the northern circuit, several circuit judges and Ben Hytner, the circuit's leader (I had a rather acrimonious conversation with him whilst telephoning his holiday house in France: he thought, wrongly, that I had accused him of putting his wish to be a high court judge before his duty to Nunan). I also spoke to a QC on that circuit whom I know from playing squash several years ago in the annual competition between our two circuits.

Some of those I spoke to said they knew nothing and could not help. Others obviously knew something but would not help. I could get nothing concrete about Nunan's alleged shortcomings as a recorder. I said, 'If there is injustice at the heart of the system of justice, then I as a judge am concerned about it.' 'Oh, so would I be,' conceded one high court judge, assuring me that his wish for promotion would not deter him. Another said that he could tell me nothing: he had handed everything over to a lord justice of appeal. I rang the latter, who − though he was very reasonable in his general attitude − said he could tell me nothing: he had handed everything over to Lord Hailsham. I did not ring him.

I felt increasingly frustrated. This was a Kafka-like world. Men who look so strong and speak so firmly on the bench were behaving differently over Nunan. Their careers were at stake and they wanted no whisper of dissent to reach the man who decides everything. I do not accuse them of bad faith or of saying anything they knew to be false. But if only one of these high judges had said, 'Yes, you're right. The system should let a man know what's blocked him. Justice has not appeared to be done, I'll back you.' When I complained to one of the high court judges about the wall of silence, this renowned man of law said, 'So far as I'm concerned, the higher that wall the better.'

On 22 September 1986 Mr Justice McNeill, who was a presiding judge of Nunan's circuit in 1981 and 1984, wrote to Nunan that he gave to Legg the same views as to Nunan's suitability as recorder on both occasions. If the views were adverse to Nunan, why was he re-appointed in 1981 without those views being put to him? If the views were favourable, Lord Hailsham over-rode them in 1984.

On Tuesday 23 September, I rang every crown court where Nunan had sat. At some courts no one was still there who had known Nunan. It was two years since he had sat as recorder. One circuit judge refused even to speak to me: he had spoken to Legg and would say no more. What a fraternity!

No one at any of the courts I contacted gave me one instance of inadequacy in Nunan, though some had sat in court with him. At one crown court I was told, 'When we were stuck for a judge, we always suggested Mr Nunan. He had a brusque manner and took short cuts, but he was efficient in getting through the work. He got the backs up of some barristers at times, but he got the right results in cases.' The chief clerk at the same court told me, 'We were very willing to have Mr Nunan, and used to ring and ask for him.'

At another crown court they could not recall any criticism of Nunan. At yet another the court-clerks were said to have spoken highly of him, and no criticism of him could be recalled. One person I spoke to said, 'Mr Nunan was very highly regarded. If the courts administrator offered him to us, we bit his hand off.' I was informed by another administrator that no court-clerk ever complained about Nunan.

A slight jarring note did come from a man who had sat with Nunan for a week. There were 'one or two odd decisions', but Nunan was a reasonably good recorder. He liked to make quick decisions. The same man added that he saw Manus Nunan prosecute in a murder, and he did a good job. (No one I have spoken to has in any way criticised Nunan's ability at the bar. Yet if he were incompetent, lacked the mental capacity or personality required of a recorder, some of that would surely have shown when he acted as an advocate.)

When Nunan was offered a meeting with Lord Hailsham, he was told that he could take one person of his choice. He asked me, and I said I would go if he insisted, but it might not help his case if Hailsham and I went for each other's throats! Any animosity of Hailsham against me would spill on to Nunan. After trying to get Lord Wigoder QC (who had retired from the bar to chair BUPA), Nunan asked Alan Rusbridger to go with him, and Rusbridger agreed.

On Wednesday – two days before the crucial meeting at the House of Lords – I decided it might be best for me to go with Nunan and Rusbridger: I had a lot of information now, or rather I had encountered a lack of it. I telephoned Oulton's office and spoke to his secretary (a man who had been a court-clerk for me years ago, though I did not recall him). When I told him that Rusbridger was to go with Nunan, he said, 'The journalist?' I said the Nunan affair was escalating and I was anxious to limit the damage to the judiciary in which I was proud to play a humble part. Should Hailsham decide, on further consideration, that Nunan ought to have his recordership back I felt sure Nunan would withdraw his comments about the Brighton bomb.

At 6 p.m. that day, Oulton rang me at home at my request. The Lord Chancellor had decided not to see me. I said the meeting should be postponed unless Nunan was to be given the grounds for his dismissal, a copy of the official notes made after the 10 September 1984 meeting and an assurance that he would get any notes made after the meeting between Nunan and Hailsham.

Then I launched into a tirade. I doubt if any judge has ever spoken to the Permanent Secretary to the Lord High Chancellor as I did. But I had no need for honeyed discretion, even if that had been my style. I wanted nothing from Hailsham or Oulton, except justice for Manus Nunan! I said the Lord Chancellor had treated him shabbily. I referred to his service to the crown abroad and as a recorder, the lack of appeals, complaints or warnings. What was he supposed to have done wrong? 'If you were sacked, you'd be entitled to know why, as is everybody else in this country.' I pointed out that the guidelines in 'Judicial Appointments', published by the Lord Chancellor in May 1986, were not followed. Under 'Renewal of Appointments', we find, 'Where the terms of the appointment have been kept, the Lord Chancellor decides not to renew a recorder's appointment only when he is personally satisfied that the recorder has failed to measure up to the standard required. *Where possible, the recorder is warned in advance of any cause for concern, so as to give him a chance to improve.* [My italics.] However, this cannot always be done.' (Nunan did not sit again after 10 September 1984.)

I went on to say that if Nunan had gone wrong, there must be people who saw it. Transcripts must have been made when defendants appealed or applied for leave to do so. What was wrong with him? Could he not sum up properly? Was he rude to people? Did he interrupt too often? How could he have done the job for nine years without an appeal succeeding? If necessary I would press Nunan's case to the extent of co-operating in an application for a judicial review, going personally to see the Prime Minister or putting the facts about the appointments system and Nunan's case before the public through the media.

Sir Derek Oulton listened in silence, then said he was only a civil servant. He had made an almost verbatim note of what I had said: presumably this was for Hailsham.

Within hours Nunan was informed that he would be told the grounds for his dismissal, and be given a copy of the 1984 notes and any made after the Friday meeting. Nothing was said about my attending, but I had said what I had to say, and in any event I had cases to try on Friday.

I have Alan Rusbridger's notes, taken by him in shorthand, of the meeting in the Lord Chancellor's room on Friday 26 September 1986. On the official side, Hailsham was supported by Oulton and Legg and a clerk took notes.

Rusbridger's notes read:

*HAILSHAM:* meeting was in response to request from Bar Council. Glad to supply as many details as he was free to supply about reasons for NUNAN's removal. Would gladly have done so two years ago if asked. Said RUSBRIDGER was here as friend of NUNAN and not as *Observer* representative. Would not want to give one newspaper a scoop.

He was always short of people to serve on bench. Only got rid of recorders on advice of civil servants, though did not always follow advice. NUNAN must get it out of his mind that he acted from his own motives, or rashly. Until December 1984 he was totally unaware of NUNAN's existence. He knew nothing of his record. It was pure illusion to suggest he might have been influenced by NUNAN's nationality. He would never have got away with it, even if he had so acted. LEGG and OULTON would have gone to Sir Robert Armstrong and HAILSHAM would have been dismissed. He found it hard to put it out of his mind that NUNAN had published the allegations he had, but, after a struggle with his conscience he thought he had done so.

He found that he had renewed NUNAN's recordership in July 81, when NUNAN had been one of 25 names.

In March 1984, though HAILSHAM was totally unaware of the fact at the time, there was an internal question-mark raised about NUNAN's suitability in the office.

In September 1984 LEGG saw NUNAN. HAILSHAM was happy to accept the notes which had now been presented to NUNAN.

In early December 1984 – but not before – HAILSHAM given list of names about which there were doubts concerning renewals, only one of which was known to HAILSHAM. Of these: four were renewed for a year; two stood down at own request; one was stood down; one was renewed for two years; one was renewed for three years. This left only NUNAN.

The summary of reports on NUNAN said that he was a bad tribunal, that he was impatient, overdramatic and something of a joke when sitting. Generally, there was a lowering of the expected standards – and these reports were confirmed on LEGG'S tour of the Northern Circuit.

HAILSHAM did not take such a summary at its face value: he turned to the material on which it was based. This was, if anything, worse than the summary indicated.

HAILSHAM, faced with such a report, could not see what any Lord Chancellor was expected to do other than fail to renew NUNAN's recordership.

He had read that the *Irish Times* had reported the Lord Chancellor's office as saying there had been no complaints about NUNAN. This was not quite true. If a recorder was reported to have behaved outrageously – such as being drunk or the Court of Appeal rejecting a case because of a recorder's ludicrous behaviour – HAILSHAM took immediate action. This wasn't such a case, and he didn't expect the regular audit to deal with specific incidents.

He couldn't see how else he could have behaved. He had been pilloried by NUNAN and by others – including Mr RUSBRIDGER himself, but he was willing to receive representations.

*NUNAN* said HAILSHAM's words were caricature. It was a false report. It was that bad.

*HAILSHAM* said he realised it was painful for NUNAN.

*NUNAN* said if specific allegations had been made against him he must be allowed to see the transcripts of the court appearances during which he had erred. It was not good enough simply to be told his court was a joke.

*HAILSHAM* said it was a painful matter. The audit was of total performance, however, not a statement of individual misdemeanours.

*NUNAN* said the allegations must refer to terminology. It must have been words used in court that had caused offence.

*HAILSHAM* agreed it did mean that, but in the nature of things he couldn't have the material. He had looked at the pieces of information as they were almost unanimous. There had been a chorus of disapproval.

*NUNAN* said that it was amazing if such impropriety had occurred on the bench that officials had not asked for transcripts.

*HAILSHAM* said a recorder held the liberty of his fellow-citizens in his hands. It was a heavy responsibility. There was a parallel with the case of Mr Ellis Smith, known as Donald Duck, a member of the Attlee government. He was a very little man, though nice. He was dismissed as a minister, just as NUNAN had been, and had asked why, just like NUNAN. Attlee said to him, 'You just weren't good enough.'

NUNAN said that he couldn't understand how there could have been a chorus of disapproval if, in September 1984, Legg had made complimentary remarks about him.

LEGG said that he spoke there in relation to NUNAN's performance at the Bar, not as a recorder. NUNAN disagreed.

HAILSHAM said he read into that September 1984 transcript a fairly clear warning that NUNAN could not be sure of a reappointment. Perhaps NUNAN could not see this. From July 1984 up to and including November 1984 there had been a series of reports as to NUNAN's performance from judges and from members of the Bar which made it quite impossible to renew.

NUNAN said Hytner [the leader of the circuit] knew nothing about the matter.

HAILSHAM said he was afraid Hytner knew everything about it. NUNAN could take it from him. This was confirmed by the documents. One of NUNAN's problems was that people appeared to like him and may have told him things which weren't in accordance with the truth because they didn't want to hurt NUNAN's feelings.

NUNAN said Judges BINGHAM and TEMPLE knew nothing of it. Nor did LAWTON, though he was now dead.

HAILSHAM said it wasn't true that TEMPLE knew nothing about it. BINGHAM did not at that stage. His knowledge ante-dated September 1984.

NUNAN said he couldn't understand how Legg said he would look for sittings in London if all the reports had been against him.

HAILSHAM said the reports were mainly after that interview and before he reached his decision. LEGG had not advised him of anything before September. NUNAN should have seen either amber or red at his meeting with LEGG. He didn't blame him for missing the signs. HAILSHAM had been in the Army.

NUNAN said he had sat for nine years and had wanted to be a full-time judge. He was the only one amongst his former colonial colleagues of comparable rank who was not a judge. He had never been overturned on appeal on grounds of misdirection or behaviour. He hesitated to mention the radical name of PICKLES in such company . . .

HAILSHAM said PICKLES was not a radical. He was somewhere to the right of Genghis Khan . . .

*NUNAN* . . . but PICKLES had phoned a great number of judges.

*HAILSHAM* thought he probably knew of most of them.

*NUNAN* said PICKLES had phoned chief clerks in every court where NUNAN had sat and had received glowing reports from them all.

*HAILSHAM* said this was hearsay from NUNAN's lips. He could not accept it.

*NUNAN* repeated that the Court of Appeal had not overturned him once.

*HAILSHAM* said the Court of Appeals's function was limited in relation to a recorder's conduct of a trial.

*NUNAN* said he couldn't understand why, after nine years' service, his behaviour should suddenly have altered.

*HAILSHAM* could not comment. He could only tell NUNAN his reasons.

*NUNAN* said he must be able to produce evidence of the words he had used.

*HAILSHAM* said he could only produce the effect NUNAN produced on the people he had consulted.

*NUNAN* said he was highly efficient and quick. He could see that some little men night be put off by this. He produced a letter from McNEILL, J. which was contrary to what HAILSHAM had said about reports from judges.

*HAILSHAM* read it and said this would be taken into account.

*NUNAN* said HAILSHAM had said McNEILL had given clear advice.

*HAILSHAM* said he had been vilified by the press.

*NUNAN* said it was inconsistent. McNEILL's letter was the end of the case against him.

*HAILSHAM* disagreed. He didn't quite read it in the sense that NUNAN did. He may have been tempering the winds to the shorn lamb. HAILSHAM would pursue this matter. He would take time to consider NUNAN's representations, which NUNAN had put warmly, as he was entitled to do. He evidently felt strongly. He would be interested to hear further evidence from NUNAN about his own supposed hostility to the Irish.

*NUNAN* said HAILSHAM had spoken out strongly against the Brighton bombing.

*HAILSHAM* said he thought he had never said anything about it, though he did think an attempt to murder the Prime Minister improper.

*NUNAN* said he had heard HAILSHAM refer to 'guests' from Ulster. As a master of language he would know what he was saying.

*HAILSHAM* said if the guests were from Ulster he would say so.

*OULTON* said he would like to ask about NUNAN's intentions. Did he intend to give up practice and live abroad?

*NUNAN* said his only concern was his reputation.

*HAILSHAM* said he had done nothing to harm it.

*NUNAN* said if reappointed he would shortly resign.

*HAILSHAM* said he had no power to make a retrospective act. That would be null and void. He would like to return to the Irish question.

*NUNAN* said that he had, during a speech to the Irish Club, said that Southern Ireland was governed by little men with a hatred of the English.

*HAILSHAM* denied having said this. He could probably produce a transcript if NUNAN wished.

*NUNAN* said HAILSHAM had called the IRA baboons – an emotional response which a lord of the language wouldn't use.

*HAILSHAM* thought this was unfair to baboons. He took a dim view of murder, as did the Pope. The IRA were servants of the devil. NUNAN must obliterate from his mind any suggestion that his behaviour was governed by feelings over Ireland.

*NUNAN* said HAILSHAM may be right about the Irish dimension, but there was still something wrong.

*HAILSHAM* realised he was beating his head against a wall. NUNAN appeared to have a higher opinion of himself than HAILSHAM had been able to form of him from the papers. He sympathised with him. He would probably find himself in the same position if he were him.

*NUNAN* repeated that he had never been appealed against. He knew his law. HAILSHAM should be able to produce one single occasion of misbehaviour in court. He must be able to produce transcripts.

*HAILSHAM* said he wished he could, but NUNAN must get it into his mind that, with the great responsibility of the office, HAILSHAM had to be sure that recorders and judges were up to snuff. NUNAN had to persuade him that he was up to snuff. He had no hostility to NUNAN, either as a man or because he was Irish or a RC. He had simply judged his capacity for holding judicial office.

*NUNAN* asked why suddenly his performance should have changed.

*HAILSHAM* said he had no reason to suppose he had or hadn't suddenly changed. It wasn't a case of what NUNAN was but of what he wasn't. It was very difficult to justify a void. He had never heard of NUNAN until he had to make the decision. His present wife was Irish. His late wife was Irish. He was himself of Irish descent, though not a RC. That was all there was to be said about charges that he had any kind of prejudice. He would consider NUNAN's representations and NUNAN was welcome to write within ten days with anything further he wished to say.

Note by the author: anyone who doubts Lord Hailsham's pro-Unionist sympathies should read chapter 35 of his book The Door wherein I went (Collins, 1975).

On 24 November 1986 Lord Hailsham wrote to Nunan that he was adhering to his previous decision not to reappoint him as a recorder.


I would summarise my views about the Nunan case as follows:
1   Nunan sat in the crown court for nine years, without any successful appeal from him or complaint made to him.
2   The notes of the meeting with Legg on 10 September 1984 do not reveal that his recordership was in danger, though minor blemishes – we all have them – were referred to.
3   In the absence of details as to why he had been dismissed and in the light of what happened at Brighton, Nunan was bound to infer that the Lord Chancellor's decision was made because he is Irish.
4   There can be no good reason for not giving Nunan full details of the complaints against him, quoting instances in specified cases, whilst not necessarily revealing the identity of the informants. He has never had those details, despite the resources of the Lord Chancellor's Department. At the meeting with Nunan, the Lord Chancellor produced nothing that could be called evidence against Nunan.
5   I am puzzled by Legg's reference in his letter of 18 February 1985 to further extensive inquiries about Nunan in October and November 1984. What triggered off those inquiries? Who decided they should be made? Did Legg make similar inquiries about any others of the recorders concerned? In the ten years I have been a judge the Lord Chancellor's office have never asked me about renewing a recordership, though Oulton and, later, Legg have asked me about applicants who have not yet been made a recorder, assistant recorder or circuit judge.
6   The present system is unsatisfactory. One man alone should not have the decision to appoint or re-appoint recorders, based on a civil servant's collation of views. The Lord Chancellor is prosecutor, judge and jury. There should be an independent tribunal. If Nunan is wrong about his Brighton theory – as I think he is – there was nevertheless nothing to

prevent Lord Hailsham acting as Nunan believes he acted. The secrecy surrounding the activities of the Lord Chancellor and his officials in this area is indefensible.

7  There should be a public inquiry into the judicial appointments system, with particular reference to the case of Manus Nunan. Obviously, no serving judge should preside over such inquiry.

I am dubious about the QC system, though not because I failed to benefit from it. (I applied three times unsuccessfully, but 'they' were right to reject me.) After ten years any barrister may apply and he has to give the names of at least two sponsors who are usually judges. Most applications are rejected. I know one man who failed thirteen times before becoming a circuit judge.

A QC wears a different gown – 'silk' as opposed to the junior's 'stuff' – and under it an eighteenth-century-type morning-coat and waistcoat. QCs only appear in important cases – where a lot of money is involved – or (in criminal cases) where the charge is grave or the facts complex. A QC is usually assisted by a junior, who does preliminary work such as drafting documents. A barrister who wants to be a high court judge has to take silk first, except in rare cases.

I see the advantage in having specialist barristers who concentrate on difficult cases, but should their elevation to silk depend on the say-so of the Lord Chancellor? This puts patronage and influence into his hands and those of the top civil servants and sponsoring judges. Conformity is promoted, as it is at the next step up. I have seen many QCs as they have approached the time for becoming a high court judge, or not. Oh, the tact and discretion, the caution, the anxiety not to say or do anything controversial, anything that might possibly be interpreted by 'them' as stepping out of line.

Originally QCs acted for the crown and had to obtain a dispensation to appear against it. Even when I began at the bar a QC had to have his chambers in London and live there; his clerk had to live outside the circuit. Those rules have gone, and I favour a further change. If a barrister wants to specialise – and take the risk that his practice might drop, as it can – the decision should be his own. Free competition should decide who shall swim and who sink.

Finally, these are the other changes I would like to see in the sphere of judicial appointments:

1  The office of Lord Chancellor should be abolished. There should be a minister of justice, sitting in the Commons, with a junior minister in the Lords. This is what happens in most other countries (except that they do not have anything so medieval as an upper chamber based in part on

inherited seats). The minister would not sit as a judge; that is inappropriate for a member of the government. The two ministers would be responsible for running the courts, appointing judges and initiating law reform. The minister would not have to preside over the upper house, or speak for the government on a variety of topics. He and his junior minister would have time to interview and select candidates for judicial posts, and civil servants would have less influence in this field. A judicial committee of the Commons would oversee the work of the Ministry of Justice, though it would not interfere in the selection of candidates. Some will hold up their hands aghast at the idea of abolishing such an ancient office as Lord Chancellor, shouting 'tradition'. I agree that tradition has its place in any long-standing institution. We naturally respect the customs and practices which our predecessors have followed. That is the essence of the common law itself. But we must not let ourselves be ruled by the dead. Tradition must be kept in its place. What matters is not whether this is the way our predecessors did things, but whether it is the best way. If the common law does not do justice, alter it. If we need a ministry of justice, make one. Addiction to the past is embedded in our national attitudes; it reduces our efficiency and makes other nations look on us as a sort of medieval antique-shop. I do not believe in change for the sake of change, but for the sake of need. If ancient customs have outlived their usefulness, they should go. If the office of Lord Chancellor belongs in a museum, let it be put there; the robes and the great seal will be splendid and admired exhibits.

2   In the selection of people for judicial jobs the Minister of Justice should sit with an appointments board, consisting, for example, of the Lord Chief Justice, the Master of the Rolls, a high court judge and a circuit judge, together with lay persons. This would prevent political nepotism or the appearance of it. There would be less suspicion of personal favouritism. Civil servants would still have to gather information about candidates, but they would have less influence and no decisive say in the final selection.

3   It should be possible for every barrister to have a go at the bar. We need a levy on practising barristers, to provide money for the financing of new sets of chambers and scholarships for promising youngsters. If necessary, public funds should be devoted to this.

# Chapter 2

## *How Judges are Controlled and Sacked*

### How Judges are Controlled

I am not here dealing with appeals from judges' decisions, but with a more subtle area. How are judges kept in line in their activities out of court, and also in the attitudes they show in court? The Lord Chåncellor and his office achieve this in two ways: by the old-boy approach ('Don't let the side down, chaps'), and by being able to withhold favours – promotion, honours, membership of royal commissions, etc. – which are all in the gift of the Lord Chancellor. In every sphere of life the old-boy approach has a pull: it is based on the loyalty we all feel to a group to which we belong. Such feelings bind together trade unionists; members of a political party; Freemasons; the bar; old Harrovians; members of any social club. All these groups contain people who share experiences and problems and help each other; they care about what their colleagues think of them; they close ranks against outsiders. So it is with the bench: no judge wants to let other judges down. This feeling of loyalty can, however, be taken too far; there are times when an individual should say what he thinks, even though he knows his colleagues may not approve. How otherwise can new ideas circulate and percolate, and improvements be made?

As for promotion and other honours or privileges, I happen to have no ambitions at all. It is easy for me to say that I do not want to be a high court judge, when I know I would never be given the chance, but it happens to be so. The life of a judge in the Queen's Bench or Family Divisions is so unattractive that no wonder they have to be given knighthoods, put up in plush mansions and provided with posh cars to take them to court or to dinner with the local high sheriff or other notables – to say nothing of a big salary and a good pension. Without those lures, who would do it? Those judges spend half their time in London; the other half is on circuit in the provinces where they go to places and lodgings which they may not like, closeted sometimes with judges and their wives with whom they may not get on, and subject to protocol. There is no popping out to the pub. I prefer to sleep in my own home. I see no need for titles, which are relics of medievalism. I do not like pomp, as opposed to dignity. Dining with and chatting to high sheriffs, mayors and masters of industry has gastronomic attractions but other limitations. The annual dishing-out of shoals of honours and titles is a cheap way for those in power to reward those who put them there, and make little folk feel not only bigger but more attached to the establishment. Some people spend years working and giving in public life in the hope of a title, a CBE or less. I know one circuit judge who hung on until statute barred him, hoping for a knighthood, but it eluded him. His MBE and DL (deputy Lord Lieutenant) were not enough. How anyone who knows the way honours are dished out, nevertheless wants one, is hard to imagine. Vanity, vanity, all is vanity – and none of us is wholly exempt.

In 1979 a radio play of mine was broadcast on 'Saturday Night Theatre', and the *Radio Times* asked me for an interview. I gave one, and let a photograph be taken of me sitting at my desk in my robes. The results were published in the issue for the week beginning Saturday 27 October 1979. I dealt with some of the topics which appear in this book. I received a rebuke through the Permanent Secretary to the Lord Chancellor and was told that it was a mistake for a judge to give interviews to the media, at any rate without prior consultation with the Lord Chancellor: 'The exercise of a wise discretion in this area is greatly to the advantage of the bench as a whole.' That was our 'old-boy' appeal, which I understand and have adhered to in the main. Unfortunately, any approach to the Lord Chancellor is normally dealt with by one of his civil servants, who is likely to say no. There may be occasions when a judge should state his views publicly, even though the Lord Chancellor might find them unpalatable.

On 25 June 1979 Lord Scarman spoke to the annual general meeting of Justice – a body which does good work on behalf of political prisoners abroad and those unjustly convicted here. He spoke on 'The Judge in Public Life' and I have the full text. Respectfully, I agree with Lord Scarman. He said there are areas of public life outside his courtroom in which a judge has a valuable role to play. He should be free to take part in the press, radio and television on major social and legal issues.

Lord Scarman has himself set out his views on such topics as the need for a bill of rights and the pros and cons of introducing into our law the European convention for the protection of human rights and fundamental freedoms. In his opinion judges could contribute to such subjects as contempt of court, the right to privacy, the development of administrative law, the ways and means of sustaining the rule of law and sentencing policy. Judges must, however, 'impose on themselves the restraints of their office'. They must be detached from political, social and economic controversies. A fine line has to be drawn. For example, in the relations between the state and trade unions, judges should be able to comment on what the law *can* do but not on what the law *ought* to do.

On 25 January 1980 Lord Hailsham wrote to all the judges. He had consulted the heads of the various sections of the higher judiciary. A majority thought that the rules laid down by Lord Chancellor Kilmuir in

1955 were correct. *Whilst Lord Hailsham had no power to give directions to 'fellow-judges' in this field* [my italics] – the reader should note that – he hoped that any judge who was invited to broadcast would approach him or his office, so that the judge could be advised on the basis of the precedents 'and so enable the judiciary as a whole to maintain consistency of practice in this sensitive field'.

What are the Kilmuir Rules? The BBC had asked Lord Chancellor Kilmuir whether judges could give a series of lectures on radio in the Third Programme about great judges of the past. In rejecting the request in a letter dated 12 December 1955, Kilmuir wrote that the overriding consideration was to keep the judiciary insulated from controversies of the day. (It is not clear how the lectures would have offended against that.) 'So long as a judge keeps silent, his reputation for wisdom and impartiality remains unassailable; but every utterance which he makes in public, except in the course of the actual performance of his judicial duties, must necessarily bring him within the focus of criticism. It would, moreover, be inappropriate for the judiciary to be associated with any series of talks or anything which could fairly be interpreted as entertainment.'

What are we to make of the 1955 rules now? Thirty years later they seem too wide. Although Lord Hailsham's 1980 letter says they are still in force, they are not in practice wholly adhered to. That letter implies that there may be circumstances in which a judge could properly appear on radio or television, and some have.

In October 1983, paragraph 77 of the Lord Chancellor's *Handbook for Circuit Judges* was amended by permitting judges to contribute articles or letters to the press on legal subjects, provided they do so with discretion. This again is vital when considering the crisis between Lord Hailsham and me. It is an example of the changes that are taking place, though Lord Hailsham seems to have gone back on that amendment.

Surely a judge could today give a lecture on radio or television about a great judge of the past without offending anybody. Senior judges have in recent years been in programmes about sentencing. Lord Denning was even on 'Desert Island Discs' whilst still Master of the Rolls, and that was entertainment. Was any harm done by them? After Lord Templeman had appeared in a Yorkshire television programme about judges in August 1986, the Lord Chancellor's office stated that the Kilmuir Rules do not apply to law lords, so he had not asked for permission to appear. They did not explain this anomaly, or state whether the rules apply to the judges of the Court of Appeal or High Court.

So far as I know, 'entertainment' under the Kilmuir rules has not been defined. Radio and television programmes must seek to entertain in the sense of holding the attention pleasurably of the listeners at whom they are aimed. (This may not apply to Open University programmes where instruction is the object rather than entertainment – though a good teacher entertains as well.)

How do the 1955 rules work in practice? In December 1981 the producer and presenter of a BBC 'Panorama' team came to see me. They were preparing a programme on prison overcrowding and sentencing policy and they wanted me in it. They had read of my speech about Mr Whitelaw (see Appendix IV). I said that I was prepared to be on the programme but they would have to ask Lord Hailsham. I doubted whether he would agree and I predicted correctly: according to the producer the Lord Chancellor refused to let me take part and so I did not. A still photograph of me was shown and a sentence from one of my speeches was read. Lord Justice Lawton was interviewed at length. He happens to be my sort of judge: robust. No harm was done by my exclusion; I would not have added anything to what he said. More recently Ludovic Kennedy did a similar television programme, but no judge took part. Surely that was not desirable: judges know about sentencing policy and angles that are not readily apparent to laymen.

Did Lord Justice Lawton consult the Lord Chancellor before taking part in the 'Panorama' programme? If he did not, then there was a technical breach of the 1980 letter. If he did, and Lord Hailsham agreed to him taking part but not me, that raises problems. A court of appeal judge has far more authority than a mere circuit judge and Lord Justice Lawton's word is weightier in every way than mine. But is this selection process right in principle? Might it not appear that the Lord Chancellor is tempted to prefer 'safe' pro-establishment judges to those who have new or dissenting notions? Might he not, in the 'Panorama'-type of programme, be tempted to prefer a judge sympathetic with government policy? Might the barriers between the executive and the judiciary, already smudged, be further blurred? I am not accusing anyone of anything, but pointing out problems.

On 5 April 1984 BBC Radio Leeds telephoned asking me to record an interview later that day. I had already rejected an approach by BBC TV. It was in connection with a radio play based on a script I had written: the play was to be broadcast on 7 and 9 April 1984. I telephoned the Lord Chancellor's department and after being directed from one person to another I spoke to the private secretary. He referred my query to Lord Hailsham and his permanent secretary, who both said that I should refuse Radio Leeds, but the Lord Chancellor would consider what I had to say on the subject if I wrote to him.

I wrote a memorandum for the Lord Chancellor. I pointed out that the judiciary should have the confidence of the public as a whole. Individual judges should have the confidence of the parties in cases they try. They should – ideally – be seen to have impartiality, wisdom, learning, common-sense and patience. It would be wrong for a judge to rush into the press, radio and television at every opportunity, airing his views on a variety of topics and appearing unbalanced in his attitudes. Lord Hailsham is right to be against that. On the other hand, there are areas in which a judge can make a real contribution to public discussion. Where is the line to be drawn?

I added that whilst a judge should be wise and detached he should not seem arrogant, remote and out of touch and sympathy with ordinary folk and their problems. A lot of people do think we have that image. So we should adjust it and we are doing so, gradually, as is fitting. We judges are no longer wholly inaccessible to the media, though we have to be about some things including, of course, the cases we try or may try. In adjusting our attitudes we should be guided by precedent but not fettered by it, or no progress will be made.

My note went on to say that Lord Hailsham's attitude might possibly be on these lines: 'I don't mind judges of the high court and above going on radio or television. I know them and I know they won't put their feet in it. I can leave it to them. I don't even expect them to consult me. But Pickles: that's different. I don't know him and what I know about him alarms me a bit. If I let him loose, where will it end? He doesn't want promotion or any sort of favour from the establishment, so we have very little hold over him. He might say something embarrassing to the judiciary as a whole. And if I let *him* loose how can I rein in the 400 or so other circuit judges? Some of them aren't all that bright. Although present practice does not fit with either the 1955 or the 1980 rules, it works all right, so why alter it?' I added, 'I see the force of such an attitude, but with respect it cannot be wholly right.'

My memorandum conceded that all judges are conservative with a small 'c', but said that I also happen to be radical with a small 'r' in some respects. I like to look at problems and try to improve things. I have views about sentencing and the need to re-think policy and also the way we run prisons; about delays in court cases; the way judicial appointments are made; plea-bargaining; the jury system. I continued: 'When such matters are being discussed in public I may have a small contribution to make. Should I keep silent or be silenced by others? I do not think so. A judge has in my view a certain responsibility to the public, and when he is approached by the media he ought not to say "No" every time. He should be as approachable as he can be without losing dignity and when he can properly assist he should.'

The note to Lord Hailsham stated my conclusions: 'I am not happy about the way in which judges seem to be selected for appearance on radio and television, but I understand the problems facing the Lord Chancellor. He may feel it is too soon to amend his 1980 letter. I am a Scarmanite. Any appearance on radio or television ought, in the main, to be within Lord Scarman's proposals. If I had done the Radio Leeds broadcast it would have been outside Scarman. It would have broken the 1955 rules, being entertainment. In practice, however, I cannot see what harm the broadcast would have done if I had answered the questions sensibly. There is an element of absurdity about a fifty-nine-year-old judge, who has some experience, going to the Lord Chancellor like a prep school boy asking his headmaster for an exeat – especially when the boy knows that the answer will be "No". I will make no more requests: I know the precedents. I shall reject most approaches from radio and television. If I accept any, what I say will normally be within Scarman. I shall try to act on the principles I have accepted in this memorandum. The chief means of expounding my views will be the written word. Of course, my attitude may well be modified by frank comments from the Lord Chancellor, which I welcome.'

Lord Hailsham referred my note to a committee of judges chosen by himself, which sought the views of all the judges. A majority favoured keeping the 'Kilmuir Rules'.

It is anomalous that whilst no one questions my submitting evidence to a royal commission or addressing magistrates, if the same material is used for radio, television or in an article for or a letter to a newspaper, the Lord Chancellor's men immediately wade in swinging clubs.

On 22 March 1985 the *Daily Telegraph* printed an article by me, 'A Place for Punishment'. It is in Appendix I. It deals with government penal policy, parole, the pressure put on judges by ministers to shorten or avoid prison sentences, and the prison system.

On the same day Sir Derek Oulton, the Lord Chancellor's permanent secretary, wrote to me. He stated that Lord Hailsham 'regards it as essential that judges should scrupulously refrain from taking part in current political controversy, interpreted in its widest sense . . . The publication of an article such as yours appears on the face of it such a flagrant breach of this convention that the Lord Chancellor must regard it prima facie as judicial misbehaviour. Before considering this matter further he has asked me to request you to send me any comments you may have on the publication of this article or the view which the Lord Chancellor takes of it . . . I would be grateful if you could reply in writing before Thursday 28 March.'

The reference to 'misbehaviour' meant that Lord Hailsham was considering whether to dismiss me. The reference to 'prima facie' meant that, on the face of things, I had done enough to warrant that. There was a time when such hints from on high would have depressed me. That may be the effect on other judges who receive such missives; I know of several instances. But I was sixty. I am not callow, cringing or easily cajoled. Any threat to dismiss me has to be taken seriously, but how seriously depends on what I know I have done and what I think those above me are likely to do when it comes to the crunch. That involves looking into their minds;

happily a judge is trained to do that and does it every day. I felt cross. 'They' have their jobs to do and they cannot be called wicked, malicious or anything like that. But this was not the way to treat me. I have worked hard, visited prisons and similar places, gone round addressing magistrates, studied, analysed, expounded on crimes and punishments, delays, bail and the like. I was concerned to do what was right for the public and especially those caught up in the process as victims or defendants. Oulton had to do as he was told, but he knew me and could have told Lord Hailsham about me. Perhaps he did and his lordship was not absorbed by the information. I do not know. But I did feel that this was not the manner in which to write to me. A reasoned and restrained rebuke is one thing; a blunt threat to sack is another. It is fair to concede that this is the way 'they' and their predecessors have used their power for generations. No one had told them otherwise.

I replied stating I was preparing my full comments but I could not possibly complete them by 28 March. I intended to go into things in some detail. On 2 April Oulton wrote asking for my comments not later than 10 April. I responded by informing him that I was going abroad on leave that very day; after I returned on 21 April I had to give an important public memorial lecture – on 23 April – but after that I would formulate my comments.

On my return there was a firmer letter for me. They had decided to pump up the pressure. Lord Hailsham had expressed 'grave concern' about my delay in providing my comments which he had expressly requested. If my comments were not in his hands by 26 April, the Lord Chancellor would 'in any event proceed to consider your future on the circuit bench'. The letter further demanded that on my return I should immediately get in touch with Oulton about the memorial lecture. 'I will wish to know what kind of occasion it will be and what you plan to say, so that Lord Hailsham can consider whether you should go ahead with it.' This is revealing. It shows how far Lord Hailsham will go to keep judges in line. It could be called extraordinary interference by the executive with the judiciary. Did he really think that after hours of preparation I would cancel such an occasion at the last minute, letting down those concerned to hear me? On no account. It is right to concede that 'they' were enquiring rather than interfering at that stage. Anyway, I ignored it. What I said in my lecture was my business, and that of the public who cared to come and listen. (In fact few did. It was an address to the Halifax Authors' Circle, of which I was a member for over thirty years, on radio drama. In introducing me the chairman held up a copy of my *Telegraph* article and said kind things about it, as indeed others have done.)

On 22 April 1985 I wrote to Oulton:

1   I am appalled that the Lord Chancellor should threaten to dismiss

me. I am determined to protect my position and reputation by any means available to me. I am prepared to apply for a judicial review, make representations to members of both houses of parliament and go to the media.

2   Since becoming a judge I have worked very hard. In all that I have done, in and out of court, I have been motivated solely by a desire to serve and protect the public. Many witnesses and documents are available to support that proposition.

3   Owing to the short time I have in which to make my representations I enclose a copy of a letter I wrote to Lord Lane CJ on 20 November 1981.

4   Paragraph 77 of the *Handbook for Circuit Judges* states: 'Judges are not precluded from contributing articles or letters to the press on legal subjects . . .'

5   In his address to the annual general meeting of Justice on 25 June 1979, Lord Scarman said that judges should be able to take part in the press, radio and television on such matters as sentencing policy.

6   For years I have been saying and writing the sort of things I wrote in the *Daily Telegraph* article. What I said was fully reported in the press on this circuit. I received no adverse comment from anyone, except that Lord Lane wrote to me in November 1981.

7   The views I hold are plain from the article in question. Having made my views known to my superiors, up to the Lord Chancellor, I felt it my duty to place certain facts before the public. There was nothing factually inaccurate, exaggerated or sensational in what I wrote. When approached by other media representatives to enlarge on what I had written, I declined. The article has not produced any public scandal or controversy, except apparently in the Lord Chancellor's office.

8   When I wrote to Lord Hailsham on 25 March 1981 sending him copies of my speeches, he did not reply. He certainly did not reply saying, 'You should not be saying these things.'

9   The extent to which a minister should threaten and harry a judge for what he has chosen to say in the public interest is obviously of high constitutional importance. It deserves parliamentary and public scrutiny.

10   The only adverse comments I have had or seen about my *Telegraph* article have been in a letter from Lord Elton [a minister of state at the Home Office] to that newspaper and in your letters to me. I have received letters in support, and I enclose a copy of an example from a judge in the USA. I cannot quote letters from lawyers in this country, lest reprisals be taken against them.

11   I have no present intention to write further newspaper articles.

12   In deciding whether to sack me, Lord Hailsham is complainant,

prosecutor, judge and jury. This cannot be right and the public will not like it. It goes against elementary principles of natural justice.

13   My over-riding duty must be to the public at large. When all the facts are put before it, I feel confident that the public will vindicate me.

Lord Hailsham waited until 21 June 1985 before replying. Naturally he had other things to do, and I must have been the least of his many problems. His letter referred to previous complaints about me. They have all been dealt with in this book, except the two referred to towards the end of the letter: they were from a local law society complaining of remarks I had made about the dilatory ways of solicitors in civil actions.

The Lord Chancellor's letter was intended to show me that he had the ultimate deterrent and was ready to use it. He wrote that it had long been considered undesirable for a judge to contribute articles to the press, particularly on matters of current controversy. (He did not refer to paragraph 77 of his own *Handbook for Circuit Judges*.) It was no part of my duty as a judge to express a motivation to serve and protect the public, save in connection with cases which come before me. I had constantly and consistently been the subject of complaints. Lord Hailsham referred to his letter following Mr Justice Jupp's resort to him in 1980, and the two recent complaints. The *Daily Telegraph* article showed I had not heeded warnings, and this must be the result of my foolishness or a complete lack of sensitivity. I had to treat his letter as a serious warning. He would not hesitate to set the necessary procedure for dismissing me in motion if I offended again.

There was no point in my beating about the bush. I thought it best to be as blunt with Lord Hailsham as he had been with me, so that each knew where the other stood.

On 27 June 1985 I replied:

1   I have no wish to be or appear to be discourteous, but it is best if I write frankly.

2   It is unfortunate that you wrote to me on 21 June 1985 in such terms. This has made the situation worse.

3   The basic difficulty is that I am a radical, and you are a conservative (like Mr Justice Jupp, and many others in the law). I believe in changes based on public need; you seem reluctant to make any changes. (I do not impute bad faith to anybody.)

4   I am more sure than ever that it is my duty to try to improve things in certain areas that I know about (from experience and study). If necessary, I should bring the defects and my proposals for reform before the public. These areas include:

(a)   Judges and the media.
(b)   The causes of and remedies for crime.

(c)   The jury system.
(d)   Sentencing policy.
(e)   The prison system.
(f)   Plea-bargaining.
(g)   Delays in court cases.
(h)   The organisation of the legal profession.
(i)   The appointment, control and dismissal of judges and magistrates.
(j)   Pressure by the executive on the judiciary for political reasons.
(k)   Whether the office of Lord Chancellor should be abolished and replaced by a minister of justice sitting in the House of Commons.

5 I realise that you may well try to dismiss me. You are certainly ruthless enough and you may be short-sighted enough. The way in which you apparently operate section 17(4) of the Courts Act 1971 leads me to think that it may be less than a perfect system. It must be hard for you to be complainant, prosecutor, judge and jury and to play all those (conflicting) roles with equal objectivity. As I understand it, the finding of a prima facie case precedes the 'summons' (see Oulton's letter of 22 March 1985). I do not know what form the hearing takes, or even if there is one; or whether representation is permitted. There appears to be no right of appeal. This is not a fair system. Justice ought to be done, even to judges.

6 As the cards may be stacked against me from the start, under your system, you will understand that I must look elsewhere in order to protect my position and reputation: representations to parliament and the media. In that way public opinion may come to my aid. Otherwise I shall be defenceless. You are better placed than I am to gauge the likely consequences to others of all that. I have no recent experience of active politics, and matters such as the likely timing of elections are outside my scope.

7 I shall do all I can to uphold the sensible traditions of the judiciary. Anything I say or write will be the result of careful thought and research and put in moderate language. The measure will always be what I think is in the public interest.

8 To demonstrate to you – should you be interested – that I have taken my work seriously and been (I hope) consistent, I enclose some relevant documents. Copies of most of them have been sent to your office as a matter of courtesy in the past.

9 I much regret that the good relations I have had with Tom Legg will now end. He does splendid work in a most conscientious manner.

10 This and previous letters to you or Oulton have been 'open', and I may publish them in full.

11  Should you suspect that I do not mean what I write, or that I lack normal courage, I suggest you consult Peter Robinson [then number two equal in the Lord Chancellor's office]. He and I have known each other for over thirty years.

Believe me, Lord Chancellor, to be, etc.

Lord Hailsham made no reply; none was needed. The documents I sent him included my evidence to the royal commissions, some speeches to magistrates and memoranda I had sent to the Lord Chief Justice and others making suggestions for reforms in procedure in various areas.

I had decided not to back down. I had things to say to the public, and Lord Hailsham was not going to shut me up. So on 7 August 1985 the *Daily Telegraph* carried a further article by me: 'Justice delayed is Justice denied'. It was about delays in court cases, why they occur and how they could be prevented – a serious, analytical article by a man who (if I may say so) knew what he was talking about. In effect the article was a summary of what I write in Chapter 5 of this book. It began by referring to the previous article and went on: 'The Lord Chancellor then wrote threatening letters to me. But I do not work for the government. I work for the public, and if I feel there are facts it should know I will not be stifled.' There was no immediate reaction to this from on high. I suppose they felt that having threatened to sack me already, there was no point in repeating the threat. They would have to try another approach.

In September 1985 I spent five days at a sentencing seminar run most efficiently by the Lord Chancellor's office. It was at a teachers' training college at Roehampton, set in spacious grounds with a lake. I had been there in September 1977 for the same purpose. It is interesting to meet judges from other circuits, from Scotland, Northern Ireland and even places like Malaya and Hong Kong. I did not find it as stimulating in 1985 as I had eight years earlier. In 1977, as a newly appointed judge, I was hammering out my ideas on crimes and punishments, but I suppose I am more blasé now; I feel I have less to learn and more to teach. Even so, I listened to the psychiatrists, probation officers, criminologists, judges and Home Office officials on both occasions with interest; there is always something new to be learned. One impression remains the same: the lottery involved in sentencing. So much depends on which judge the defendant gets. When judges discuss, at Roehampton or at meetings on their circuits, sets of real but disguised facts and say what sentences they would pass, the range is vast: say from probation to two years' imprisonment, in an extreme case. The Court of Appeal (Criminal Division) is there to try to bring about uniformity, though the prosecution cannot appeal. (Why not? I see no logical reason for this. The objection seems to be merely that historically the prosecution in the UK has never involved itself in sentencing. It does not suggest a sentence, nor object to one that has been passed. Whatever the precedents, this could and should be changed. There are too many lenient sentences, often because a judge or recorder is afraid of appeals which he – wrongly – thinks might harm his prospect of promotion. The proposed change, giving the prosecution the right to appeal, would help to redress the balance.)

On 17 September, as I was dining, one of the Lord Chancellor's men came to me discreetly and said that Lord Justice Watkins would like to speak to me by phone after the meal. I had an idea what was coming, and I was right. Lord Justice Tasker Watkins VC assists the Lord Chief Justice administratively. Unusually, Tasker Watkins went to a grammar school (in South Wales) and did not go to university. Obviously he had a highly distinguished war record, though he modestly explains his VC by saying that as he rushed the German machine-gun nest – or whatever it was – the bullets went over his head, he being so small. On the phone he said that the Lord Chief Justice wished to see me at the Royal Courts of Justice at 9.30 next morning. An official car would take me both ways. It was about the speeches I had been making: that is what he said, though in fact the two articles in the *Daily Telegraph* had brought things to a head.

A uniformed woman chauffeur drove me to the Law Courts – in a British car, of course. I had had time to think about the line to take. I had never met Lord Lane (Shrewsbury and Cambridge – where he took firsts in classics and law; he also had a distinguished war record in the RAF, being awarded the AFC) though I knew he was a good judge, rather shy socially. I had thought it right to stand up to the Lord Chancellor, but to antagonise the Lord Chief Justice in the process might be taking things too far. There is courage in jumping off a cliff, but it is hardly commendable. I valued my substantial salary and the pension which another six years on the bench would earn. Dismissed, I would have no right even to a pension. This could be the start of the sacking procedure, for all I knew. Who would come to my aid? Public opinion was an unknown quantity. The media might be interested for a day or two, but what about the years to follow? I had no wish to end my days in penury, parading up the Strand, holding a protesting placard. There were things to do and enjoy; things to say to the public. Who would listen to a disgraced judge?

In the controversies I have had at the bar and on the bench – most of which are detailed in this book – I have never sought allies. That is one reason why I was a failure as a politician. When I was at university I wanted to get into parliament early and combine that with the bar. My record, however, is abysmal. I was on the Brighouse council from 1956–62, first for Labour and then as a Liberal. I was prospective Labour candidate for the old Barkston Ash division (Wetherby, Selby, Garforth) from 1957–9. I stood as Liberal candidate for Brighouse and Spenborough in the 1964 general election and managed to save my deposit. Then, at the age of thirty-nine, I slid out of active politics. I would have been of little use in parliament. I am not good at intrigue or flattery. I could not have attached myself to a leading figure, sycophantically worming my way into his list of future cabinet ministers. The other reason for my failure as a politician was that I could not espouse, in public, causes which I privately rejected. But this is a diversion I cannot further enlarge on here.

I suppose I am essentially a solitary person. I can be gregarious and enjoy addressing a large meeting or speaking after dinner. But I am not clubbable. I find it hard to identify too closely with groups to which I belong, whether family, sporting or professional. I do not instinctively rise to defend a group against criticism merely because I belong to it. If I am in crisis there are very few that I go to for advice or support. I listened to my late father – an intelligent, wise, subtle man who knew how to deal with people, and did so less aggressively than I have been known to. I listen to my wife, who has common-sense and an instinct for what is right – I do not mean 'the right thing' in the conventional, stuck-up sense. As I think about it I have few if any really close friends, certainly among men. I am not 'a man's man', as normally understood.

As the official car crawled through south London suburbs I knew that I had to have the Lord Chief Justice on my side. I had pushed things far enough. In future I had to take things up through him and hope improvements could be made that way. I was not too confident about that. After I made my speech to Inner Manchester magistrates on 14 October 1981 (see Appendix IV) I had two understanding, reticent letters from Lord Lane, and I had left it to him for four years to stand up to the government on penal policy, but he had been seen to do so only rarely, tentatively. His speech at the Lord Mayor of London's annual Mansion House dinner to the judges on 9 July 1985 was one such occasion. On the whole, though, he had seemed to fall in with Home Office attitudes.

I left the car and went in by the judges' entrance for the first time. I had never been behind the scenes in that great neo-Gothic cathedral known as the Law Courts. I had been through the front entrance to do cases at the bar. And my great-grandfather George worked as a stone-mason when the place was being built; it was opened in 1882. Whilst in London he met Louisa Cornaby, a cockney from Bow, and brought her back to Halifax and married her. The mix of cockney wit and Yorkshire grit produced Fred, my grandfather (a most amusing man) and his three sons included my father Arthur, and my uncle Wilfred Pickles. But this is not an autobiography, and I was not thinking of my forebears or the past as I climbed the stairs. I was thinking of myself and the future, especially the immediate future.

The Lord Chief's courteous clerk showed me where to sit in the corridor.

Workmen were clambering about and things were in a bit of a mess. Perhaps there was dry rot in that ancient place? Lord Justice Watkins passed by and, after introducing himself, told me that the Lord Chief would be ready to see me soon. Tasker Watkins struck me as a pleasant, well-meaning man, as did Lord Lane, when I went in to meet him. In his shirt-sleeves he stood and extended his welcoming hand. Lord Justice Watkins sat at the back and did not say anything during my interview. I like and respect Lord Lane, and our few minutes together that day strengthened my feeling. He is everything a judge should be – in court: patient, fair, courteous, tolerant, yet firm when necessary; Lord Lane must have few if any enemies. I have reservations about his out-of-court work (see Appendix VII), well-intentioned as it is. But I was in a court-type situation then: in the dock, before the great man.

The Lord Chancellor's office had supplied the Lord Chief with the correspondence I had had with them, and also details of previous complaints about me – as already referred to in this chapter. Lord Lane did not say, and I did not ask, precisely what he had been asked to do with me. I did not know whether it was to approve my dismissal, or merely to get me to shut up. The question of dismissal was never referred to; it was not that sort of interview. Lord Lane did say I should not have written the *Telegraph* articles. He said he had read the documents sent to him, with increasing concern. Things really had gone too far in the correspondence between Lord Hailsham and me, and it would harm the judiciary if the press got hold of it.

I decided to declare my attitude. I said I was sorry I had embarrassed Lord Lane – as I was, because although I had written the articles in good faith, and think now looking back that I was right to say what I did in them, I had nevertheless embarrassed my 'boss'. He was a good man, so it had to be regretted. I gave my undertaking not to write further newspaper articles until I retired. I thought it best to volunteer that rather than have it forced out of me, however gently.

Lord Lane was visibly relieved. He accepted my apology and undertaking. He would inform the Lord Chancellor, who would be glad to hear it. But was there anything I wanted to say? I raised the question of court delays, which were scandalous, and I saw them almost daily. The Lord Chief's reaction had, I feel obliged to record, more than a touch of complacency about it. He urged me however to raise with him any problems that might worry me. I could write or phone or even go to see him. I was prepared to leave it on that reassuring note. The interview cannot have lasted longer than about a quarter of an hour. A few more nice words from Tasker Watkins and I was on my ruminative way back to Roehampton. It had not gone badly. It had been a civilised meeting. Lord Lane and Lord Justice Watkins could not have treated me better. My flag was down, but I had lowered it honourably. I would do things the other way now; I would take them up privately with the Lord Chief, and get results that way. And in the months that followed I wrote to him several times. Things did not work out as I had hoped.

The office of Lord Chief Justice is a difficult one. The holder is in charge of the criminal law. He presides over the Court of Appeal (Criminal Division) and so gives a lead on the level of sentences for crime or for particular types of crime. He meets the judges of the Queen's Bench Division, and the twelve presiding judges from the circuits. He is in touch with the Home Secretary on such matters as sentencing policy, and with the Lord Chancellor on appointments to the high court bench and above. The strands of the establishment all meet at the top, too cosily I fear. The old-boy attitude must dominate at times: for example, when Hailsham (Eton) met Whitelaw (Winchester) and Lane (Shrewsbury).

The first Lord Chief Justice I appeared before was Lord Goddard. A judge I met when sitting at the Old Bailey said something interesting about him. (I do not sit at the fascinating, ancient, tradition-encrusted Bailey now: someone apparently blackballed me. I have my suspicions, and the reader may share them. It does not matter. I am happy to sit at Inner London crown court for two or three weeks a year. I am certainly not going to go crawling to anybody, asking to go back on the Old Bailey team.) Goddard's methods would not be tolerated today, said my friend, who is now a high court judge. He meant the refusal to let the accused have a fair say, if Goddard thought there was no defence; and his failure sometimes even to consult his colleagues on the bench in the Court of Criminal Appeal or Divisional Court, before giving judgment. But I liked Lord Goddard. He was frank and straight. Robust is the word. I never found him unfair. He certainly had no malice; there was humour and humanity just under the surface. 'Show us your best case,' he would say, as I rose in the Court of Criminal Appeal for some optimistic appellant, a pile of law reports in front of me. He said what he thought. There was no cold, careful calculation of a man anxious to please the establishment, or anybody. He was an establishment man – he loved his old school Marlborough and revelled in his success in the 100 yards at Oxford. But if he were in the job today and thought, say, the Home Office too soft on parole – as he might well – he would take it up with them forthrightly, pointing out that the public had to be protected, and judges' authority was being undermined. If that did not work, he would get up in the House of Lords and speak his mind. We live in less robust days now, welfarist days. I would not agree with a resurrected Goddard on everything – for example, his belief in capital punishment. But we miss that man. The criminal law, and the morale of those who administer it, has not been the same since he left.

The rot set in with his successor, Lord Chief Justice Parker. He was an excellent lawyer and a good and fair judge; probably an efficient administrator. But there was no robustness. He could not speak for the people, as a man of the people. Goddard had the common touch, had dealt with criminals when at the bar. Parker had not been brought up in the hurly-burly of crime. He was a civil lawyer. It was said that the first summing-up he ever heard was his own! I would be surprised if he ever encountered a criminal before he became a judge.

The slide into misplaced leniency had begun. It accelerated under the next Lord Chief Justice, Lord Widgery. He was a brilliant solicitor before the war; he did not go to university. Demobilised as a brigadier, he came to the bar. I went to lectures he gave at Gibson and Weldon's law school in Chancery Lane in 1947, as I prepared for the bar final examination. Widgery was elegant, smooth, detached, superior, with an excellent, lucid brain. He soon built up a large practice in planning law and the like. For all his good qualities, he was the wrong choice for Lord Chief Justice; he was another judge who probably never met a criminal, except perhaps in the army. The idea that top civil lawyers are superior to others in every way has some force, but Widgery showed that it can be taken too far. Intellectual brilliance is not enough. Lord Widgery came to the 1977 seminar at Roehampton, but there and afterwards he slid meekly into line with the simplistic Home Office attitude that prison sentences had to be avoided or cut because prisons and other custodial places were full. We working in the engine-room kept hoping for a message from the bridge that a new course was to be taken. But no word ever came on that; few words on anything. We drifted on.

I accept that – until near the end – Lord Widgery decided cases in court with crisp accuracy. But he seemed oblivious to the drift into weakness. As an establishment man – every Lord Chief Justice has to be that – he may have felt obliged to go along with the Lord Chancellor and the Home Secretary. And it is right to acknowledge that one who has been chosen for that high job by no less than the Prime Minister must find it hard to turn and stand up to his fellows in the establishment, even if he feels he should. Biting the hand that has selected one; stepping out of line; letting the side down: establishment people do not do those things. It simply is not done, except by outsiders. Eventually the spectacle of Lord Widgery on the bench embarrassed all who knew he was ill, and must have puzzled those who did not know. His intellect had been damaged. He went on too long, but who in the establishment was going to be cad enough to tell him or say so publicly?

Lord Lane is an improvement on Lord Widgery. He has a firmer hand on the tiller. In court one could not find a better Lord Chief Justice for individual cases. He is a strong sentencer when sitting in the crown court, as he showed when he came to Leeds. I have reservations about Lord Lane, however, and it is pointless to conceal them. I refer to his failure, as I see it, to be seen to stand up to the government on penal policy; his reticence to speak up on that in public; and his apparent complacency – I must not shrink from the word, much as I like him as a man and a judge – on such matters as court delays and the flood of bail applications which increasingly weigh on all circuit judges.

I have to go into all this in order to explain why I withdrew my undertaking not to write more newspaper articles, and why I wrote my *Guardian* article of 14 February 1986, 'Kilmuir Rules – OK?', which has had such an effect on my life.

Before I give details I must in fairness set out what I assume would be Lord Lane's case, were he to be asked for it and to reply: 'It's all very well Pickles talking. He does a lot of that, and he's embarrassed me more than once. Mine is a very hard job. I wasn't ambitious for it – sitting in the Lords is a lot easier – but they asked me, so I thought I ought to take it on. Pickles only sees part of what I have to do. I start work at the Law Courts at 8.30 a.m., five days a week, and I don't push off when the court rises at 4 p.m. I take work home. How often does Pickles do that? I sit in court for most of each day, but there are dozens of other matters to see to – administrative matters. I have to keep an eye on a lot of things, and a lot of people. Everything that happens in every crown court is my responsibility. I don't enjoy pontificating in public. Nor is it part of my job to get across with the Home Office. I have to get on with them, so far as I can. They have a hard job. It's not their fault or mine that crime has mushroomed over the last twenty years. Pickles is good at criticising people and falling out with them, but that isn't my style. It isn't the way to get results. I get them by slow, quiet, patient effort. That doesn't take me into the headlines, but I've no wish for that. Tell Pickles to pipe down and leave things to me. He's only a very small cog in the machine. It's time he realised it. He isn't even a high court judge, thank God. How he got to be a circuit judge is beyond me, but we have to put up with him for a bit yet, I suppose, till he retires and hopefully goes abroad, to somewhere distant, and writes plays or something harmless like that.'

After I gave my undertaking to Lord Lane I wrote to him on several occasions, raising various matters. Increasingly I felt unhappy with his response. The main effect of my undertaking had been to shut me up. Raising things by writing to Lord Lane had not worked. Then on 23 January 1986 I listened to a programme by Hugo Young on BBC Radio 4 about the bar, one of a series 'Pillars of Society'. On the same day Young wrote an article in the *Guardian*, 'Voices you can't hear under the Woolsack'. In both, that able commentator lamented Lord Hailsham's efforts to prevent judges from speaking in public, including his radio programme: several had been ready to appear until warned off by the Lord Chancellor's office. On 27 January the *Guardian* published a letter in reply by Lord Hailsham. I had correspondence and phone-calls with

Hugo Young. I realised that – to quote the beginning of my *Guardian* article – 'I have things to say that must be said.' But I had first to withdraw my undertaking.

On 5 February 1986 I wrote the letter to Lord Lane that is in Appendix VII. I lavished gallons of midnight oil on my article. I had to get it right, or there could be disaster for me. I was defying a man who had the power to sack me and had already threatened to use it. I had to set out my case in a responsible, judge-like manner, or I would give ammunition to my detractors. It would have been easy to say to myself, 'What does it matter? Let the Lord Chancellor and his men have it their way. Have an easy life, like most other judges. Carry on for another five years, then grab your pension and your tax-free gratuity and do and say what you like, go where you like.' But I am not made like that. I hesitate to dignify it by calling it conscience. I am no more moral than the next judge. The public had to know what was going on: that is what drove me on into the cavern of death, as it might turn out to be. The law and the way it works; the way judges work: the public had a right to know. We do it for *them*, or should. Lord Hailsham is not running a secret society or private club – though at times I feel I am a member of both.

A few days before my article was due to be published, Mr Justice Taylor, the senior presiding judge of my circuit, rang me. I have known Peter Taylor for many years, and there is a lot I could write here, but he is at the moment my immediate superior, so I shall restrict myself. He is an interesting character. From a Jewish family in Newcastle, ability and effort took him to Newcastle Royal Grammar School and Cambridge. As his burly frame confirms, he played rugby for his county. He also plays the piano well. The flame of ambition burns fiercely within him, and why not? It is said he is being groomed to be the next Lord Chief Justice, and that does not surprise me. He was a very capable advocate at the bar: hard-working, firm, fair. He always grasped the facts, and his grasp of the law is adequate though probably not outstanding. I never appeared before him when he was a recorder, but I hear and believe that he is a very good judge. If he does get the top job – and no lack of effort or discretion will hinder him – he will be in the Lord Lane mould, both in and out of court. Excellent in court, but not so good behind the scenes. I have seen Peter Taylor at work, presiding over us circuit judges at meetings and dealing with points we have raised. Frankly, he has disappointed me. To my mind, he lacks imagination and drive.

When he rang me, Mr Justice Taylor said he understood I was going into the press again. I said I was. Had it been sent off? Yes. So it was too late to stop it, he lamented. (He even knew the day on which the article was to be published. I assume that his information came via someone in the Lord Chancellor's office. But where had *they* got it? Is there a mole in the *Guardian*?) My local boss went on to say that he had read the correspondence I had had with the Lord Chancellor, who could not be expected to back down. As I read that, the Lord Chancellor's office were trying to stop the article by yet a further threat. I said that if Lord Hailsham did try to dismiss me, the public fuss might be bigger than Westland. 'Oh, who's threatening now?' asked the judge.

When the article appeared, the reaction to it was immediate and torrential, but not in the way I had in bleak moments feared. I was prey for the judge-hungry media. At last, a judge who would talk to them. TV, radio and the press were on to me. My address in *Who's Who* is – because of threats to my life – 'c/o Leeds Crown Court', and I happened to be sitting there, so it was easy for them to ring. Some were surprised that they got through to me immediately (at first; I had to put up the shutters eventually). I rejected most approaches. I gave a telephone interview to *The Times*, which on 21 February printed a story on its front page in heavy type headed 'Judge Challenge to Hailsham over "gag" ', with my photograph in full-bottomed judicial wig – taken when I was sworn in. That same day BBC TV 'News at Six' and 'News at Nine' – different groups, surprisingly – both wanted me on, with Lord Hailsham, if possible. I do not know what his lordship's office told them when they said they could offer (as I remember) twelve million viewers, but I said that publicity was not the name of my game. I was trying to push forward the frontiers of judicial availability, but it had to be done gradually, responsibly. I turned down Eddie Shah's *Today:* they wanted me to do an article for the first issue. I also rejected BBC TV's 'Out of Court'; they had never had a judge on, and would soon close down until October. I said that I might be able to do it in October, but if I was not careful people would think I had gone completely over the top.

I did an interview for BBC Radio 4's 'Law in Action'. Amiable Joshua Rozenberg, with the silver voice, came to stay overnight at my house, and we did the recording there. That was my first time on radio. The only time I had been on television was in the 1964 general election, when I had to speak, 'live', for two minutes: I found it terrifying. I enjoyed the radio recording; I did not find it hard. Perhaps this was a medium I could use to discuss ideas. I was soon able to arrange that as BBC Radio 4 from Manchester came to see me and read some of my writings. I agreed to do two programmes (see p.68). On 7 March I addressed the British Legal Association, a solicitors' pressure group, at their annual meeting at Cheltenham. They had telephoned on the day the *Guardian* article came out, suggesting 'All power corrupts' as a subject. There was a report in *The Times* on 10 March 1986 and in the *Guardian*'s 'Out of Court' feature on 14 March.

Another thing that came directly out of my *Guardian* article was this book. I had a letter from a member of my publishers and within days he came to stay overnight and discuss the project. Material I had already written had to be re-shaped and added to. A contract signed, I began the work with relish on holiday in Ireland at Easter 1986, getting up at 4 or 5 a.m. – and going to bed about 9.30 p.m. There is no more contented time for me than writing when it is (apparently) going well.

The only hostile reaction to my article that I saw or heard about was Bernard Levin's piece in *The Times* demanding my dismissal. I hope no one ever dismisses Bernard. I would miss those sinuous sentences that go on for ever. He has a lively mind, and we need him in this tradition-encrusted, sclerotic country. I have never met him, but I have now met many media representatives, and it has been as stimulating as bathing in a mountain stream. Here are lively, alert, inquiring, unstuffy people – my sort of people. In the law I sometimes feel we are ruled by the dead: men like Lord Kilmuir. I prefer people like Alan Rusbridger, who had a long profile on me in the *Guardian* on 26 May 1986.

There was speculation in the press and elsewhere that I was about to be sacked. At 11 a.m. on 21 February my court-clerk brought an ominous sounding message, which presumably came from the Lord Chancellor's office via the circuit adminstrator (who, until recently, used to work in that office, and will presumably go back there later. He went to Marlborough, and though he is not yet in *Who's Who* I guess he is Oxbridge). In an hour the Lord Chancellor was to issue a statement about that day's report in *The Times*. But no word came. All the publicity arising from my article produced not one word from above. No curt, threatening letters, nothing. That was significant, and supported my theory. Going fully out into the public arena had looked dangerous, but seemingly had brought safety. I had a hot-line to the media now. Ministers and bureaucrats who fume and threaten behind blind windows go silent when the light is let in. The media, and so public opinion, are influences they fear.

I had heartening letters from lawyers and other members of the public. A member of the Royal Commission on Criminal Procedure wrote that when they were sitting, the Lord Chancellor's department told them, 'Whatever else, read Pickles,' referring to my evidence. Lord Hailsham's name kept cropping up in letters. The grievances against him are, for all I know, unjustifed, but it is the complainants' feelings of impotence that worry me. They have dealt with a man whose power seems boundless and his decisions beyond question. There is a case for an ombudsman in this area, and some correspondents think I can be that, but I cannot.

What about the Kilmuir Rules now? Boiled down, Kilmuir had two objections to judges appearing on radio or television and so (logically) in any other medium. One was that judges might be 'brought within the focus of criticism'. The other was that judges could not take part in 'entertainment'. The Kilmuir letter did not refer to preserving judicial independence.

In his letter to all judges of 25 January 1980 enclosing the Kilmuir letter, Lord Hailsham wrote: 'The independence of the judges depends on their immunity from direct criticism,' which could not be preserved unless judges refrained from expressing opinions, off the bench and to the public at large, on matters of current interest. But Lord Hailsham allows some senior judges to express their opinions. And why should judges be immune from criticism? We should welcome it, as should everybody also in official positions. That can be an antidote to the complacency which grounds so many of our national ills. If criticism is rash, I ignore it; if it is sense, I act on it. What is wrong with that? But how can criticism make me less independent? That question lies at the heart of the Kilmuir controversy, and I have not seen an answer. Who are going to take my independence from me? How will they do it? The only persons who have threatened my out-of-court independence are Lord Hailsham and Sir Derek Oulton.

As for Kilmuir's reference to entertainment, it was a bit priggish. I hope listeners to 'Law in Action' were entertained in the sense of being interested in what I said. Such entertainment cannot be wrong today. We need more of it. The public are entitled to know why we judges do what we do.

There is the further anomaly that Lords Kilmuir and Hailsham have both said that a lord chancellor has no disciplinary power over judges. So when the media approach us, we have a discretion whether to accept. Yet lord chancellors have tried to snuff out that discretion by getting a majority of judges to agree to go to the Lord Chancellor's office for 'advice', which every circuit judge knows will almost certainly be in his case, 'Don't do it'. That 'agreement' cannot bind the judges who did not, in fact, agree. There is no way in which an informal counting of judicial heads can alter the constitutional position that judges do have a discretion. I intend to hold on to mine. I decline to surrender it to anyone – though I have a duty to act responsibly.

The Kilmuir letter is a dead letter now, so far as I am concerned. Its rules are illogical and against the public interest. I shall make no more approaches to the Lord Chancellor's office. I shall use my discretion, discreetly. But there have to be rules, whether imposed by oneself or by others. The rules I shall act on, and commend to other judges, are:

1   In or out of court a judge should act so as to retain or gain the confidence of the public, including those whose cases he may have to try.
2   A judge should only go into the media if he feels he has something important to say on a topic he knows about from experience and study, and which he should communicate to the public. He should be dignified (not pompous) in manner, and balanced in content.
3   A judge must avoid party politics, and reference to cases he has tried or may try.

I shall spread myself thinly, but I shall spread myself as no circuit judge has done before. I work for the public and I am accountable to them. I have things to tell them that they are entitled to know. Some in the law will disapprove, but the public must be the judges here. If I sense that they want me to shut up, I shall.

## How Judges are Dismissed

High court judges can only be removed from office on an address by both houses of parliament to the crown. This was first laid down in the Act of Settlement 1700. It makes them virtually irremovable. For some reason, parliament has not given the same protection to circuit judges, who can be removed by the Lord Chancellor for misbehaviour or incapacity: section 17(4) Courts Act 1971.

Incapacity must mean mental or physical incapacity, disabling a judge from doing his job properly. What does misbehaviour mean? So far as I know, it has not been defined. My friend Bruce Campbell QC – he was at Roehampton in 1977 and sat at Inner London crown court – was understandably dismissed after pleading guilty to a customs offence. Even with criminal offences, however, it is not clear what amounts to misbehaviour. A parking or speeding offence would not. But suppose there were ten speeding offences, leading to disqualification? Driving with excess alcohol has not been treated as judicial misbehaviour: two court of appeal judges and more than one circuit judge have been convicted but remained in office. What about causing death by dangerous driving? Would it depend whether the judge went to prison? There should be guidelines. As we have seen, Lord Hailsham's view is that writing a newspaper article – albeit carefully written and closely argued – can be misbehaviour.

Over twenty years ago a county court judge, who had been on my circuit whilst at the bar, resigned when he was divorced for adultery with one woman. (Fortunately he had private means; and a few years later he was 'rehabilitated' by being made a circuit judge.) That would not happen today. But suppose a judge committed adultery with twenty women, or his wife's petition alleged repeated physical violence? Can it really be that the Lord Chancellor is free to decide what is misbehaviour, unencumbered by rules except those he chooses to lay down? The answer is yes, apparently. It used to be said of Equity that it was 'as long as the chancellor's foot', but even Equity settled down into established rules. Parliament should define misbehaviour, but how could parliamentary time be found for the benefit of a few judges? And how can the Lord Chancellor be expected to introduce or advocate procedure limiting his power?

There is the further injustice that no procedure or appeal are provided for; I certainly know of none, though I have not enquired. The Lord Chancellor is complainant, prosecutor, judge and jury. Justice should be done, even to judges. One hopes that a judge's dismissal will arise rarely. But one circuit judge has been dismissed; I have been threatened with it. What does a disgraced judge do for a living? Any pension is discretionary, and proportionate to time served on the bench. Though I might earn some money, uncertainly, as a writer, most disgraced judges would be hard put to avoid penury. An ex-circuit judge is not allowed, so I believe, to return to the bar, even if that were practicable.

I know one recorder whom the Lord Chancellor disqualified after a contested divorce in which the recorder appeared unbalanced – though when he has appeared before me as a barrister he has not been like that. I can understand the decision in that case, though again: there is no procedure or independent tribunal. What about lay magistrates? A few years ago a man and a woman were magistrates on the same bench; each was married to another. For years it was known to many that they were having an affair with each other. When it became public knowledge – through a divorce, I assume – Lord Hailsham dismissed them. I know only what I saw in the press, and I am sure that the Lord Chancellor listened to them. But I believe they feel aggrieved, understandably. They were tried and convicted by their prosecutor. Lord Hailsham is no longer young; he is known to have strict, orthodox Christian views. He may be out of touch with current public opinion.

What are my recommendations, then? Misbehaviour should be carefully defined, and procedure laid down for deciding whether it has been established and if so what the penalty should be. For what it is worth, I would define judicial misbehaviour thus: such conduct as is likely substantially to reduce the confidence of the public as a whole in a judge's ability to reach correct decisions in the cases he tries. The Lord Chancellor should 'prosecute', but a board or committee similar to that suggested for making judicial appointments, consisting of judges and laymen, should be set up. There should be a right of appeal to another body. None of this would be hard to arrange.

# Chapter 3

## The Role of Judges in Society

I am here concerned with the role we judges ought to have. No one who knows and cares and looks at things impartially could be satisfied with the present position. Judges are chosen by a government minister, mainly from barristers. They are not trained to be judges, except superficially. Their independence of the establishment, although it exists, is limited: most judges have conservative backgrounds and all go in fear of the Lord Chancellor and his senior civil servants. Most judges see their function as trying cases put before them, then going home. They rarely open their mouths in public outside court. They do the job as it has been done for centuries. Yet it could be done so much better.

Our judges ought to be the supreme guardians of the people. At present that role is mainly filled by parliament and the media, but imperfectly by both. The media have a key role in a democracy. They expose injustice and corruption, and the threat that they may do so inhibits some who would otherwise be tyrannical. In recent years investigative reporting by the press, television and radio has been a useful corrective. *Private Eye*, despite its excesses, has led the way in exposing public scandals. But there are limits to the media's powers: the law of libel is hard on and can ruin those who seek to expose misdeeds; the Official Secrets Act ties their hands, as does the obsession which official decision-makers have to operate in secrecy.

Years ago I was on Brighouse Council, and I learned a lot. All committee meetings were in private. Committee minutes were given to the local press on the strict understanding that they were not to be commented on before they went to the full council for confirmation. What arrogance, one may say. Yet the aldermen and councillors were not villains. They were ordinary decent Brighousers, doing what came naturally. (I protested, but I was a lone voice.)

Are politicians the guardians of the people? Imperfectly. Even in a so-called democracy they can be the people's oppressors. In this country the executive is so powerful that we are approaching an elected dictatorship. A prime minister with a large majority in the House of Commons, as with Mrs Thatcher in her second term, can virtually have his or her way on any matter of policy if she keeps the support of her party in the House. This is unhealthy.

The UK needs a written constitution incorporating a bill of rights, as

Lord Scarman has proposed. At present a simple act of parliament, rushed through in a day, can make or unmake the law to any extent. It could, in theory, set up a dictatorship. A written constitution would give more power to judges, who would even be able to declare a statute invalid as contrary to the constitution. This happens in the United States, as part of their system of checks and balances.

Increased power for the judiciary would have a steadying influence in constitutional affairs. Judges would be public guardians by reason of their independence.

But how independent are our judges? Under the present system, only those without ambition can claim full independence. I shall never come up for re-election, not having been elected in the first place. I am not weighed down by the stone that hampers politicians who have or seek electable office or prime-ministerial favour. That stone prevents politicians from saying what they really think. They need to curry favour with others; in the polling booths, or the back-street corridors where fingers are pointed at or hands held out to those selected for ministerial posts. A politician who knows what is good for him cannot lift his head defiantly and speak his mind about anything. He must always look craftily over his shoulder at those who perpetually peer at him: voters and party bosses.

At present, ambitious judges have a stone that may be heavier than a politician's. I mean those who seek something from the Lord Chancellor. A judge is entitled to look for promotion, a title beyond the one that goes with his post, membership of a Royal Commission, a job on the parole board, or any of the many favours which 'they' can give with a nod of the head or the scratch of a pen. But it should not entail the sometimes cringing conformity I have seen in judge after judge. An MP, arguably, may even be freer than a judge. He is answerable to thousands of electors, and more than a few party workers. A judge only has to offend one man, or his chief cohort, and his prospects may be for ever blighted.

The bench is not equipped yet to play the full role I foresee for it. There are other necessary changes in addition to a new system of selection and promotion. We judges are not well trained. It is not enough to have studied and practised law: we need to learn more about sociology, psychology, criminology and penology; we should know more about how criminals are dealt with abroad. The English bench as a whole is too ignorant, isolated, and, of course, self-satisfied.

According to an article in the *Listener* on 24 July 1986, Lord Scarman thinks on similar lines:

> In many ways, Lord Scarman is encouraging lawyers to prepare for a more central role in society . . . He wants legal practitioners, academics and students to look at what other disciplines have to offer and at what is best in the American and European legal traditions. In short, he is

intent on breaking down barriers in society, whether between lawyers and politicians, *judges and the public* [my italics], Protestants and Catholics, police and citizens, black and white.

Lord Scarman has shown what an enlightened judge can do, even under our unenlightened system. If Britain is to drag itself out of its present slothfulness, there must be reasoned discussion and argument, in which we judges can assist.

Early in 1986 I was asked by the BBC to take part in two radio programmes, and I agreed, much to the disapproval of the Lord Chancellor and his top advisers and – though they did not say so to me – many judges, I feel sure. (One colleague did say to me, however, 'I am with you all the way, Jimmy – *anonymously*.') The first programme was about the permissive society. I interviewed a prostitute in the 'red light' district of Leeds, and we discussed her way of life, its earnings and dangers and the need for licensed brothels. I discussed 'page three' girls with Clare Short MP, who had introduced into parliament a bill (which failed) to ban such photographs. The second programme was on punishment. I met three men I had sentenced in the past, and discussed how far they thought prison was a deterrent. I discussed deterrence further with Professor Terence Morris JP. The broadcasts were not an outstanding success, though they were something new. Looking back, we tried to do too much. We could have had a whole programme on prostitution, another on 'page three' and a third on drugs. As it was, there were only twenty-five minutes in each programme, which required very tight editing. There was not enough time to explore all the arguments. But we showed what *might* be done, and I hope one day to resume the experiment. I certainly found it fascinating work.

When I sit in court, or express myself outside it, to whom am I responsible? For whom am I speaking? In a narrow sense, I apply or explain the law as laid down by parliament and superior courts. More broadly, I see myself as representing the public as a whole, or at least its right-thinking members who are, one hopes, still the majority. I am doing it for them. Not for the establishment, the Lord Chancellor or the politicians, but for the public, the men and women 'on top of the Clapham omnibus', as judges sometimes put it when referring to the reasonable person.

But what do those on the top of that bus think of us judges? That is the question. In the eyes of many, it is a 'them and us' situation. Judges are thought of as remote, august beings, to be feared, certainly; to be respected, one hopes; but not to be identified with. For we come from a narrow, privileged class, as they see it. We are inaccessible. Even probation officers have complained about that, to me, referring to judges generally. They want to meet us and get their views across to us, but they can see no way.

But judges can never be entirely 'of the people'. We are not 'common' people, and it is no use pretending we are. We must remain a bit like surgeons, for example, to those who do not know us. Those in both professions are the subject of mystique, making life-and-death decisions, using skills that others do not have or understand. The patient being wheeled into the operating theatre and the litigant being directed into the courtroom are submitting themselves to those who can make them or mar them; heal them or destroy them; enrich them or impoverish them; release them into light or lock them into darkness. The victim in both situations should feel confident that he is in hands that are safe, directed by supreme skill and learning. To see a surgeon drunk – even off-duty, or a judge urinating in the street – necessarily off-duty, would detract from such confidence. An onlooker would say, 'I wouldn't like to get into *his* hands. He's no better than me.'

This feeling of 'otherness', however, must be kept within bounds. If the trade unionist thinks of the soberest of judges, 'He is from another class altogether; the ruling-class, the bosses, the ones who own it all and run it all, mostly for their own benefit,' then he can have no confidence in the judge's impartiality and so, in his mind, there can be no justice.

How should a judge behave to those who appear before him? With dignity, but not pomposity. I am for an unstuffy, down-to-earth style; I try to use simple, homely language, but not slang. Lord Denning has demonstrated that even the most complex points of law or sets of facts can be broken down and put simply. Admirers of plain English should read any reported judgment of his. Lucidity can be taken no further, though he over-does it at times – too many sentences without verbs, and so on. Behaviour out of court by a judge should be on similar lines: sensible, sober, unstuffy, no strutting or condescending.

Judges differ in their outlooks, their attitudes, and this is bound to be so. We have all had different experiences; we all look at life through our own lenses. I see as one of my aims the need to protect the oppressed weak from the oppressive strong. There is a problem here. The establishment itself – even the government – can be oppressive. Yet a judge is part of the establishment, so how can he stand up to it? The answer is that he should be able to; if he cannot, he is unfit for his office. And he is more likely to stand up if he does not come from the institutions which feed the establishment: public schools, Oxbridge, and – let us be frank about it – Tory households. This is not to accuse anyone of anything they know to be wrong, nor to condemn all Tories as unfit to be judges – that would put most of today's bench in the dock!

What *is* this thing we call the establishment? It is a certain type of mind. It reads *The Times* and the *Daily Telegraph*, but not the *Guardian*. It instinctively aligns itself with the Church of England, but not the nonconformists, and most definitely not with the agnostics or aethists. It sympathises with the leaders rather than the led, in the forces, industry or any other institution. It expects to eat in the directors' dining-room, not the workers' canteen. But life is not as simple as that, of course. There are trade unionists who join the establishment by gaining a peerage. Thus does the establishment strengthen and renew itself, as does the aristocracy (part of the establishment). The aristocracy does it by admitting some of the rich and — less reluctantly — the expensively educated sons of the rich.

It happens that I do not identify with the establishment, whereas most judges certainly do, even though they may not have done so when they set out in the law. Perhaps the true distinction is between those who are on the whole satisfied with things as they find them and resentful of those who suggest otherwise, on the one hand, and those who see and urge the need for changes, on the other hand. The older I get, the more radical I feel, like Gladstone (though I lack his high qualities), who began his political life as 'the rising hope of the stern, unbending Tories' and went increasingly to the left. He probably could not explain that, any more than I can explain my own inclinations. Gladstone would probably have attributed it to God; I do not.

What about wigs and gowns? They symbolise tradition. Some would say they stand for all that is antique in the legal profession. Barristers and judges wear wigs because in the eighteenth century all 'gentlemen' did, and we went on doing it when the rest had stopped. It is said that barristers wear dark suits and black gowns because the courts went into mourning when Queen Anne died, and nobody told them to go back to whatever was worn before. Former British colonies, such as Australia, New Zealand and the new African nations, still have wigs and gowns. Wigs are not worn in Canada. In the United States, judges wear gowns but advocates wear ordinary suits.

Some say that barristers dress up as a symbol that they are only playing a part, putting forward a case in which they do not have to believe, like an actor. That cannot apply to a judge. The regalia worn by barristers and judges must have an intimidating effect on lay people which goes beyond the need for dignity. If one were thinking it all out afresh, there would be a thin case for wearing wigs but a much stronger one for gowns. Should we make the change, then? I would agree, but a lot of people would object, fiercely. They would see the break with tradition as a revolutionary act. They would assume that, if we threw wigs out of the window, other things of more value would go with them. All in all, it is probably not worth arguing about; it would cause too much fuss. There are other things that matter more. Wigs are a bit like royalty: an imperfect system, lacking logic and embodying false values, but it is probably best to let it be and turn to more important areas.

# Chapter 4

# *Why Crime has Increased*

This is a difficult area: why has a man gone wrong when his father and grandfather never did? The man does not know; nor does his father. Such notions as they have are likely to be superficial, such as 'He fell in with the wrong crowd'. Statistics can tell us that crime has increased enormously since the 1939 war, but not *why*.

I have thought about the causes of crime in the light of my experience over the years with criminals. I have prosecuted them, defended them and judged them. Have I got the right answers? Who can be sure? I cannot. My ideas tend to modify all the time, so my propositions have to be tentative. I am concerned mainly with crimes of dishonesty and violence rather than with bigamy or dangerous driving, for example.

The post-1939 war increase in crime has not been confined to one country, continent or social system. It has happened – though figures are hard to get – in communist countries. What is it that has swept across the globe, turning harmless people into harmful ones? I can only deal with this country; I have lived through it and seen the levels rise year by year.

I think this is the key. As new generations have grown up they have thought about things differently from those who went before. This is not bad in itself. Stagnation is bad; change is to be welcomed. We are all affected by the trends in thinking, in attitudes of mind, of the groups in which we live. There is the family group. There are working groups; mine has been the legal profession. There is the group formed by society as a whole, welded together in its attitudes by the modern media. When very young our thinking is influenced by those who bring us up – ideally our own parents in a family setting. The influences on us there are the strongest and longest lasting. As our contacts widen we meet teachers, other children and neighbours; we watch television, read newspapers and books. All this is shaping and re-shaping our attitudes.

Why do some trends of thought replace others? Why is religious belief replaced by agnosticism, and acceptance of authority by rebelliousness? Why does the hand that doffs the cap become in the son the hand that hurls the ripe tomato? Why does restraint become in the next generation a search for sensation? The answers are to be found partly in the questions. In a free, alert, questing society, children react against those of their parents' attitudes which they think outmoded. My own three children have done in some ways, and I respect them for it. I sometimes think I have learnt more from them than they from me. The thought of living with a woman, unblessed by marriage, would have sent my parents into apoplexy. I would never have done it when young. My own children and their generation think differently and I now agree with them. It is the quality of the relationship that matters, and not whether one has gone through a ceremony and obtained a piece of paper. It has taken me decades to stand back and look at the attitudes I had when I grew up, and to modify them.

In this chapter I shall try to isolate some of the changes in thinking that have taken place, and which seem to me to have caused increases in crime. I am not saying that all these changes or trends are bad in themselves, but some of their side-effects are. Although I must deal with the changed attitudes separately, they interweave and overlap and cannot be disentangled from each other.

## The Decline in Religious Belief

If I had to pick one event as contributing most to the decline in religious belief (by which I mainly mean belief in the Christian religion) which we have seen in the UK in this century, I would select the publication of Charles Darwin's *Origin of Species* in 1859. Whatever some Christian apologists may say, the theory of evolution began to undermine confidence in the church and its teachings. Previously there was general acceptance that the Bible had been inspired by 'God' and held eternal truths. Darwin showed that the world did not begin as the Bible says; parts of that book are no more than allegory at best. This is the first step towards total scepticism. Most people in the UK are probably sceptics today. I do not say that most people are total sceptics; only a few think deeply enough to be that. But the attitude towards religion that most people have is very different from that of their grandparents.

My parents were born at the turn of the century, 1900 and 1901: my mother is just a Victorian and my father was just an Edwardian. When they were children Sunday was a special day; they wore their 'Sunday' clothes and were forbidden to play games. When I was nine – in 1934 – I went to stay with my maternal grandparents to escape the scarlet fever which had seized my mother and my four sisters. My grandparents lived in a through terraced house near to a public playground in Halifax. The WC was outside and they had a front room as 'the room', which was only used and warmed by its open fire on Sundays and other special days like Christmas. On other days it was cold, silent and unwelcoming and had a fusty smell.

Every Saturday evening a man from the council came to padlock the swings and chain the slide in the playground lest a child break the sabbath;

on Monday morning he came to do the unlocking. This must have stopped during the war, which brought many changes including the playing of light music on Sunday by John Reith's BBC: the troops had to fight on Sundays and so deserved to listen to their sort of music on that day too. This presumably went against the grain with god-like Reith.

The sabbath was not strictly observed in my family when I was young. We did not have to put on our Sunday best or refrain from games. We went to the C of E at Christmas and for christenings, weddings and funerals. I seem to remember going to Sunday school for a time. My parents taught me to say prayers, and until I was about thirteen I said them and believed there was someone listening at the other end. I got large doses of 'divinity' at my boarding-school. We all went to chapel every evening, marching in and out in a line; we went twice on Sundays. There was one Jewish boy: he was allowed to sit in the organ-loft. I can still taste the wood of the pew in front as I knelt and bent my head as if in prayer. I found church services boring and I watched the clock throughout. I still do, on the rare occasions when I go. It is all so predictable, repetitive and empty.

I was christened when a baby but my wife was not. We were married in Halifax parish church. My parents and grandparents would have been shocked by the thought of a register office. Illogically I also would have found the ceremony there less impressive than in that fine old church. Our three children were not christened when babies; we let them decide for themselves. We did not press our agnosticism on them. Two have become committed Christians and the third has followed Indian mystics sporadically. They all behave well; they are kind and thoughtful, like their mother.

By puberty I had become sceptical about the historical soundness of Christianity. I was not prepared to conform with doctrines which I could not accept intellectually. At the age of sixty-one that is still my attitude. I cannot accept the Christian account of the making of the world, the existence of an all-knowing, all-powerful personal God or the sending to Earth of his son. The virgin birth of Jesus seems most unlikely. As for the Holy Ghost and the Holy Trinity: hard to grasp and unlikely to have any existence outside men's minds. Religions have been made by men. They cater for human needs: to explain why we are here on this planet; to cushion us from the fear of death and oblivion; to foster hopes of immortality and reunion with dead loved ones. It must be comforting to believe; a believer must have a happier life than an agnostic. God will look after the believer; the priest will wash away his sins; there is no need to worry about life's tragedies. But to see the practical advantages of 'faith' is not enough to make me embrace it. Perhaps it is the lawyer in me, but I cannot shut my eyes and take the leap into the dark that faith requires in those in whom it was not instilled from the cradle by parents, teachers and priests.

Some people ask me: 'Do you then not believe in anything?' Of course I do. One has to have values by which to live one's life. I start with what I know to be true: that life exists on Earth and that its highest form is man. All life has the means to reproduce itself. This has gone on for millions of years. Who am I to interfere with or go against that? It seems logical and right to protect and enhance life, and especially human life. What does that is good. What does not is bad. There is no need to be mystical about it, however satisfying that may be to one side of us: the theatre is the place for that. There is certainly no need for fanaticism. Those zealots who believe they have the one true faith and that God is on their side have always been a menace. Such religions give men excuses for cruelty as with the Aztecs, the Inquisition, the Nazis and the mullahs of modern Iran. The cruel streak in men should be suppressed, and the life-enhancers can do that. Nor do we need to build an organisation, a priesthood or a caste. Such bodies become ends in themselves. Those who run them tend to do so in their own interests and to the detriment of their followers.

The point I have been leading up to is this. There used to be a feeling in most people in this country – and in other Western countries – that to break the Ten Commandments was a sin, wrong in itself regardless of the consequences to others. Other religions have similar codes and similar attitudes towards breaches of them. My grandparents, although they did not go to church regularly, regarded theft as morally wrong. God was looking over their shoulders and could call them to account later. Meanwhile it would be on their consciences. Who thinks like that today? Not many. Take stealing at work, which is very common now; I try such cases. I sometimes feel that every employee of a large firm who gets the chance does it. This is too cynical, but those who do it – and how many get detected and prosecuted? – see no shame in the deed but only in its discovery. Similarly with the army of shoplifters.

There are other factors as well as the decline in religious belief. Such thieves do not see themselves as criminals or as doing anything very wrong. Lots of people do it. It is covered by insurance. No one individual in the firm or shop will suffer. The bosses have their own fiddles – income-tax, work being done at home by the firm's workers. An employee may feel he is being exploited, and in stealing is only getting back part of what should rightly be his. Those who steal at their work or from shops would in the main never pick a pocket or burgle a house: they would regard that as *really* wrong. This is the state that we have got into, after abandoning belief in absolute religious values.

I sentenced a woman in her twenties who had shoplifted repeatedly, taking over a thousand pounds worth of goods by clever means. She worked for a local authority and her parents were both professional people. Her unhappy marriage was said to have contributed to her wrongdoing. I said to her young counsel that at one time such a woman would not have done such things: religion would have inhibited her. He did not seem to understand what I was talking about.

A few years ago I called at a Scottish port in a small boat and I needed diesel. I was directed to a tanker lorry and the man in charge drew off six gallons. When I asked him how much it was he said, 'Oh, just give the boy something,' referring to his young companion. His employer would not miss the six gallons. He was ready to do me, a stranger, a favour and get no advantage for himself, and the notion that he was stealing from his employer was of no importance to him. This shows how low our standards of honesty have sunk. That man's grandfather would never have acted as he did. To his surprise, I insisted on paying the full price. No doubt he thought me a fool as he pocketed the lot. I suppose I should have told his employers, but I had neither the heart nor the time.

## Egalitarianism

The statement that I am for equality will not surprise anyone. Who would publicly advocate or defend inequality today? We are all egalitarians now. We all *say* we are. How is equality to be defined? Equality of opportunity is the most important aspect. In the UK we do not have even that yet; bright children can climb the educational ladder to the top, even if they come from families which have little money. But parents with money can ensure that their mediocre children get to the top, educationally and otherwise. One sees many examples in politics, at the bar, on the bench and in the City. Those who came from the 'right' families and went to the 'right' schools and universities have got on, despite in many cases the lack of real talent. We have a long way to go before we catch up with other European countries and the USA, where privilege and class distinctions mean less than here.

Even so, in the last, say, hundred years there has been a great levelling-up. In all previous times in this country, and many other countries, most people were kept down, their backs bent in work when they could get it, their bodies hit by ills when they could not. It was hard to exist from day to day. The many could not hope to enjoy what the few had, and this is still so in many lands. In the UK, despite high unemployment and all the waste, anguish and deprivation involved, the masses have in the main been freed from evils like starvation, lack of medical care, gross lack of educational opportunity and no roof over their heads. *The masses have also been freed from the acceptance of their own inferiority.*

In former days most people like my grandparents never hoped to have the standards of life which are taken for granted today, with many who live on state benefits having a colour television set and often a video recorder too. They accepted their lowly lot in the old days. I remember my grandma Crampton saying about something, owning a car perhaps, 'Such things are not for the likes of people like us.' They were ordinary folk and could not expect to live like those in fine big houses. Most people do not think like that today. Jacks feel as good as their many masters. They want the good things of life *now*, and if they cannot get them by work or state handouts – well, some Jacks help themselves by theft and do not feel bad about it. They are not willing to stand back from the bran-tub, meekly working and saving and waiting as their forbears did. They want to dip their hands in deep today.

The common man has come into his inheritance at last. He is asserting himself and let those who stand in his way beware. This new assertiveness leads to violence; we often see the results in the crown court, as after a sudden confrontation between two or more people in a pub or club. We get arguments between motorists after a near miss. I remember one middle-aged businessman driving a Rover who argued with and struck another motorist as the latter still sat in his vehicle. Bottles or glasses may be seized and used, if they are not already in the hand at the start. Knives come out sometimes. When he feels thwarted the modern tendency is not for a man to think twice and back down. He lashes out.

When the police come, things may get worse. In my experience most officers are tactful and pacifying. But some assert themselves too much and throw their weight about. Men who resist the police often find themselves facing several officers whose anger is reflected in the cuts and bruises they cause. We are all affected by the trends I am dealing with.

The enfranchisement of the common man is probably the most important phenomenon when considering why crime has increased. We have not seen the worst yet and there is no easy solution. The genie is out of the bottle and there is no forcing him back.

## Anti-authority Attitudes

Here is a trivial example of how things have changed. An ex-police constable, now a sub-postmaster, said he would not be able to come to a crown court to testify for the prosecution in a criminal case on the due day as he would be too busy; if we wanted him to come we would have to arrest him. Thirty years ago would such a man – still a public employee – have said that? I could have ordered his arrest, had he failed to come to the trial. Instead I invited him to come before the day, and I reasoned with him in open court. I told him that we in the crown court have our problems too, and we could not fix every case to fit in with everyone's convenience. We would do our best to help him by calling him first and then releasing him, but he *must* come or it would be serious for him. He came and we parted on good terms. I did only what most judges would have done, but there is a moral. More people than formerly question or even defy authority, but most people still know what is reasonable and respond to reason. It depends how authority handles them.

In the county court I had an application by a local authority for possession of a council house. The defendant, being homeless, had gone to squat in the house. He was in his early twenties and his father came to court to speak for him. The father was indignant that the council was giving houses to people from Bangladesh or some such place. I pointed out that I had no control over council lettings. That was done by elected councillors who had procedures: committee meetings, points for priority, and so on. I told the father that homeless people could not be allowed to move into and retain others' houses: 'Suppose someone moved into your house.' In the end the father was virtually telling his son that he had to go.

Anti-authority feelings are increasing. I am not for blind, unquestioning obedience to those set over us. Scepticism about politicians, judges and police officers is healthy. We should all welcome scrutiny and criticism and be prepared either to justify what we do or act differently. But there are those who would demolish authority altogether and this can cause trouble, including crime. Those of us who are in authority have to be careful how we respond. There are more serious cases of defying authority than I have so far instanced, but the principles remain the same. Large trade unions sometimes refuse to obey the law as laid down by Parliament and the courts. This is to some extent because of the spread of extreme political ideas. Thousands believe that our society is based on injustice, with one class dominating and exploiting another; that the scales are weighted in favour of the few who run everything as against the many who have no free choices. There is no point in angrily dismissing such views; there is something in them. Our society does have injustices, which any progressive person wants to remove. Too many people are still born with silver spoons in their mouths; sometimes golden. Some people make money by clever manipulation rather than hard work. Others have money which they have not earned and which insulates them from the need to work. Unscrupulous businessmen sail through the sections of the companies acts, enriching themselves while leaving their victims penniless and without remedy.

Some extremists want to overthrow society as we know it, by stealth at first and by violence if necessary. This has a bearing on crime. Such people are unlikely to condemn violence in the streets or stealing from employers. They hate the police and judges as symbols of the authority they would overthrow. We know what one militant said about judges and other authority figures: the revolution would sweep us away. Whether the 'dictatorship of the proletariat' would bring benefits to any but the dictators, and what would happen to freedoms of the press and of the ballot-box, are matters for speculation by others.

Extreme ideas have a strong hold in some trade unions and have influenced workers who do not look on themselves as political beings. The trade unionist who defies the law by picketing illegally or refusing to obey a court order to stop that or any other illegal conduct, cannot be reasoned with if he is an extremist: he is doing his bit to bring down society. If he is not an extremist – and most trade unionists are not – he can be reasoned with. The government and the courts could do more than they do in this regard. The approach should be on these lines: 'We have a democratically elected parliament, which is free to make or alter laws. We all live under the protection of the law. Without law, there is anarchy. In a free society no one is justified in deciding which laws to obey and which not. If an employer defied safety legislation or refused to honour an agreement as to pay or conditions, the union would rush to court asking that the law be upheld; the employer would be made to obey. Why should a trade union try to have it both ways, enforcing the laws it likes and defying those it dislikes? Is such a union saying (as Hitler did) that might is right? And that imprisoning thousands of trade unionists is impractical?'

What about the Greenham Common women? The motives of most of them are admirable; they are for life and against death. But again, when they break the law they lose my sympathy and that of many others. One of their leaders has said that a particular missile is contrary to international law, and so CND supporters are morally justified in disobeying national laws in campaigning against its installation. This is arrogant. No individual can make such a decision. It is an anarchic stance. If it were to be allowed in this sphere, why not in others? A line between what is lawful and what is unlawful is easy to draw and should be adhered to by campaigners in any field. The law is one structure, and any attack on it weakens the protection that it gives to all. It is like a tent: every time a guy-rope is loosened or removed the tent is brought nearer to collapse. Peaceful demonstrations; propaganda by spoken or written words: these are lawful. Obstructing or trespassing upon the rights of others are unlawful acts and cannot be permitted.


## Intolerance

When I was a student we listened to anyone who had anything interesting to say. The more we disagreed with the speaker the more eagerly we listened. Today there are politicians of high intellect or eminence or both who cannot speak to any audience of students without violence erupting. Eggs or paint are thrown. How far this is spontaneous and how far it is organised by extremist groups is hard to say. There seems to be a new strain of intolerance in our society; this links up with some of the things I have referred to above. Adolf Hitler was the foremost exponent of intolerance in modern times. He used violence on the streets as a technique for gaining power. Intolerance and freedom do not go together. It is for the courts to uphold the rights of those who obey the law and to move against those who break it. This guarantees freedom for all and not only for the exponents of force.

This is where the conduct of some young English and Scottish football supporters fits in. I have to deal with it somewhere. These people have terrorised every capital in Europe. When English or Scottish teams are playing, the shutters go up and the police don their riot gear. Why is this? Very young children have a destructive streak. I remember when I was about eight and with an older boy, rolling coping-stones down a hill on to hen-huts. A man came and chased us. I hope I soon grew out of it. Do the young football supporters have the same tendency at a later age? Do we all harbour hidden violence and destructiveness within us? The cruelties which all armies show in wartime suggests that we do. Most of the time we control it. An individual who would never be violent on his own finds it easy when he is in a group. Anonymity lends boldness. The one is swept along by the many. But the short answer in the case of our football supporters is probably that they have not been brought up properly. Of all the foreign countries I have visited I know West Germany and Eire best. Their children seem to behave better than ours. They seem to have a stronger sense of 'family', and religion – certainly in the case of Eire – has a firmer hold.

## Materialism

A monk in a monastery has, or should have, few material needs; those he has are catered for by others. So he has little incentive to steal, even if he were minded to. There are some other ascetics in our society, but most of us are materialist mad. That may be putting it a bit high, but ours is certainly a materialist society. Most of us want to raise our living standards, add to our comfort and gadgets, travel around. We are not happier for our search for satisfaction, but we continue even so. We have a car that goes but we want a better, more impressive one, then a second, then one for our son and daughter, then one each for them. There is always a finer house, better electronic equipment, more exotic holidays. The hunt goes on. Some religions tell their followers that the search for materialism is wrong. Christian churches do not seem to do that. The Roman Catholic church can hardly do it, being so very wealthy and ostentatious itself. What is left of the Church of England does not show or preach asceticism.

I mentioned happiness. Who is truly happy? A true monk and a true artist. They both lose themselves ecstatically in their work and have little time for self-pity. The monk prays to God and helps others (in some orders he only prays to God); the artist loses himself in creating words or paintings or figures. Neither man has time or need to dwell on his petty, selfish problems; these hardly exist in the mind of one moved to creative activity. The word creative is important; a man cannot get the same satisfaction from tightening bolts. Joyce Cary wrote a novel *The Horse's Mouth* about a painter, Gully Jimson. That artist cared nothing for material things, and wanted only to paint. Poor though his circumstances were in the eyes of others, he was happy.

In a democracy a good test of what voters long for is what politicians offer them to get their votes. All political parties today promise a better material life, higher wages. We must not blame the politicians but ourselves. We get the politics that we want, just as in our capacity as readers we get the press that we want. Sensationalist tabloids flourish as in no other country because they appeal to the majority. Some people, especially some young ones, react against the brash search for money and goods and go for Greenpeace, ban-the-bomb or Eastern mysticism. We older ones tend to stick to our comforts. We are too staid for fresh thinking. While there is this accent on materialism in a largely agnostic society, crimes of dishonesty are sure to be rife.

## The Permissive Society

Here too there is overlap with what I have written above. The churches still tell us how to run our lives, but most of us no longer take heed. 'God' and the 'devil' are unreal, remote, unlikely notions. The ban on sex outside marriage was religious in origin. When I was young, feelings of sin and guilt, added to the more practical pre-Pill fear of pregnancy, inhibited many of us. My father told of an uncle who had never married and who boasted that he had never 'fallen', never slept with a woman. A man who said that today would be laughed at. How many parents now tell their children that sex outside marriage is morally wrong? Barbara Cartland preaches that a girl should save herself for marriage, but she does not say the same about men, so it cannot be based on morality. There is a double standard. (Similarly, it was made plain in royal circles that Prince Charles could not marry a sexually experienced woman, but it was never said that he should remain sexually inexperienced.)

With unpaid and paid sex being so freely available, it is surprising there are so many rapes and indecent assaults. (Or are more reported to the police now? In any age many crimes are unreported.) But permissiveness leads some men to think that sex should be available to them, and if they cannot find a willing woman when the urge is on them, they take it from an unwilling one. There is a complication, however: some such attackers get their satisfaction from violating an *un*willing woman.

The permissive age has brought a liberated attitude towards books, films and plays. Stage censorship has rightly gone. Books and films are more daring. Some video films dredge the depths of depravity, disgusting even those who think themselves enlightened. Some say that books and films cause crime, and there is something in this. Some weak or young people can be excited into doing wrong. But we must be careful here. I do not believe that anyone is changed for the worse by what he sees in a book or a film. He goes for what he is already inclined towards. His character is formed before he is old enough to read. I do not believe in censorship. Adults should be free to behave as they like, if they do not harm others.

Pornography is a dirty word. But what do we mean by it? A display of words or pictures or both which is likely to arouse some people sexually but disgusts *me*. So it is subjective, it is in the eye of the beholder. Efforts to have an objective test, on the lines of a tendency to deprave or corrupt others, have failed and merely brought the law into disrepute. Most men have some interest in what some others call pornography. I like to look at page 3 of the *Sun* newspaper. Though I would not buy it for that or any other purpose, if I see a copy left in the train I do not pass by with my nose in the air. Attractive women do attract men, by definition. Pictures of nubile naked women do attract most men, and to suggest that they do not or should not is hypocritical. Women are not generally attracted by the sight of male nakedness, in the flesh or on the page. Men are more superficial in this respect. We are easily aroused and captivated by the physical appearance of a woman. Women are more sensible and tend to go for subtler qualities such as strength of character, reliability and, above all, kindness.

Where should the law draw the line with 'pornography'? Ideally, it should not draw it at all. Every adult should draw it for himself or herself; every parent for his child. Some books and magazines I have seen in court cases have disgusted me. What disgusts cannot harm. Suppose they are seen by the young or weak-minded? Children who have been brought up properly should be immune from harm. Although some people are excited into crime by literature or films, the number is small and this may be the price we pay for a free society. The argument that the young and the weak must be protected by the law from bad influences has the paternalist approach which dictatorships accept, as in the Soviet Union and Nazi Germany.

There is a case for a law against attempting to induce a child to act to his or her physical or moral detriment. For example, showing pictures to an under-sixteen with a view to illegal sexual activity with the child. But that is covered by the existing law, as an incitement or attempt to have unlawful sexual intercourse, gross indecency or make an indecent assault.

It might nevertheless be desirable to tighten up the law in that area. Such legislation, taken with the existing law against the display of indecent material, should be adequate, without paddling in the muddy-bottomed pond of pornography.

I am not advocating that we all run riot, indulging every fancy, or that every party should become an orgy. But the teaching of good behaviour is for parents, not the state. The idea that sexual behaviour itself is in some way wrong is a hangover from Christianity. Sexual excitement is part of a normal healthy life and so is sexual activity. It only becomes criminal if imposed on an unwilling person or an under-sixteen.

The attitudes included in the notion of a permissive society have played a part in crime. There are some who think, 'No matter what, I am going to indulge myself, enjoy myself, have all the women and booze and other entertainment I can cram in. It's the good life for me, and I don't care what I do to others in getting it.' But the permissive society can no more be closed down, by propaganda or decree, than the Severn bore could be.

## Women's Lib

I am for it. For centuries women had to take a back seat. Men denied them the vote, entry into Parliament, universities and the professions. Most families treated daughters as inferior to sons, and some still do. Women were expected to stay in the bedroom, the nursery and the kitchen. They were paid less at work and still are in many instances. I have seen a small business virtually run by a woman employee who gets a fraction out of it compared with the male owners. Women at the bar are still discriminated against. No wonder women have asserted themselves, demanding equal rights. They have been pushed out for too long and their struggle is not over yet.

As with some other trends this movement for liberation is good in itself, but it has inevitable side-effects which are not as welcome. Thirty years ago we saw very few women in the dock at assizes and quarter sessions. There are more now, though women are very much in the minority in courts and prisons. The increase in crimes by women was bound to happen when women began to assert themselves instead of staying meekly at home.

This may sound 'sexist' to some, but my impression is that when a woman stands in the dock at a crown court it is usually because of her association with one or more men. (I except shoplifting.) Brothel offences are obvious cases. A woman who is up for burglary probably got involved by trying to ingratiate herself with a man or because of feeling loyal to him. It is rare to find a woman planning a burglary and doing it on her own or with another woman. Similarly with handling stolen goods; the initiative usually comes from a man. Women are not as hard, aggressive or predatory as men. They are more sensitive of others' feelings. A woman who gets on to drink and drugs often does so because her relationship with a man has gone wrong. The male quest for conquest, sensation and change is more likely to cause unhappiness than the female quest for affection, children and a stable home life. But some women want more than that now.

## Family Fragmentation

Marriage is less popular than it was. With religion removed, many couples see no need to go through a ceremony and obtain a piece of paper in order to show their commitment to each other. Pregnancy may alter things if the parents are free to marry. The law, which has not yet caught up with modern attitudes, gives several advantages to those who marry rather than merely cohabit. A deserted wife is in a better legal position in claiming money and a share in property. On the other hand, divorce can be a long and messy business; simply saying goodbye and parting is easier.

Marital discord was never more widespread than now (or was it hidden before?). In the UK one marriage in three ends in divorce. We and Denmark head the European divorce league. One in five of our children sees his parents divorce before he is sixteen. As a divorce judge I have to see divorcing parents of children who are under sixteen, or under eighteen if still in full-time education. I have been struck by the number of divorcing couples who now have very young children, sometimes babies. Many must have married feeling that if it does not work out, divorce is easy. I have come across a few women under thirty who have gone for a second divorce and are about to marry for a third time. One finds couples who have children from *her* former marriage, some from *his* and some from the marriage that is being dissolved. This unsettles and confuses the children.

Spouses soon seem to feel unfulfilled. They want all they can get out of life, and if this partner falls short of the ideal they are eager to try another, inside or outside marriage. The excitement and satisfaction gained from sex with a new partner lose their edge after a time, and unless shared experiences and respect for each other's qualities build up love as opposed to sexual infatuation, a marriage may be in peril. Some women lose interest in sex after a time, and if the husband is still keen on it and finds a similar partner – it is a familiar story, posing real dilemmas. Should he stay with his wife out of loyalty for her and the children, or seek and hope to find real fulfilment elsewhere? Or can he hope to straddle both worlds at once?

Most young people who come before the courts for crimes are from broken families. Time after time one finds in social inquiry reports: separation; divorce; mother lived with various men; child went to live with relatives; he was taken into care and went into a local authority home; behavioural problems. Then the slow climb up the penal ladder: supervision order; conditional discharge; attendance centre (say, for twenty-four hours – a few hours on Saturday afternoons, under police supervision, doing physical exercises at the double and other less exhausting tasks like making purses); detention centre; youth custody; prison.

In the early years of his life a child needs two united parents who care for each other and for him. If he cannot have his natural parents, two parental figures – preferably one of each sex – are the next best thing, provided there is not much shuttling from one home to another. A child needs love and stability in the tender years when he is forming his attitudes and developing his emotions. If he does not get these it may take years to untwist him; or he may forever remain twisted and a menace to others. One day he may be a parent himself: what effect will all this have upon his children? When parents are divorced, young children suffer, though this may be better than living with parents who are at each other's throats most of the time.

The position is certainly different from my grandparents' time, when divorce was almost unknown. Families spent more time at home then. Whether they were any happier is difficult to judge. Children had harsher discipline; too harsh sometimes. Today things have gone far the other way. I tried a case in which a prosecution witness happened to say that his son of nine had been watching television at 10 p.m. 'Hasn't he a set time to go to bed?' I asked. 'Oh no, he stays up till he feels tired,' said the father. 'Did *you* have a set time?' 'Oh yes,' he replied, 'but times have changed.' I told him that they have indeed changed and that daily we saw the results in that very courtroom. How can a nation's parents be taught to bring up their children better? It is like lifting oneself up by one's boot-straps.

Recently I was in a public library waiting to be served. The girl next to me, who looked about fifteen and had a cold-spot on her lip, said something to her friend about being 'pissed off' at having to wait. 'Not a very ladylike thing to say,' I remarked. 'I can say what I like. It's a free country,' was the reply. 'Yes, and a very unruly one,' I countered. I was unwise to say anything, and if the person next to me had been male I probably would not have spoken, for fear of being knocked down, challenged to go outside or knifed.

If I have to point to one place where criminals are made, it is the home. Those who are damaged by parental neglect cannot easily be put right by teachers, judges or social workers. Children brought up with firm concern and united love are unlikely to go wrong. Some do, of course. In the last twenty years, several children of prominent people have committed crimes such as those involving drugs, or come to early deaths or both. This seems to be connected with the parents' eminence. Happily, my children have not had that disadvantage.

## Welfarism

I tried a robbery not long ago in which the victims were a man and woman who lived together. They were both unemployed but they were hiring a video. There are more videos per head of our population than anywhere else in Europe – or is it in the world? It is common to see unemployed couples who have a colour television set, and some look on it as higher in their list of wants than carpets or curtains.

I am in danger of being misunderstood. I am not against the welfare state. In this country the foundations were laid by Liberal governments of 1906–1916. The Labour governments of 1945–51 established the complex network that we know today. The welfare state is based on a noble ideal: that no one should fall below a minimum standard of life through misfortune such as unemployment, illness or being a one-parent family. In the thirties welfare aid was much less than it is now, and it is surprising that there was less civil strife and much less crime than now. Today, with current attitudes and high unemployment, there could be revolution but for the welfare state. Political extremists would be in their element.

In court I sometimes refer to 'perverted welfarism'. Some of the old virtues have been pushed out. There is much less emphasis on self-reliance, on the need for people to make their own way in life, to stand on their own feet and accept responsibility for what they choose to do. In the minds of those who have known only the welfare state there is a feeling that there is always someone to help them out of problems, some way of cushioning them from real adversity.

About fifteen years ago I went to York Assizes to do a defended divorce for a husband, who won. Afterwards he asked me, 'Where do I claim for my loss of earnings for today?' His automatic reaction was that if he lost a day's pay through no fault of his there must be some way of claiming it from the state. I told him that it was his case, the state had supported him under legal aid by paying his legal costs, but he must bear the loss of pay himself. I said to my pupil, after the client had gone, 'There goes homo welfariensis. He got free education, he gets free medical treatment, he wears national health teeth and spectacles. Later he will get a state hearing aid and a state wig.' (I realise that he paid taxes, and would probably have to contribute to teeth, hearing-aid and wig.) It is all very fine, helping lame dogs over stiles, but we are in danger of breeding a nation of lame dogs.

There is something wrong in the way we run our welfare state. Germany has a system that is as extensive as ours, but they do not run it as we do.

In the ten years I have been a full-time judge I have seen defendant after defendant who have done no honest work for years and see no need to, when the state is so generous and crime is so fruitful. Unemployed men with large families dig deep into the nation's resources and often *drink* deep into them, while the children go hungry. Yet there are others who do not get enough state help. When doing divorce work I see many one-parent mothers who live thin lives. They cannot easily get work if they have young children; work as barmaids or cleaners is poorly paid and leaves them little better off after deductions from social security payments. They hardly ever go out; they never have a holiday except to stay with relatives; for clothes they go to sales of second-hand goods. When they give me details I cannot understand how they manage. Some of them must be tempted to prostitute themselves and some do – though they are unlikely to tell me about it unless the divorcing husband raises it.

I did a case in the county court where a shopkeeper who owed about £800 in income-tax had been committed to prison for twenty-eight days, suspended upon his paying £50 a month. He had made one payment of £25 and after over a year was applying for the £50 to be *reduced*. 'Have you brought your toothbrush?' I asked. 'Why?' 'Because you're in danger of going to jail today. But before I send anyone there – and I send a lot – I like them to be represented by a lawyer. I'll give you an hour to get one. Don't leave the building, but there's a phone you can use.' Within the hour he came back, not with a solicitor but with £800 in cash! 'You've been playing the system,' I told him. And so do a lot more who get away with it.

In another county court a local authority was applying for possession of a council house for non-payment of rent. The tenant owed over £500; he had been receiving rent money from the DHSS and spending it on other things. When the rent-collector called he put out the lights, turned off the television and refused to come to the door until the official had gone. He had not even troubled to come to court, probably thinking that at the most a suspended possession order would be made. I made an order for immediate possession. 'Get him out today,' I said, 'and if he has to sleep outside tonight, I shan't be sorry.' The eyes of the housing manager's representative lit up. The council's solicitor said this was a most refreshing though unusual judicial approach. Next day at another county court a social worker held back after an adoption application and thanked me for what I had said on the previous day – it had been reported in the press. 'It strengthens our hands with these people.' I can say and do things that politicians cannot; I shall never come up for re-election. That does not mean I can be irresponsible; I always try to choose my words carefully and refer to the other point of view, if I can find it.

## Drink and Other Drugs

As a nation we are going to the drugs. In case after case in the crown court defendants are said to have been drinking before they committed offences. Sometimes they drink to give themselves courage to do a planned offence, such as a robbery. A weak, drifting type may drink too much and then do an offence without planning. He is on his alcoholic way home when he sees a shop window and decides to take something from it, so he hurls a brick. He may get something trivial or nothing at all. I have known such men cut a hand on the glass and leave a trail of blood to their homes.

An alarming number of teenagers drink too much and are said to have a drink problem. Under-eighteens regularly drink in pubs or clubs. Recently, a defendant of twenty-two, charged with assaulting a club doorman, was said to drink ten or eleven pints of beer on about three evenings a week. The use of drugs such as cannabis, heroin and cocaine by young people is increasing. In the United States four out of ten serious crimes are drug-related: defendants steal drugs, or steal in order to buy them, or commit offences whilst under their influence. We are presumably following the US in this disturbing trend.

The sentencing aspect of cases involving drugs worries me. Apart from drugs that have been prescribed medically, the only drugs I have ever taken are alcohol and nicotine. I drink alcohol in what I hope are moderate quantities; I smoke occasional cigars. No one has ever offered me cannabis or any other illegal drug: I have never met them at parties or elsewhere. My children grew up in a different environment. All three went to university, where it is usual to try and not unusual to smoke cannabis. I feel sure that none of them takes such drugs today, and none of them ever had a drug problem. Whether they ever tried drugs is something I have not cross-examined them about. Cannabis is smoked widely in the UK today, and not only by those with West Indian connections. How harmful is it? In small quantities, probably no more harmful than alcohol. In large quantities, both are harmful. In the USA some states have legalised the possession of small quantities of cannabis of certain qualities. Should we do the same here? This is worth study, especially if the existing law is being widely flouted. What is accepted and practised by a large section of the community should be made lawful, especially if it does no harm. Searches and arrests by the police for cannabis can make law-abiding people anti-police.

But would legalisation look like approval? Not necessarily. The state does not approve cigarette-smoking and goes to timid lengths to disapprove it by banning television advertising and requiring packets to carry a warning.

There is a quandary about the banning of drugs. Despite strong efforts to stop them they continue to get into the country and probably always will. By banning them the state sends up the price. This gives scope for racketeers. It also makes it necessary for those hooked on drugs to get a lot of money for their purchase which they cannot earn by work – they have to get it by unlawful means.

If it were lawful to buy drugs, prices would fall, rackets would disappear, and it would not be necessary for addicts to get money for drugs by dishonesty. *But* would the use of drugs rocket? Would people think that their use, being lawful, was acceptable? The idea of going into a chemist's and asking for an ounce of heroin certainly startles. But how far should the state protect people from themselves? If an adult wishes to abuse his body by alcohol, nicotine or other drugs, should the state interfere, provided he does not harm other people? There again, if one country legalised drugs, it might become a mecca for addicts. Whatever is done should be by international agreement, and step by step. Consideration of legalising the possession of small quantities of cannabis for one's own use is the first step.

When I spoke recently to magistrates on the sentencing aspect of drug-related offences I got some disturbing information from other speakers. Drugs are available in some prisons. They are taken in by visitors and 'bent' prison officers. Cannabis is the most common drug, and in some overcrowded prisons the prison officers are apparently prepared to turn a blind eye in order to keep the prisoners contented. A murderer in Parkhurst prison is reported as saying that he was able to smoke opium every day. Another man said that he was able to get more drugs whilst in prison than he had been able to get outside. At one prison the bus that brings visitors is known as the 'dream bus', as it brings so many drugs. Sometimes a wife kisses her husband and passes into his mouth a male contraceptive containing drugs; the prisoner swallows it and later vomits it up. A solicitor has told me that a client at a long-term prison said that he was going off 'to have a few jars with the IRA lads', referring to beer that the prisoners brewed in prison. All this information has opened my eyes; I always assumed that by sending a man or woman to prison I was ensuring abstinence from drink and drugs. I have passed all this information to higher authority, but I do not know with what results. The Home Office should tighten security in prisons.

Finally, why are drugs so prevalent and their use increasing in Britain today? The answers lie in what I have written above: lack of proper parental care; the search for quick sensation; the need, felt by many, to fly from or cover up worries caused by unemployment, unhappiness in relationships or even fear of the Bomb.

If the above trends or changes in attitudes are the main causes of the increase in crimes, are we powerless? No. The trends cannot be reversed as a result of the decisions of governments or courts. The seas of change have a momentum of their own; they make their own channels and eventually they will make new ones. We are seeing reactions against former attitudes; our children and grandchildren will see reactions against present attitudes. We must not assume that everything always gets worse. And if enough people think, for example, that the welfare state ought to be trimmed and improved, or that our society has become too permissive in some respects, then there will be changes. Let those who seek to influence others do their best by any lawful means.

But what about the courts? Are judges and magistrates powerless in the face of these mighty forces in society? Must we shrug our shoulders and say that whatever we do things will go on getting worse? No. What is said and done in court does have some influence on the way people think. Some criminals or potential criminals are affected in their actions by what they think courts will do to them. Criminals are not automata; they are people with minds and can choose to act in one way or another. This is a difficult area, but I will try to grapple with it in Chapter 9.

# Chapter 5

# *Justice Delayed is Justice Denied*

No area cries out more loudly for reform than this. None is so infested with complacency and conservatism. In my evidence to the Royal Commission on Legal Services in 1977 I wrote: 'Justice delayed is justice denied. Yet delays increasingly disfigure the work of the legal profession. In civil claims it can take many years to get to court. This is usually the fault of solicitors. The delays in hearing crown court cases in London are scandalous.' Things have not since improved with civil cases. In many crown courts the delays are gross. There have always been delays in civil cases, and all lawyers know about them, as does anyone who has been caught up in litigation as a party or a witness. When appearing for plaintiffs at the bar I often had to start a case by explaining the delay. Sometimes the blame was placed on a clerk who had left or had a nervous breakdown. Sometimes a solicitor was frank enough to admit that he had simply filed the papers away and forgotten about them. I had one solicitor client who had unexpectedly won an old case; after that he thought that cases improved with age – matured, like wine!

I will deal with my judicial experience in the county court, though the position in the high court is even worse. Justice in the county court *can* be swift. I hear many applications by women for injunctions based on domestic violence: these can be heard within hours. On two occasions I have gone to court on a Saturday when a man has been arrested for breach of an injunction: normally he has to be dealt with within twenty-four hours or released. The delays take place in actions for damages, as for breach of contract or for personal injuries arising out of an accident at work or on the roads. The situation is appalling. The average time, from a solicitor coming into a case for the plaintiff to the trial, is probably about three years; sometimes it is much longer. Most of the blame attaches to solicitors. I can only refer to what I see. Some solicitors do not do court work at all and so I know nothing about them. Most civil claims are settled before they get to court, and I do not see those. I am sure that some solicitors are efficient, within the limits of the system as it has been operated for generations. *But* the general picture is bad, and many parties leave court wishing they had never become involved with the law.

In civil actions the parties set out their cases in what are called 'pleadings'. The plaintiff files particulars of claim (called a statement of claim in the high court). The defendant then files a defence and in some cases also a counterclaim. The plaintiff then files a reply and defence to the counterclaim. The defendant may blame a third party and bring him into the action by a third party notice. The third party files a defence to that. The other side may ask for further and better particulars of any of these pleadings, and this causes delay. Requests and replies usually take up a lot of time. Neither side harries the other: there is a kind of mutual back-scratching. Every step, every letter, is of course charged for. The costs in some county court actions mushroom out of all proportion to the amounts being sued for, and in the end nobody gains except the lawyers. I would never go to law unless it were a matter of life and death; I know too much about the hazards and expense, and the dilatory and inefficient ways of many solicitors.

I tried a case of breach of contract. The relevant dates of the stages of the action were as follows:

| | |
|---|---|
| 23/2/77 | Particulars of claim filed. |
| 25/4/77 | Defence. |
| 1/11/77 | Amended defence and counterclaim. |
| 5/9/79 | Amended particulars of claim. |
| 13/9/79 | Request for particulars of particulars of claim. |
| 14/1/80 | Amended defence. |
| 15/4/80 | Third party notice. |
| 25/7/80 | Fourth party notice. |
| 29/9/80 | Defence of fourth party. Defence of defendant further amended. |
| 8/4/83 | Registrar strikes out third party notice for want of prosecution. |
| 16/6/83 | Judge restores third party notice on appeal. |
| 26/11/83 | Third party notice withdrawn. |
| 22/2/84 | Action tried before me. |

I do not know all the reasons for delay in that case, but it cannot be right for seven years to pass between the start of an action and its trial. Such delays harm plaintiffs more than defendants. The plaintiff has to prove his case, and this becomes more difficult with time. A plaintiff in an accident case whose evidence differs from his case as pleaded usually loses, yet there may have been no deliberate falsification. Mulling over the details month after month can distort memory. I cannot blame a defendant for letting an action go to sleep; if he does nothing it might die. The court does not take action of its own motion; it only acts when a party makes an application to it.

I had a written application to adjourn a hearing date at short notice, which both sides agreed to. The reason was that the plaintiff's expert witness would not be available. The claim was for breach of contract, and the relevant dates were:

9/2/82      Statement of claim filed in the high court.

| 5/3/82 | Defence. |
| 17/5/82 | Case transferred to county court. |
| 13/12/82 | Amended statement of claim. |
| 6/3/84 | Notice of hearing sent by the court. |
| 2/4/84 | Projected hearing date. |

At my request the plaintiff's solicitor's clerk came to see me in my room. His firm is a large one with a good reputation; I did some of my early cases for it thirty-five years ago. The clerk said that when the notice of hearing arrived he was away ill and it was merely put on his desk. He did not see it as soon as he returned to work and had only seen it recently. He rang his expert witness, who could not come at a few days' notice, having other appointments. (I have noticed in other cases that some solicitors do not have an efficient 'diary' system and so overlook hearing dates.) I asked the clerk why cases take so long to get to court. He said that he has between 500 and 600 files of on-going cases. He goes through them once a month, but tends to give priority to clients who ring or write asking about progress; also, I suspect, to those who have 'clout'. This may be the key to a lot that is wrong. I suspect that some litigation clerks are overworked, underpaid and insufficiently supervised. Most of their clients – certainly plaintiffs in accident cases – are 'little people' who are diffident about nagging at or complaining about solicitors and are easily fobbed off with explanations. Such a client is unlikely to bring further work to the firm; there is no incentive to 'pull out all the stops' for him. He has to wait his turn. If he has a legal aid certificate – as most plaintiffs have – he is even more hesitant to throw his weight about.

What is the attitude of the solicitor's profession as a whole about delays? The most appropriate word is complacent. I tried a case in which a plaintiff had sued a nationalised body over two years previously. The defendants were applying to bring in a third party, but I refused leave as it would have meant further delay. I also said, according to a press cutting: 'Solicitors proceed at such a leisurely pace that they seem to forget about the people awaiting remedies. People wait three years for a simple dispute to come before a court of law. Solicitors are leisurely, meandering and forget about the real interests of their clients. Litigants need to have actions brought before the courts within a few months – not years.' I added that the Law Society was not a very effective body, and the only help it gave to complaining litigants in such cases was to tell them that they could change solicitors and, if they have suffered through the negligence of the first firm, sue them. (So the plaintiff who is already sick with one lawsuit is told that he can start another.) The local newspaper published a leading article welcoming my remarks and stating:

The Law Society exercises considerable powers in the regulation of the profession, and laymen often wonder whether it is unable or simply unwilling to do more about complaints from the public against individual solicitors and law firms. Criticisms like that made in —— county court must bring closer the day when, unless the Society does live up to public and even judicial expectations, regulation of the profession will be put into other hands.

I received a letter from the honorary secretary to the local law society stating: 'The committee feel that your remarks must have been taken out of context, and we will be grateful for your confirmation that this was indeed the case.' I replied that I had been accurately reported, but that my remarks were not confined to the solicitors in that locality – they extended to all the places where I sat. That produced a tart acknowledgment.

Solicitors will never put their own house in order. They are much too complacent. They are well represented in parliament. Judges – who whilst practising at the bar received all their work from solicitors – feel a natural diffidence about taking steps against them; there is even something of a 'dog does not eat dog' feeling. 'We are all lawyers together and must *stand* together.'

Standards in the profession are much lower than they were, especially amongst young solicitors. Spelling is poor with some of them; some come to court without their robes or with screwed up bands; there is a slovenly approach to their work. The young women are better than the young men; they dress more smartly and are more conscientious and attentive to detail. There is not enough incentive to be efficient. The Law Society gives me the impression of being a solicitors' protection society. A notorious case in which an influential solicitor guilty of gross misconduct was protected by the society is an example.

It might be expected that cases in which plaintiffs are supported by a trade union would have less delay, but that is not the case. Delays caused by the trade union itself makes things worse.

It is sometimes said that in a personal injuries case it is necessary to wait until the final prognosis for the injuries can be arrived at. This is not so: liability can be tried separately from the quantification of damages, though this is hardly ever done.

The legal aid system causes some delays. There are two aspects of an application: consideration of the merits, and assessment of the applicant's means by the legal aid assessment office of the DHSS. I had one case investigated, and these were the dates:

| | |
|---|---|
| 27/5/83 | Application received. |
| 3/6/83 | Statement of means sent to DHSS. |
| July/83 | Application approved on its merits. |

| 10/8/83 | Information as to applicant's domestic circumstances given to DHSS. |
| 29/8/83 | DHSS state that a property valuation is being obtained from the district valuer. |
| 7/2/84 | DHSS state they are awaiting a statement of earnings of applicant's husband. |
| 29/2/84 | Legal aid offered to applicant. |

I was informed that in 1982/3 the average time taken nationally to issue a contributory certificate (i.e., the applicant has to make payments) was eighty-four days, and for a non-contributory certificate forty-one days.

There should be a rule that both sides shall file a certificate of readiness within, say, six months of an action being started. Failure to do this would entail appearing before the court and giving an explanation. The court would give directions – striking out the claim, extending the time for good reasons, etc. The court would have to be firm, and able to order that a recalcitrant solicitor be deprived of his costs. There should be a body with power to order solicitors to pay compensation to their clients.

The Lord Chancellor has set up an 'in-house' inquiry into civil litigation, with a view to streamlining procedure and reducing delays. It is due to report at the end of 1987.

As for delays in criminal cases, in June 1985 I sat for two weeks in a Yorkshire city. At the end of June 1984 the number of trials outstanding for more than twenty-four weeks after receipt from the magistrates' courts in that group of courts was 141 – eleven per cent of the whole. By March 1985 the figures had risen to 233 and sixteen per cent.

One man waited nearly two years from his arrest, for hiring out obscene video films, to his trial. Another, charged with arson, waited nineteen months. They were on bail but a third man, charged with burglary, waited nine months in custody: equivalent to a sentence of twenty-seven months, with remission and parole. He had served his sentence before he got it. He had served it whether he was convicted or acquitted.

The iniquities of delay are: witnesses forget; sleepless nights for defendants; dilemma for courts over bail; risk to the public if bail is granted because of delay; pressure on remand accommodation; lack of confidence by defendants, witnesses, jurors and the public in the system and those who run it. And the sentencing process is distorted. I could not sentence the arsonist to the time in jail he would have deserved fresh after the crime. He set fire to an office, doing several thousand pounds worth of damage, when two men were in the same building. The normal tariff was about three years, but I felt I could not sentence him to more than eighteen months. (With remission and parole he would be free after six months: inadequate for what he did.)

There are three stages at which delays occur: during police inquiries and the decision whether to prosecute; in the magistrates' court; and in the crown court.

Delays at the first stage occur because police officers are sometimes slow in interviewing witnesses, obtaining statements and preparing files. The files spend too long on senior officers' desks on occasions. There is not enough incentive for speed.

In the magistrates' court delays are caused by too many adjournments, too lengthy adjournments and a shortage of staff. In 1980 the Vera Institute of Justice in New York did a report for the Home Office on waiting times in magistrates' courts. The report states that some solicitors take on too much court work and rely on adjournments to help out. Under legal aid, solicitors are paid for each hearing, so there is no financial incentive to reduce their number. A slow approach gives police officers more time to interview witnesses, get statements typed, conclude investigations and complete the file. Prosecuting solicitors have no incentive to complete the file, and may want adjournments in order to review the file or get further evidence. Delays may help a defendant to find a job – a strong mitigating factor in these days – and to show that he can stay out of trouble. And successive adjournments may 'wear down' prosecution witnesses, making them less willing to testify and less able to remember precisely what happened. Busy magistrates and their clerks may welcome adjournments as a way of getting through their lists. The Vera Report stated that, in most of the courts visited, unopposed adjournments were typically granted without reference to the number of previous adjournments, the reasons for them or the overall age of the case: 'At its worst the end result of these practices is a kind of "churning" of cases, in which a significant amount of time is spent simply putting off action to another day – often a day on which nothing of substance will occur except a further adjournment.'

A magistrates' clerk wrote to me on 17 December 1982:

At the present time a person who pleads guilty on a criminal charge, unless in custody, can expect his case to be adjourned until about the middle of March 1983 for a trial date. This is, of course, most unsatisfactory, but these delays have arisen as a result of a lack of sufficient prosecuting solicitors and sufficient court clerks and administrative staff in my office.

If a case is to be committed for trial at the crown court, the sooner it gets there the better. When I began at the bar, prosecution witnesses had to give evidence before the magistrates in every case which was to be sent for trial at assizes or quarter sessions. Now that happens rarely and only when the defence asks. In the other cases the magistrates do not look at the evidence; there is a formal handing over of documents. Why wait for months when that is all that is to happen? As soon as the prosecution is ready it should be able to send the statements direct to the crown court. The magistrates would merely have to deal with bail and legal aid. A submission by the defence that there was insufficient evidence could be made to a judge at the crown court.

Delays in the crown court are caused by a shortage of circuit judges and the unavailability of witnesses or defending counsel. Under the system on the north-eastern circuit a plea of guilty is normally dealt with five weeks after the case has been committed to the crown court by the magistrates. Some defendants 'play the system'. Although they intend to plead guilty eventually, the longer they remain unconvicted the longer they retain privileges: more visits, food sent in and no obligation to work. One ploy is to ask for a change of solicitors and counsel under legal aid, saying they have lost confidence in their present ones: it is hard for the court to resist such an application, especially if the lawyers now feel too embarrassed to act for the man. (A solicitor has told me, however, that some men prefer to be convicted early: otherwise they are locked in their cells for most of the time, away from the other men.)

In a contested case with a lot of witnesses, delay is inevitable at holiday times: if only one witness on either side is to be away, the case cannot start. Little can be done about this, except to try to ensure that notification comes in time. I have had cases in which news of police officers' holidays comes to the court listing officer a day or two before the date for trial: there is no excuse for that.

A trial is often delayed because the defendant's counsel is engaged in other cases. We should be stricter than we are: no barrister can do every brief with his name on it. A defendant should be satisfied with competent counsel who has had time to prepare the case.

There is a shortage of circuit judges on the north-eastern circuit. This may apply elsewhere too. I understand that money is not the problem here – though it is in other areas of delay. There are said to be insufficient barrister and solicitor applicants of the required calibre. I find this hard to accept, based on what I know. It is true, however, that some QCs and senior juniors earn so much that they say they cannot afford to take a circuit judgeship despite the over £42,000 a year salary, a relatively relaxed life, a large tax-free capital sum on retirement and a £21,000 a year pension, index-linked. One solution might be to hint to certain barristers that it is 'now or never': the supply of applicants might suddenly increase.

Maximum periods for the three stages, with extensions only granted for strong reasons, are essential. In the United States the Federal Speedy Trial Act 1974 requires a defendant to be tried within a hundred days; ninety if he is in custody. Several states in the USA have similar rules. In the federal system, periods can be ordered by a judge to be excluded for several reasons. Unfortunately the statistics do not show how long such excludable periods are in practice.

The useful Home Office research bulletin dealt with the federal system in number 17 for 1985:

> While time limits have played a part in setting standards or targets according to which courts assess their performances, the real key to success lies in judicial control over a wide ranging programme of delay reduction. A commitment on the part of the court to enforce reasonable deadlines is viewed as an essential prerequisite of such a programme. In addition, the court should monitor the extent to which time limits are met, and set up consultative machinery to ensure co-operation from the defence and prosecution on the goals of the programme. On the other hand there is reason to believe that measures to speed up case disposition which lack effective sanctions will have little impact if, as seems often to be the case, the interest of practitioners and their responsibilities to their clients are better served by maintaining the status quo.

Scottish Law has time limits. The Prosecution of Offences Act 1985 empowers the Home Secretary to prescribe these for the rest of the UK. I hope he does so soon: dates in red on files will concentrate minds. The dates will be known and will have to be worked to. If there are no dates and no public fuss is made, delays get worse.

To show what happens now, take the video case. This is not typical; it is a bad case for delay but there are others like it, some worse. In London and the south-eastern circuit many are worse. I was told in July 1985 that one crown court in the south had informed the defence that their trial could not start there until 1987. (It was moved to another crown court.) The relevant dates for the video case were:

| | |
|---|---|
| 27/7/83 | *Arrest* of defendant for hiring out obscene video tapes, as part of an otherwise respectable business. |
| 10/11/83 | Advice by prosecuting solicitor (1). |
| 7–8/12/83 | Magistrates viewed tapes. |
| 14/12/83 | File to divisional police HQ and prosecuting solicitor. |
| 16/12/83 | Advice by prosecuting solicitor (2). Defence asked to view tapes. |
| 28/2/84 | Appearance before *magistrates*. Adjournment at request of defence. |
| 10/4/84 | Adjournment agreed to by both sides, to await result of another crown court case. |
| May/84 | Other case heard. |
| 20/5/84 | Defence requested 'old style' committal. Advice by prosecuting solicitor (3). |
| 7/9/84 | *'New style' committal* to crown court. |

| 9/11/84 | Pre-trial review at crown court. Estimated length of trial: three days. Thereafter, case kept out of list as defending counsel unavailable. Case was in many provisional lists put to barristers' clerks by Listing Office. |
| 12/6/85 | Plea of guilty at crown court. |

So the total period was nearly two years. The three stages took seven, seven and nine months respectively. Parts of the waiting period in the crown court were attributable to the defence, especially because their counsel was not available. (In the end another counsel took the brief.) The sentencing process was distorted. After all the agony of not knowing whether his business and personal life were to be ruined, I ordered the defendant to be conditionally discharged. He had suffered enough. (There were other factors: the tapes were not of the worst type and were confined to adults who made a request – they were not displayed.)

I decided to set out my views on delays in the crown court for my superiors and colleagues. I quoted some of the cases and points I have dealt with above. I wrote:

> Hindrances to reform in this and many other areas of our national life include conservatism and complacency. We tend to shrug our shoulders and get on with our daily work, though we all know how bad things are. If we do not put our house in order – for which arguments should not be necessary – we may find public opinion being brought to bear on us.

I went on to suggest a pilot scheme for our crown court, which has the longest backlog. A team of circuit judges would sit continuously for, say, six months. Each judge would have a group of cases allotted to him. He would tackle his load in co-operation with his court clerk and the listing officer, reading the papers well in advance and sending for both sides and hammering out sensible solutions where practicable. Old, weak or trifling cases would be thrown out: delay destroys any point they ever had. The aim would be to reduce the delay between committal and trial to a maximum of ten weeks. Any extension would entail a special application to the judge. More circuit judges will have to be appointed.

My paper advocated experimental evening sessions, say from 5 to 8 p.m., starting with cases which do not require jurors or lay witnesses. Some officials would have to be paid overtime and be glad to earn it. More money would be required, but we must get our priorities right, and the present situation is intolerable.

My proposals were considered at a meeting of judges on my circuit in July 1985. They got a cool reception. The chairman, Mr Justice Taylor, seemed mainly concerned about my reference to complacency, which he did not like. My words fell stillborn from the typewriter. Then in October 1985 I went to sit again at Inner London Crown Court. I could not believe the change that had taken place during the previous twelve months. Instead of trying cases where the crime had taken place eighteen months previously, the cases were only a few months old. I asked what had happened. Judge Peter Mason QC had set up a 'ginger committee' under Judge Suzanne Norwood; the other members are the chief clerk and the listing officer. The crown court speeded up its own processes. Papers are received from the magistrates' courts earlier, and then processed and dispatched to both sides quickly. Indictments are prepared much earlier than before. Cases are listed for trial at the earliest opportunity. Any application to the chief clerk to delay a case is dealt with by the chief clerk personally and scrutinised carefully. Applications for adjournments to the judge on the day of the trial are often dealt with severely, with financial penalties if a solicitor is at fault. Information from the police as to holiday dates of police officers is looked at carefully: it was discovered that the court was being told that an officer would be away 'in August and September' when he would be away for two weeks or not at all: some officers faced disciplinary charges for giving wrong information.

The chief clerk, John Earnshaw, informed me that 'every case is scrutinised regularly at a high level, decisions are taken thereon and stuck to whenever possible. There has been a period of re-educating the professions, and most are now aware that at this court delays are intended to be a thing of the past. We in turn have to reciprocate, and all our processes, including payment of costs, are dealt with expeditiously.'

When I reported all this to the north-eastern circuit judges, a similar 'ginger committee' was set up at Leeds. It is too early to say how successful this will be. But Inner London has shown what can be done by using existing resources. The Lord Chancellor's department should keep its finger on all crown courts and require similar measures. But there seems to be a lack of will and drive. Circuit administrators should be 'business managers' with wider powers.

Here is an example of one case I dealt with. It shows how delays can build up in a case, when there is insufficient effort to keep a constant check on cases:

*Monday, 13th January, 1986.*

*Mr Goss:* May it please your Honour, I appear for the Accused in this case. Your Honour, I understand this case has been listed at the request of the Court.

*Judge Pickles:* It has, because the Court – that is to say, the Court staff and I – are very worried about cases like this. Can you understand our concern?

*Mr Goss:* I can indeed, your Honour, yes.

*Judge Pickles:* Do you share it?

*Mr Goss:* I do, your Honour.

*Judge Pickles:* Perhaps that is unfair. What have you to say in the circumstances?

*Mr Goss:* I anticipate that the Court will primarily be anxious to know when it is that the Defence say they will be in a position to proceed to Trial.

*Judge Pickles:* It is not as simple as that, Mr Goss. The Court must look carefully at what has happened thus far and I do so now because I have the advantage, which you may not have, of having looked at the record which the Court keeps in these matters.

Mr X is charged on an Indictment alleging that on a day between the 1st June 1982, and the 1st January 1983, he stole £6,930.00 in money belonging to the Committee and Members of Y Polytechnic Students Union. I have not scrutinised the papers in this case with the greatest particularity, but I note that it is said on sheet 3 of A's statement that the Defendant was the Treasurer of the Students Union general accounts and Rag account. That is how it is put. In other words, he was a student, I apprehend?

*Mr Goss:* No, your Honour, I think he was employed by the Students Union.

*Judge Pickles:* Oh, I am sorry, he was employed by the Students Union. He was a full-time employee?

*Mr Goss:* Yes.

*Judge Pickles:* Well, there it is. But the dates are these, after the ones in the Indictment: the Defendant was first seen by the police as long ago as the 19th August 1983. He was committed for trial to this Court by the Magistrates on the 5th September 1984.

*Mr Goss:* Yes.

*Judge Pickles:* On the 8th October 1984, he appeared before this Court and pleaded not guilty and there was a pre-Trial Review.

*Mr Goss:* That is right.

*Judge Pickles:* On the 20th December 1984, there is a note that the case was not to be listed until January. That, I apprehend, was at the request of the Defence?

*Mr Goss:* Yes, I would imagine so, your Honour.

*Judge Pickles:* On the 7th January 1985, just over one year ago now, the Prosecution informed the Court that they needed to serve further evidence, which would be done shortly.

*Mr Goss:* Yes.

*Judge Pickles:* On the 11th January 1985, we were asked by the Defendant's solicitors that . . . (*His Honour confers with the Clerk of the Court*) . . . that is right, the Defendant's solicitors had no instructions from the Defendant and could it be listed for mention. On the 8th February 1985, it was mentioned. The Defendant failed to attend Court. A Bench Warrant backed for bail was issued, with a condition that he should instruct his solicitors in the matter. On the 12th February – that is four days later – there was a letter from the solicitors saying that the Defendant had failed to attend for conference with them and the Court, I think, told the solicitors – or rather there is a note that the Defendant was to be told to attend such conference or meeting.

*Mr Goss:* Yes.

*Judge Pickles:* On the 26th March 1985, the Accused failed to attend the Court.

*Mr Goss:* Yes.

*Judge Pickles:* A Bench Warrant was issued which was not backed for bail at that time. He was arrested. On the 28th March – that is two days later – he was bailed by this Court. We were told the case was to be contested.

On the 24th May 1985, the Defendant, we were told, was applying, or the solicitors were applying, to the Legal Aid Area Committee for authority to employ an accountant. We were asked not to list the case yet.

On the 14th June 1985, the Defendant's solicitors said that the accounts had not yet been seen by their accountant. We were asked not, or a note was made not to list the case until the Court was told that the Defence were ready.

On the 11th September 1985, it was decided to list the case for the 26th September 1985, but it was taken out that day because the Defence were still not ready, as on the 26th (on that same day) there was an appointment between the police and the Defence accountant, whereby the Defence accountants were to spend some three days looking at the documents and the accountant apparently thought he would need more time than that.

The next date that appears is the 25th October 1985, when there was a letter from the Defendant's solicitors, which I have here, saying, 'In order to keep you informed of the present position in relation to the above matter, we were informed by County Prosecuting Solicitor that our accountant should contact Chief Inspector Dodds to make arrangements to inspect the relevant papers, only to discover that the Chief Inspector had left and had been posted elsewhere. After some difficulties, arrangements were made and Mr Butterworth,' that is the accountant, 'will be attending at the police station with our client from the 30th October for a number of days. This was the first occasion that the police and our accountant together could fix a suitable time. We shall contact you further as soon as the necessary work has been completed.' Well now, we had heard nothing – the Court heard nothing further from the Defendant's solicitors. What they were doing or not doing, we do not know.

*Mr Goss:* Yes.

*Judge Pickles:* No doubt they were doing something and no doubt we shall be told what.

*Mr Goss:* Yes.

*Judge Pickles:* And why there has been such lamentable delay in this matter. But, on the 12th December, nothing having been heard from the Defence, the Court decided to list the case for mention and I apprehend that is why we are here this day, which, be it noted (I hope I am right), is the 13th January 1986, when we are looking back over a period which begins with the first date in the Indictment, the 1st June 1982.

Mr Goss, my views about delays in Court cases have achieved a certain currency. They have aroused a certain amount of opposition, even vehemence by some people, including some solicitors, but this is the sort of case which makes me extremely worried and I want now to hear from you all you have to say about the reasons for the delay and, in particular, how far they are attributable to those persons who have been representing this Defendant.

*Mr Goss:* Your Honour is obviously intent on conducting a detailed inquiry into this matter and had those instructing me been aware that it was to be such a detailed inquiry, then I would have particularly wished your Honour to see the full bundle of correspondence. It may be possible for that to happen now.

*Judge Pickles:* Mr Goss, you see, one can only put one's finger on these delays which besmirch what should be the fair face of English Justice – and I say 'English' advisedly because it does not happen in Scotland where they conduct themselves with far more efficiency and expedition that we do. Our system – one may use the analogy – it is an old, clanking, carthorse of a system and yet, when one raises these matters with certain people, one gets the sort of remark, 'English Justice is the swiftest in the world.' And that comes from people who know nothing about any other system. But, I digress.

One can only find out why these cases happen if one looks day by day at dates, and one can only investigate this case and try and look to the future conduct of it in the light of what has happened in the past, and I am not prepared just to say blithely, 'Oh, well, it's here now and the past is the past, let's get on with it.' If we are to improve things, we can only do so by seeing what is going wrong and trying – I, in my humble, halting way; there are others far higher than me who have far more power and authority than I have – I have very little, but we can only do what we can, each of us, if we know what is going on and why.

*Mr Goss:* Yes.

*Judge Pickles:* I have to be fair to you. I say, 'to you'. I hope no one would suggest I would be anything else to anybody – certainly not to you. You have done nothing wrong; it is not your fault. I suppose you came into this case last night?

*Mr Goss:* No, your Honour. I can give your Honour certainly quite a lot of information today. Whether it would be sufficient for your Honour's purposes . . .

*Judge Pickles:* Let's be fair to everybody – anybody who has been mentioned – the accountant, the solicitors, the police . . .

*Mr Goss:* Yes.

*Judge Pickles:* The Court is certainly not at fault. You see, we are at the receiving end. We wait for others to act, we in the Court, the staff and I . . .

*Mr Goss:* Yes.

*Judge Pickles:* And that is really the trouble. The Court – and I say this because I have thought a lot about it; I have written a lot about it and I am still on about it with the highest officials in the land – and I mean that – the very highest. The trouble is, the Court ought to take things into its own hands and give directions to people at an early stage. It is the only remedy, and it is all right us waiting and being told, 'Don't list; wait.' But, you see, the trouble is that the listing officer has not got the power of the judge, and judges are going to have to take hold of these cases much, much earlier. Time limits are going to have to be laid down under the Prosecution of Offences Act. The Home Office can do it tomorrow, but they have not done it yet. Judges are going to have to be much firmer and, in my own way, I am going to try. Whether I can change the system . . . However, Mr Goss, if you feel – and you may well properly feel that you and those instructing you should have more time to consider what I have said – I will adjourn it until such time as you wish and I will then carefully consider everything you want to say. If you want it to be adjourned until later today, it will be, or later this week, it will be, but not too long, otherwise I shall be accused of delay.

*Mr Goss:* May I start, your Honour – and if you feel I am providing insufficient information, or there are gaps your Honour requires further investigation into, then perhaps it could be stood down until later today or sometime later this week . . .

*Judge Pickles:* I will do whatever you want, Mr Goss.

*Mr Goss:* May I begin by referring your Honour to the depositions in the first case, and this is a case where it is alleged the Accused has stolen money from the Students Union, at which time he was the Treasurer. Your Honour may have observed from the witness statements, if you have looked at them . . .

*Judge Pickles:* Not in detail. It is my fault. I did not have enough time this morning.

*Mr Goss:* Your Honour, no accounts whatsoever or documents were exhibited and the witness statements contained a great deal of hearsay evidence.

*Judge Pickles:* I see.

*Mr Goss:* Or conclusions of fact drawn from documents which were not produced, and was, therefore, not the best evidence. So, at pre-Trial Review on the 8th October 1984, the first day on which I appeared before the Court, I sought an Order and was granted an Order by His Honour Judge Hallam that the Prosecution provide copies of all documents, schedules and accounts referred to in the witness statements, which the judge agreed.

*Judge Pickles:* That was which date?

*Mr Goss:* 8th October 1984.

*Judge Pickles:* Yes.

*Mr Goss:* Which seemed a reasonable request, seeing as the Defence was denying the allegation that was being made. It was then ordered that the case was not to be listed for at least four weeks.

Your Honour will have seen that nothing was forthcoming – and, indeed, nothing has ever been forthcoming – from the Prosecution by way of copies of documents. What it has been necessary to do has been to inspect those documents at the police station – not, in itself, unreasonable, but obviously mechanically much more difficult.

There came a difficulty in early 1985 – by which time it is right no inspection whatsoever had taken place because no documents had been produced at that stage – when the Accused was not co-operating with his solicitors. Your Honour will have gathered that from the fact that the solicitors were requesting that this case be listed for mention because the Accused was not keeping appointments with them and they were not getting instructions from him, and, your Honour, that took place in February/March 1985.

On the 26th March, your Honour knows, a Bench Warrant, not backed for bail, was issued. He was arrested and released two days later and it is thereafter that I anticipate your Honour will require detailed information as to what took place.

On the 23rd April, last year, those instructing me – and I can produce the copy letter if your Honour wishes to see it – wrote to the Crown Court, requesting extension of the Legal Aid, or confirmation of authority under the Legal Aid Certificate, to appoint an independent firm of accountants to consider the various papers relating to the Y Polytechnic Students Union. My instructing solicitor was told by the Crown Court on the 24th April (obviously the day on which the letter was received) that it would be necessary to apply to the Law Society for extension of that Legal Aid, and there followed over the next few months correspondence with the Law Society, endeavouring to obtain their authority for extension of the Legal Aid, which was finally granted in a limited sum up to £300.00, on a letter dated the 12th August 1985. Thereafter, my instructing solicitors enquired of the Law Society the precise terms of their extension on the 16th August.

On the same day they wrote to the Prosecuting Solicitor's Department, asking for facilities for an accountant, who was now authorised to act, to inspect the documents, saying that it would take more than one day.

On the 21st August there was a conversation with an Officer of the Crown Court, explaining the difficulties that had been encountered extending Legal Aid and the attempts that were now being made, with the assistance of the police, to inspect the various documents.

On the 21st August those instructing me wrote to the Chief Superintendent, West Yorkshire Metropolitan Police, having been told that they should contact him to make facilities available for inspection of the documents.

There followed correspondence with the accountant through September, the accountant indicating that because of holiday commitments he could not carry out the audit until the 24th, 25th and 26th September.

On the 13th September those instructing me wrote to the Crown Court, the Chief Clerk at this Court, explaining in detail what was being done and the problems that were being encountered and your Honour will no doubt have the original of that letter, concluding, 'We trust that you consider that we have done everything in our power to avoid delays, and it is essential to the Defence case that the books are studied by an independent accountant.

On the 30th September the accountant, who had then looked at the books, wrote to those instructing me, saying that he attended at the police station. 'After much searching amongst the boxes of evidence, I came to the conclusion that there were no items on any accounts covering the period after the 28th February 1983, and all activity on Rag accounts occurs in the latter end of the year and almost certainly dies out by the 31st December.' He was saying that he must not only speak to the Accused, but he should have access to the documents in the presence of the Accused.

The Crown Court were kept informed. Those instructing me wrote on the 3rd October, explaining the difficulty that was being encountered.

There followed correspondence with the Prosecution and the police about facilities for inspecting thse documents. Those instructing me were told on the 9th October to contact Chief Inspector Dodd. Of course, it then transpired that Chief Inspector Dodd was not at the police station. It was arranged between the accountant and the police that the only convenient time upon which these inspections could be carried out would be from the 30th October.

On the 29th November the accountant wrote to those instructing me, saying he had examined the documents in question in the company of the Defendant and that he was compiling a report, but, unfortunately, it had been delayed due to illness. He at that time was apparently ill and the delay since then has been caused by his absence from the office due to illness. He simply has not been in to work. I have seen him this morning and this is the first day that he is going to be working again.

On the 19th December those instructing me wrote to the accountant, not appreciating that he was still absent through illness, informing him that the case was listed for mention at this Court on the 13th January this year, and indicating that it was, indeed, before your Honour and that 'this particular judge will make his feelings known in no uncertain terms if we are not ready to proceed'.

*Judge Pickles:* Who wrote that?

*Mr Goss:* My instructing solicitor; a perceptive man, your Honour may think.

*Judge Pickles:* Well, he certainly had an element of foresight . . .

*Mr Goss:* Yes.

*Judge Pickles:* And accurate predictability, from what you say.

*Mr Goss:* Yes.

*Judge Pickles:* I say now that I did not know that I had seen this case before when I looked at it fairly quickly this morning, but I am interested about what you have just recorded. Yes, I am sorry to interrupt.

*Mr Goss:* Yes, and then the information came through, by a telephone memo dated the 20th December, Mr Butterworth has been ill; he came back to the office too soon and was found to have a virus infection and that he was not working. Later that same day, attending the accountant Mr Butterworth, who said it was impossible for him to let us have the report by the 26th December. He said he had had another session at the police station with Mr X and that the evidence was incomplete, that he was nevertheless going to attempt to compile a report, and there are other matters that I do not think it is right to disclose in public about what he is saying about the nature of the evidence.

So, your Honour will see that it is, of course, an unacceptable delay, but it is due to a variety of reasons and I think really none of them could be laid at the doors of those instructing me, who have pursued this matter and chased up wherever possible. I think blame can be laid at various doors, but those instructing me have certainly – and if your Honour wishes to see all the file it can be done . . .

*Judge Pickles:* Yes, thank you. What do you say, Mr Sigsworth?

*Mr Sigsworth:* Your Honour, the correspondence I have in front of me is very limited correspondence, I think, between those instructing me and those instructing my learned friend. It relates entirely, I think, to October of last year when there was a request made by the Defendant's solicitors to take away the documents from the police station so that they could peruse them at leisure, as it were, and presumably with the Accused. They found it difficult to work at the police station, examining the documents there, but Chief Inspector Dodd felt that it would not be appropriate to let the documents leave the police station and refused that permission, but offered to supply the accountant with the most suitable accommodation that could be found at the police station where he could work uninterrupted and thereafter – that was a letter dated the 9th October in reply to the Defendant's letter of the 3rd October – and there seems to be on my file no further correspondence between the Prosecuting Solicitor and the Defence Solicitors. So, I do not think I can assist the Court very much, I am afraid.

*Judge Pickles:* Thank you, Mr Sigsworth. Is there anything else you want to say at this stage in reply to that, Mr Goss?

*Mr Goss:* No, your Honour. I have just received further instructions about the adverse working conditions. Apparently they were placed in the corner of an office in which other people were working in a busy office and it was virtually impossible, when they have to study documents, take instructions on documents, comment on documents, for Mr Butterworth to take proper instructions. I quote from a letter that is dated the 30th September to those instructing me: 'I feel very strongly that it would be in Mr X's interest if he could have access in my presence to the 2 boxes of evidence. In view of the adverse working conditions in the police station and the necessity to be handling continuous computer printouts, it would make life far easier if the evidence could be released to our offices for a period of time,' but obviously I can understand why that was not agreed to, but the facilities that were being afforded were obviously not satisfactory – in itself, of course, not the cause of the delay, but it is one of the factors that contributed to the cause of the delay.

*Judge Pickles:* Thank you, Mr Goss.

*Mr Goss:* May I simply add the position the Defence are in now?

*Judge Pickles:* Yes, because we have got to look at the future in a minute.

*Mr Goss:* Exactly. I have received an assurance from Mr Butterworth, the accountant dealing with it, and from the Accused, that full instructions will be given, a report will be compiled, and the Defence will be prepared for Trial commencing in four weeks time.

*Judge Pickles:* Mr Goss, I think it essential now to fix a specific date when this Trial will definitely start, unless, of course, something which we cannot foresee should intervene.

*Mr Goss:* Yes.

*Judge Pickles:* What is that date to be? The sooner the better.

*Mr Goss:* Yes, I anticipate that the Court Clerk will wish to liaise with Wakefield, because it will be a three-day Trial.

*Judge Pickles:* Can I say now then that, all those involved having been consulted – in particular, Counsel, or Counsel's Clerks – and the availability of witnesses having been checked, every effort be made this day to fix a definite date on which this Trial will commence, and I say now that, should there be any application to un-fix that date, it should be made to me personally because I know about this case, not some judge who will not have that advantage – through no fault of his.

Before I part with this matter, I think I should make one or two observations. First of all, I thank you and Mr Sigsworth for placing before me all the facts that you have been able to. You, Mr Goss, who have had the greater burden in that regard, have, as usual, discharged your duties pleasantly, frankly and in an efficient way. I do not think it would be right, on the facts that I now know, to apportion blame to anybody. It is the system that is wrong and anybody – I apprehend any member of the public who has heard the history of this case, or may hereafter learn of it, I think will share with me my deep concern because, despite the fact that many of these steps that have taken place over the years now may have plausible reasons, in the end it is now three years since this offence is alleged to have taken place and it is, on my calculation, just over two years and four months since this man was first seen by the police about the matter and, although some of the delay is attributable on the face of it to the Defendant himself – let us add, in all fairness to everyone, we do not know the reasons, but he does not appear to have done all that he might to keep in touch with those representing him.

There are other factors, in addition: the worry and sleepless nights afflicted upon waiting Defendants. Witnesses forget, and we have to consider this: the view taken of the law and the way it works by ordinary members of the public is very important because if ordinary people do not respect the law and regard it as inefficient in its working and unjust in its working, then what we do in these Courts fails.

In all the circumstances, I have decided, as this is a case in which we have managed to get, I think, all the relevant dates and details on record, I have decided to ask for a transcript to be prepared and I will send it to my superiors, as an example of what is going on, with my appropriate comments, one of which, of course, will be that this is not typical, all cases do not happen like this, but this is one of the worst, but this is not the only one. There are some worse still in some areas, I know. I say no more this day. Thank you very much.

*Mr Goss:* I wonder if your Honour feels that you can, to send the matter on further, whether your Honour would wish to append to it a copy of the correspondence of those instructing me?

*Judge Pickles:* I will append to it anything that you will put before me on behalf of those whom you are instructed by, Mr Goss, yes, certainly. Either side is free on any day this week to send to the Court any documents which they think in all fairness ought to be appended to the transcript, so that all matters can be before those high persons who will, I trust – in fact, I am sure will scrutinise this with the anxiety which you and I share.

There is no need for long delays in crown court cases. I have pointed to the changes that I think are needed. Inner London Crown Court has shown what can be done by using existing resources. The Lord Chancellor's department should keep its finger on all crown courts and require similar measures. The Home Secretary should bring in statutory time-limits. At moment there is a lack of will and drive at the top; we are not business-like enough at any level. Too often matters are left to judges who have insufficient interest, and staff who feel they have insufficient authority. Yet hundreds wait in jail or lose sleep at home, for month after month, anxious to know their fate at court.

# Chapter 6

## *Too Many Prosecutions?*

At all times there are many cases on their way to every crown court, as on a moving conveyor. Most of the load is sound – the cases were properly commenced. But there is a proportion – say between five and ten per cent – which should not be on the conveyor. Months ago someone put the poor stuff on, and ever since it has creaked and trundled its way to the crown court. No one has had the duty, or even the right, to take it off. If the judge sits by it will end on the lap of the jurors, whose reaction could have been predicted many months and several hundred pounds ago.

Mrs C. was fifty-six and had a good character; she earned £21 a week in a food factory and her husband had £25 from an invalidity pension. In 1977 she came before me, having chosen trial at the crown court for stealing a tin of salmon and a packet of gravy salt from a supermarket: she was seen putting them into her mackintosh pocket. She paid for items in her wire-basket. To the store detective who followed her outside Mrs C. expressed surprise at having items she had not paid for. She gave a false address but gave the correct one when told that the police were to be called. To the police officer she said, 'I can't remember what happened. The things were in my pocket but I can't remember paying for them. I'm on tablets from my doctor, I'm not thinking straight.' She made a written statement to the same effect ending, 'I am under my doctor for nerve trouble and I am taking sleeping-pills – valium – which make me feel drowsy until late in the morning. I am very sorry for what I have done wrong.'

At my suggestion the prosecution agreed to drop the case. Mrs C. had waited months for her trial, which must have meant extra worry and sleepless nights. Even if she had been found guilty after an expensive trial, any penalty would have been nominal. Should she have been prosecuted at all? A warning should be enough in such a case, where a suspect has a good character and the value of the goods is trivial; even more so when she is on tablets. I have no sympathy with gangs of shoplifters or defendants who do it repeatedly. On the other hand, stores choose to operate a system which economises on labour and makes theft temptingly easy; they could do more to protect themselves if they wished, as by requiring the use of a wire-basket and refusing to let customers take their own baskets and bags into the store itself.

In 1986 a young man and a young woman appeared before me charged with stealing a jacket from Woolworth's. They selected the jacket, the price of which was £29.99, and substituted for the price-tag a tag which had £24.99 on. When stopped they offered to pay the extra £5. It is true that the defendants elected trial at crown court, but what need was there to prosecute them at all? In fact they pleaded guilty and received a trifling sentence. It is hard to see what the case achieved.

England and Wales are the only countries I know of where the police, in addition to collecting evidence, decide whether to prosecute. They tend to be too close to the action and to take the view that if there is substantial evidence the court must decide. But policy should come into it. Whoever decides whether to prosecute should ask whether it will serve any practical purpose. Prosecutions are costly, time-consuming and, in some cases, can have a traumatic effect on defendants.

One such case concerned a local Jubilee Fund which had been started. The accused, a housewife, had agreed to look after the cash which came in many tiny sums. Some of the contributors thought she had taken money for herself. Her accounting system was as crude as theirs; they were all enthusiastic amateurs. The accused had a good character and denied the allegations. There was no evidence of excessive spending by her. A glance at the papers on the day before the trial told me that she would not and should not be convicted. I sent a message to both sides indicating my concern and the case was mentioned in open court. Prosecuting counsel, who had only just come into the case, agreed with me and the unfortunate woman was released after months of worry to her and expense to the public. Afterwards prosecuting counsel, a clerk from his solicitors and a senior police officer in the case came to see me in my room at my request. I was not so much concerned to find whose fault had spilt the milk as to protect future consignments. The police attitude was: 'Several members of the public said this woman had stolen charity money donated by them. We knew we hadn't a strong case but we thought it best to let the court decide. We didn't want complaints from councillors or MPs that we were neglecting our job. So we decided to run it. We aren't surprised it's been thrown out and we don't mind in the least.' Someone removed from the police would surely have told them: 'No action. Tell the woman that if she takes on a job like that again she'd better get some advice on book-keeping. Tell the complainants to sue her in the county court if they want to, but we can't waste public money on it.'

Years ago I tried a case at Leeds quarter sessions where two male student teachers had been at a rowdy party. Neighbours' complaints brought officers in a police car. The two students, fortified by the liquid part of the festivities, went out and pushed the police car round the corner as a prank. The enraged and humiliated officers charged the men with taking the car without consent. Technically there may have been no defence but I thought it unnecessary to put such a conviction on their records. I took the initiative, they were cleared and I gave them words of advice which should have come from a senior officer in the first place and been enough. Was I right, or should I have sat back and let the case go on?

A judge has to be careful in a situation like that, for several reasons. He ought not to interfere too much in a contest which is essentially between prosecution and defence, with himself as referee. There may be hidden reasons why the prosecution want to press on. As an example of that, take another case I tried at Leeds sessions. A sixtyish woman who worked in a hospital kitchen was up for stealing a piece of chicken: about enough for one person at one meal – we had a photograph. She had a good character and had suffered through all the waiting. I can see her now, sitting forlornly in the dock in her old raincoat. All those people there, to try that woman for that! I confess I said to myself, 'Convict *her*? Not if I have anything to do with it' – which of course I had. She got off. Yet the prosecution had a point of view, though it did not bear directly on this accused. Because of thefts from the hospital kitchen, one day all the workers there were searched. Those who had property they should not have had were prosecuted, and all pleaded guilty before the magistrates – except this woman. Letting her go did not worry the prosecution in itself but they thought it unfair to the others. So one has to try to find all the angles and do what is right. I still think I did right in that case.

A man of good character was indicted for causing wilful damage to a process-server's car. The defendant had refused to accept a writ and when the process-server touched him with it – so technically serving it – he was so cross that he kicked the car once, causing £25 worth of damage. I suggested that if the accused paid £25 to the process-server the indictment could lie on the file and this was agreed to. In another case, a man of good character was indicted for stealing about £800. He and his father kept a shop; they were agents for a travel firm and kept cash from bookings in a tin. Periodically the travel firm called for the cash. It had become the practice for the defendant to 'borrow' the cash, replacing it later. Eventually he could not replace the £800 because the shop was in financial difficulties. I doubted whether the prosecution could prove dishonesty at the time the money was taken. Defending counsel had the £800 in court in bank-notes. I suggested that the cash be handed over and the indictment lie on the file; this was done. In both those cases justice was, I hope, achieved; the time and expense of a trial were avoided.

I happen to have the transcript of what took place when two young men, S. and W., were jointly charged with stealing a purse and its contents in a night-club. The purse was missed at about 11.10 p.m. About ten minutes earlier the doorman had seen the two defendants standing in a cubicle in the men's toilet. They were facing the cistern and apparently sliding the porcelain lid back into place. When asked what they were doing S. said, 'I'm having a piss'. He did not reply when he was asked why he was messing about with the cistern. The purse was found stuck in the top of the cistern clear of the water. When questioned by the police soon afterwards S. said that he was in the toilet when W. brought the purse in. H. appeared for the prosecution. W. pleaded guilty. M. represented S.

The transcript reads:

| | |
|---|---|
| *Judge Pickles:* | Mr H., what is the evidence against S. on which you rely? |
| *Mr H:* | Your Honour, firstly the two were together in the vicinity of the stolen purse and handbag; secondly that they were found together, as it seemed to the witness – the doorman – replacing the lid of the cistern in which the purse was found. |
| *Judge Pickles:* | They were not both replacing it. |
| *Mr H:* | Well, let me just . . . |
| *Judge Pickles:* | I do not see how there would be room for them. |
| *Mr H:* | Well, they were both in the cubicle. The witness C. says they were both sliding the porcelain lid of the cistern back on, as if it had been removed. Anyway, the prosecution case is that they were both acting in concert, from start to finish. |
| *Judge Pickles:* | But when seen, did he make any admissions? |
| *Mr H:* | No, your Honour; he denied it. |
| *Judge Pickles:* | He said he had just gone in for a 'piss'. |
| *Mr H:* | Then, later, he altered the nature of what he had gone in for – he told two stories of what he had gone in for – saying that W. had just come in with the purse while he was using the toilet. He claimed, your Honour, did S., that he was using the toilet at the time, but there is no evidence from the witness about that. In fact, your Honour, S. says at the middle of page 7 that he was in the toilet with his trousers half way down his ankles when W. came in with the purse but, in contrast to that, the doorman says what I have told you all ready, that they were at the cistern, putting the lid back on. |
| *Judge Pickles:* | It seems a bit thin against S., doesn't it? I mean, say what you think. If you think it is strong, say so. |
| *Mr H:* | It is not a case I am minded not to proceed on. |
| *Judge Pickles:* | All right. |

| | |
|---|---|
| *Mr H:* | He may well be acquitted, your Honour; that is another matter. |
| *Judge Pickles:* | If he probably will, there is no point in going on with it. |
| *Mr H:* | On the evidence, there is a case against him. |
| *Judge Pickles:* | There is always a case against people, otherwise we don't proceed. The question is how strong is it? He is a man of good character. |
| *Mr H:* | Your Honour, with respect, so is every shoplifter until he is convicted. |
| *Judge Pickles:* | Of course, that is right. But if the case were strong it would be quite irrelevant; if it is very thin, well, it is a fact that weighs, isn't it? |
| *Mr H:* | Oh, your Honour, certainly. I mean, so far as penalty is concerned, even if he were convicted, little would flow – little penalty would be imposed. But, your Honour, I have considered this case; I hope your Honour will think that I have. |
| *Judge Pickles:* | Of course you have. |
| *Mr H:* | So far as I am concerned, although any comments from your Honour are extremely carefully considered and treated with respect, I feel that this is a case where there is evidence. |
| *Judge Pickles:* | He wasn't seen to take it. The first time he really comes into it, so far as the purse is concerned, is when he is seen in the toilet, and there is some dispute about what he was precisely doing. The person who saw him in the toilet is a twenty-year-old night-club doorman. |
| *Mr H:* | Yes – whose evidence, your Honour, suggests that whatever they were doing, they were doing together. I mean, if the doorman's evidence is accepted, then the defendant's evidence about using the toilet for his own relief cannot be; it is as simple as that. |
| *Judge Pickles:* | How can two men apparently stand side by side in a toilet and fiddle about with the cistern? There isn't room, is there? |
| *Mr H:* | I have not seen inside of this toilet, but there is room in most toilets for two men to stand together, one on each side of the bowl. I must not give evidence |

|  |  |
|---|---|
| | myself! |
| *Judge Pickles:* | It would be a bit cramped! Anyway, you say you want to go on? |
| *Mr H:* | I ought to make the point it is not the prosecution who have elected trial . . . |
| *Judge Pickles:* | Certainly not, but the prosecution have elected to prosecute. |
| *Mr H:* | Certainly, your Honour. |
| *Judge Pickles:* | Anyway, I don't think it is very strong. On the other hand, it is for you to say, and if you want to run it, all right, you have got that right, I can't stop you; and it is right there is a case, yes, there is, it is right, but I wonder whether it is worth spending hundreds of pounds on finding yea or nay whether he did it. |
| *Mr H:* | There is also the point to consider, if the defendant is guilty – and there is evidence to support the case against him – it would be unfair on the defendant who has had the honesty to plead guilty . . . |
| *Judge Pickles:* | Yes, but there is more evidence against him, you see, because he has admitted it, in terms; that is the difference. |
| *Mr H:* | I agree. But so far as acts are concerned, your Honour, all the evidence is they acted together. |
| *Judge Pickles:* | I know, but a confession adds some weight. |
| *Mr H:* | Oh, yes, your Honour. |
| *Judge Pickles:* | I say no more. |
| *Mr H:* | I would ask for bail for him. |
| *Judge Pickles:* | Yes. Mr S. can go. Keep in touch with your solicitor, and come back ready to be tried when you are told to come. Mr M., have you given us the list of prosecution witnesses you will require? |
| *Mr M:* | I will hand it in now. |
| *Judge Pickles:* | Length? |
| *Mr M:* | Three-quarters of a day. It is unforunate, I think, I have got to ask for all of the witnesses. |
| *Judge Pickles:* | Anyway, Mr H. is going to have another think about the matter. |

*Mr H:*          I am not, with respect, your Honour. The position is
as I have indicated.

*Judge Pickles:*   He is not. His mind is made up. All right.

At the trial, before another judge, another prosecuting counsel offered no
evidence against S.

A national prosecution service came into full operation on 1 October
1986. With others I recommended this to the Royal Commission on
Criminal Procedure, and their report favoured it. Under the old system,
not every area had a prosecuting solicitor's department. The police did
not have to take the advice given to them where they had solicitors. As I
understand the new system, the police still usually decide whether to
prosecute, but the prosecution department, staffed by lawyers, then takes
over. These are early days. I have not so far noticed any difference. We
will see how it works; it is bound to bring some improvements. There
will, nevertheless, be a need for judges to play a more active, positive and
constructive role than is usual. The judge is the referee, but the analogy
is not apt all the way through. There are times when a judge should not
only stop play but even kick the ball. He must, however, keep his clothing
clean and not get rolled in the mud. His authority comes from impartiality
that is not indifference; dignity that falls short of pomposity; help which
does not patronise; suggestions which do not dominate.

As the law stands the judge cannot stop a case until the end of the
prosecution evidence, when he can rule that there is insufficient evidence
and direct an acquittal.

Some cases are so trivial that trying them achieves little except the
expenditure of public time and money, to the detriment of substantial
cases. A judge should be able to order that an indictment lie on the file,
even though the prosecution want to go on. He would do so if he
considered that the public interest did not require a trial. The indictment
would lie on the file, but if during, say, the next six months new circumstances arose, such as that the defendant had 'done it again', the judge
could order the indictment to be taken off the file and the case tried. The
prosecution would have rights of appeal against the judge's decision to
file the indictment or to refuse to take it off the file, and a defendant could
at any stage ask the judge to direct an acquittal.

The filing of the indictment would be recorded for the guidance of any
future judge who might be considering what to do with a further indictment. An accused could not normally expect to get the benefit of this
procedure more than, say, once every ten years. There are potential drawbacks. Care would have to be taken not to encourage an accused to go to
the crown court merely to obtain an advantage he would not have had
before the magistrates. If all shoplifters of good character could be sure
of a pigeon-holed indictment they might all go for trial at the crown court.

But they could not be sure. And crown Court sentencing tariffs are – or should be – stiffer than magistrates'. In any event, why not give to magistrates similar pigeon-holing powers with similar safeguards?

The legal process is expensive, inevitably. Every crown court case costs the public hundreds of pounds. There are many important cases to be tried, yet they are delayed by the inclusion of relatively trifling cases, the prosecution of which does no discernible good to anybody. In the past, prosecuting authorities – usually the police – have not been flexible enough in deciding whether to take people to court. Their discretion should be used more wisely and less woodenly in 'useless' prosecutions. One hopes that the new national prosecution service will achieve that, eventually. Giving some discretion to judges, as I have suggested, would let them play 'long-stop' in those cases which still slipped through.

# Chapter 7

## *Juries*

We have the jury system because we have always had it. If we did not have it no one would think of inventing it. No one would suggest, as a means of settling a dispute, going into the street and choosing twelve over-eighteens at random. Jurors were originally witnesses: they knew what had been going on in the area where they lived. Over the centuries the English common law and those legal systems based on it have attached to the jury a certain mysticism. The jury system has its good points but it is illogical in its selection and uncertain in its results. I have seen hundreds of juries at work, and one of the advantages from a defendant's angle is that they let many people off whom lawyers would not. This certainly introduces a sporting element, but whether that is in the interest of society as a whole is doubtful. In most criminal trials there is tacit acceptance by both sides' lawyers that the accused is guilty. The only uncertainty is whether the untrained jurors, bringing to their task minds that are not used to analysing calmly or thinking logically and are easily swayed and unbalanced by prejudice, will see what to lawyers is obvious. Some defendants get away with stories that to me seem not only fictional but farcical. In 1984 I tried a man for burglary of television sets and the like valued at £11,500. He was alleged to have said to the police, 'I've got to take a chance with a jury. If they convict me that's my bad luck, but some of the decisions they hand down these days, I'm bound to stand a chance. I've got to, I've nothing against you lads, you've been as right as rain with me, and I appreciate that. I'm going to have to call you liars when I get to court. I can't risk this on my own, especially when I've got nothing out of it.' (The defendant must have thought this was off-the-record – though the police could have invented it, 'putting on the verbals' as the criminal fraternity say.)

It is true that the jurors usually do not know all that I know about the case, including the defendant's background and any previous convictions. If he has a good character he can tell the jury so, but the prosecution's hands are usually tied. It is fair to say that a man may be innocent even though appearances suggest otherwise, and letting that man go free is some justification for our system, even though many more go free who should not. One of the anomalies is that during a trial we go to great lengths to do things properly in court, excluding what is irrelevant or unfair, and then we lock up the jurors on their own with no outsider to guide them or ensure that their discussion is orderly. When jurors return to court to ask the judge a question it is often apparent that they have not followed a clear direction on a simple point of law – why should they, they are laymen? – or that they have latched on to things that do not matter. It is well that juries do not give reasons for their verdicts or there would be an appeal in most cases. When I happen to meet people socially who have served on juries (not in cases I have tried) they say such things as, 'I didn't really agree with the verdict, but I went along with the others,' or, 'The discussion was a shambles.'

None of this is surprising. Members of other lay tribunals – magistrates, general commissioners of income tax or lay members of industrial tribunals – are carefully chosen for their proven qualities. Magistrates get detailed instruction in law and procedure before they are allowed to adjudicate. Jurors are picked blindly from lists of electors and get no training; they are pitched straight into a case. Or – more likely – they have to wait about for a long time, and some of them must feel cross about this. Some waiting is inevitable: we have to call more jurors than we will probably need because at the moment every defendant can challenge three jurors without giving reasons and the prosecution has a similar right. It is imposs-ible to foretell precisely how long a case will last. A defendant may change his mind and plead guilty or not guilty when not expected to; or plead guilty part way through a case. Even so we in the courts do not always consider jurors' convenience as we should. If they have been kept waiting I like to tell them why. I have seen more jurors called than was necessary. Jurors have no option; they have to come or be fined, unless they ask to be and are excused for having a one-man business, being ill or deaf or the like.

There is nothing to guarantee that illiterates or mental defectives do not get on a jury. A man who cannot read says, 'I've left my spectacles at home,' and the oath is read to him. A severely subnormal person would probably be noticed and objected to by the prosecution. Nothing is known about the panel except their names and addresses. Their occupations used to be on the list but several years ago the Lord Chancellor stopped this, no doubt because of the sort of practice that I took part in once. A QC and I were defending a man charged with receiving goods by buying them from a lorry-driver who had stolen them from his employers. The defendant said he believed the man was buying and selling honestly on his own account, using the lorry as transport. My main job in the case was to go through the list of jurors beforehand, as we did not think it prudent to have on the jury those who might know too much about the trade in question or lorry-driving. The defendant was acquitted, rightly I assume.

Some judges from the provinces, including me, sit in London crown courts for a few weeks a year to help out: there is a backlog of cases caused partly by a shortage of judges. It is interesting to see how things are done there, by juries and others. In London the bar is subtly different. Metropolitan Police prosecutions go to those on a list and they do not normally defend. In the provinces it is usual for barristers who do crime to take both sides' briefs. This tends not make them either prosecution-minded or defence-minded. The criminal bar in London is more cosmo-politan, with more coloured counsel than the north-eastern circuit has. There is an increasing and understandable tendency for coloured defend-ants to ask for coloured solicitors and counsel, and this boosts many a practice, sometimes out of proportion to talent. Some counsel from different cultural backgrounds find it hard to think along established lines; some identify too closely with their clients and clash frequently with the bench. Coloured accused properly try to get as many coloured jurors on to their jury as they can, and this is easier in London where there seems to be a higher proportion of coloured jurors than on my own circuit.

The challenging of jurors is done more often in London than in the north, and it is common for the defence to use all their rights of challenge. If there are four defendants, all the jurors can be replaced. If the charge is house-burglary, 'respectable' looking jurors tend to be challenged; not so young, casually dressed or unshaven ones. If a man called for jury service does not wish to serve he should go in his best suit, carrying a rolled umbrella and the *Financial Times:* he is almost certain to be challenged in London. Crime is more professional there, and the legal profession – parts of it – tends to be more pro-criminal in the sense of exploiting every lawful device and, I suspect, some that are unlawful.

In my evidence to the Royal Commission on Criminal Procedure in 1978 I wrote this about defending solicitors in criminal cases:

If a solicitor gets a lot of criminal defences, whether legally aided or paid, there is good money in it. Criminals tend to go to and recommend those they think are 'sympathetic'. The temptations are obvious. One solicitor admitted to me that he had invented the client's story. I had reliable information about another solicitor who wrote to an alibi witness asking for his account and enclosing the accused's proof of evidence. How typical are they? I do not know. There is privilege of communication between solicitor and client and neither usually has any reason to reveal malpractice. One does get signs though. When trying a case I saw a letter which had been intercepted on its way out of prison: the accused had written to a prosecution witness who was friendly, telling her how to change her story, what to do when the police went to see her and which solicitor to go to, adding, 'I think he's bent' (I don't think he is). Most solicitors are honest, some bend the rules a bit – sometimes to compensate for similar police practice – and a few are as crooked as any client but cleverer.

In one case I tried in London all the rights of challenge were used. The defendant who had most to explain chose to make an unsworn statement from the dock (a right since abolished) so that he could not be cross-examined. Another defendant in the case sacked his lawyers so that he could, for example, make attacks on me that his barrister would not have made. The barrister began his final speech to the jury: 'You may ask how I can defend a man if I know he is guilty. The answer is that I don't.' This could mean 'I only defend innocent people'. In releasing one of the defendants from prison early the Court of Appeal referred to a letter offering him a job. I read this with a certain cynicism. The letter may well have been genuine, but not all such documents are, as I have found in several cases.

I had an appeal by a man who had received three months' imprisonment from the magistrates. His counsel urged us not to uphold the sentence, as he was working in a job for the NCB. A document was produced giving a date for an interview. When I had it checked it came out that the appellant had not worked there for a single day. The magistrates sitting with me and I doubled his sentence: that is justice, doing what fits the case. A man who has the effrontery to try to mislead a court deserves extra punishment. In another case a defendant's wife brought a doctor's certificate saying the defendant was unfit to come to court. When the police went to his house at my request he was away at a football match in another town. His deception did him no good in the end. Magistrates and judges should always check such documents and pleas. It is odd how many jobs are offered just before a man is due to be sentenced, and it is not hard to obtain documents from 'employers'.

The jury is not essential to the legal process. An appeal from the magistrates is heard by a judge and magistrates without a jury. Until the 1914 war we had juries in civil cases in the high court and county courts, but since then juries have gradually been eclipsed in civil cases and are now confined to such cases as defamation and false imprisonment. In other civil cases the judge decides everything, facts as well as law. I have only twice been in civil cases with juries: once at the bar and once as a judge. In the latter case it was in the county court, where a jury has only eight members; we had to look everything up. To have jurors in every contested county court case would soon jam up the works. As it is I can get at the facts in common-sense, short-cutting ways that would be impossible if everything had to be explained to jurors. Criminal trials are lengthened for that reason: counsel have to go into everything with tedious repetition. They cannot know what is going on in the jurors' minds, whereas they know a judge and how his mind works and he can, if necessary, tell them. A jury has no collective mind before it retires at the end of the case; even nods and grimaces are only from individuals, and may be misinterpreted.

A nod in apparent agreement with counsel's point may in fact mean, 'I thought you were going to say that but it's nonsense.'

Another factor against the jury system is the colossal use of manpower. An unemployed person or housewife with no outside job may find the experience fascinating; but what of the busy executive whose office is clamouring for his return? Do we need as many as twelve jurors? In the 1939 war eight sufficed except in capital cases. In Scotland they have fifteen but a bare majority is enough, whereas in England and Wales the verdict must have at least ten in favour. Jury-nobbling is becoming a problem in London though I have not heard of it happening elsewhere. Bank-robbers may have enough money to tempt impoverished jurors. It is more difficult to bribe a judge and I have never heard of its being tried, even in London. A colleague of mine, now a judge, did arrive at the Court of Appeal to be shown by his appellant client a suitcase full of money on the principle that every judge must have his price, but the client was swiftly disabused.

Now for the good points about the jury system: there are some. If defendants in the crown court were tried by 'professionals' – judges only or judges and magistrates – they would say, 'You don't stand a chance with that lot. They know it all. They've heard it all before.' The 'sporting element' is not to be sneered at. The main object is to leave a defendant feeling that he has had 'a fair do', win or lose. If he feels he has not, he becomes alienated from the system. As it is, if he loses it is at the hands of ordinary folk like himself – not from 'them', the clever privileged people who know it all. It is also good for jurors to play an essential part in the process. They do not say to me what they think about it at the end of two or more weeks in the crown court. They may have come reluctantly, hesitantly like children going to school for the first time, not knowing what to expect or how those in charge will treat them, half fearing and half looking forward to a new experience. Some must resent a potential waste of time. I hope that by the end they all feel some respect for the way we do things and confidence that should they come back one day and sit in the dock instead of the jury-box, they will have a fair trial.

Jurors reflect public opinion. When I first practised, in pre-breathalyser days, they usually acquitted defendants in driving under the influence of drink cases, presumably on the basis of 'There but for the grace of God'. Many jurors did it themselves and thought it hard luck for those who got caught. Even before the breathalyser the conviction-rate increased, as jurors realised how dangerous drink-driving was. Parliament has now removed breathalyser cases from juries altogether. (When I first sat as assistant recorder most of my work was trying such cases.) A further factor in favour of the system is that jurors are a safeguard against oppression by judges or policemen. A judge who tries too hard for a conviction may get a nose-ender from the jury, and this restrains most judges, whatever they feel about the facts.

It is difficult now for the prosecution to get a conviction based on the evidence of police officers only; in London it is virtually impossible. Jurors know how many officers, some of very high rank, have been convicted of serious misconduct in recent years. Some officers misbehave when dealing with potential jurors as members of the public. Not long ago I was stopped for speeding in my little sports-car. It was late one Saturday evening and my son and I were casually dressed. The observer in the police car may have thought we were two tearaways as he came to the passenger door, opened it and said brusquely, 'Got your licence?' 'Yes.' 'Then bring it.' He marched over to the police car followed by meek me. I sat in the back and only spoke when spoken to. The driver was polite, but not so the observer. He was angry. 'I expect you know why you've been stopped; you should do,' and so on. I should not have been speeding; a judge ought to set a good example; I was properly prosecuted and fairly fined.

A bit later I decided to ring the observer's police station and speak to his superior. I pointed out the folly of dealing with the public like that; if I had had a larger chip on my shoulder than I have I might have shown resentment and been rude back, and before long there could have been blood all over the place and many flashing blue lights. That would happen to that man eventually. I try such cases in court, when each side blames the other. I suggested that someone have a quiet word with the man; I did not want to make an official complaint. He was spoken to in due course by his divisional commander. Such experiences are useful for a judge: a peep into a life he hears about but does not normally see. Police-men are not all angels, and some go too far, but it is wrong to be prejudiced against them all, as some jurors undoubtedly are.

These are my proposals for altering the jury system in criminal cases:

1 Juries should consist of nine persons in criminal cases. Majority verdicts should be 7–2 or 8–1. A jury should not be reduced below eight for illness, etc., the majority required then being 7–1.

2 Anyone convicted of an offence of dishonesty in the past fifteen years should be disqualified. Failure to disclose such a conviction should be an imprisonable offence.

3 A jury should only be vetted under an order made by a judge after hearing both sides. The defence should be able to apply. The test: whether a class of juror is likely to be biased.

4 A defendant should have the option of trial at the crown court by a judge, two jurors and two magistrates, the judge retiring with the others, all to have one vote, majority verdicts to be 4–1.

5 A judge should be able to direct trial as under 4 above in cases of unusual length or complexity and to order that the jurors be chosen

from special panels – of accountants and persons experienced in business in the case of company fraud trials, for example.

# Chapter 8

## *Plea-bargaining*

Plea-bargaining has become a dirty word in some people's minds. They think it is something sordid; part of a selfish game played by lawyers and judges at the expense of defendants. This may be partly because the term comes from the USA, where things go on which we condemn. It might be better to use another term but I know none. English law has got into an odd state. The Court of Appeal has said that plea-bargaining does not exist; that it is impossible for a defendant to bargain with the court about sentence. Yet it happens every day and it is in the interests of all concerned that it should.

There are three principles in this area. First, a sentence must fit the facts; a defendant must get what he deserves and it is wrong to shorten a case if it involves his getting less than he deserves. Second, we judges must earn public confidence by acting openly, fairly and with dignity. Third, we need to limit the contested parts of crown court trials, so saving time and expense and shortening delays in other cases. The taxpayer usually pays both sides' costs and crown courts are expensive to run when everything is included: officials' salaries, lawyers' fees, jurors' and witnesses' expenses and maintenance of the buildings.

What *is* plea-bargaining? Years ago at Leeds Assizes I was defending before a jury and a high court judge, who later became a law lord. I forget the facts but at an early stage the judge adjourned and asked both counsel to go to his room, where the talk went like this:

*Judge:*    This defence won't come off, Pickles.
*I:*    I know the difficulties, my lord, and so does my client.
*Judge:*    Well?
*I:*    Frankly, he's worried about going to prison.
*Judge:*    Yes. Well. Understandable. Let me see. He hasn't much of a criminal record, has he? (Document examined.) Oh, on that, no, I don't see why he should go down. A substantial fine.
*I:*    (brightening) Just give me five minutes with him, my lord.

My client now had the one bit of information that had been lacking. Soon he had changed his plea to guilty and he was on his happy way home. All concerned were satisfied. No one thought there was anything wrong. Yet it was a plea-bargain: an offer by the judge to allow the defendant his liberty if he pleaded guilty, which was accepted by the defendant when he pleaded guilty.

The key to understanding plea-bargaining is: imprisonment. I mean an immediate sentence (not a suspended one), and I include detention centre and youth custody orders. By comparison most defendants shrug off any other penalty as tolerable. Prisons are unpleasant places and must remain so. On his release a man who has not been before may suffer further humiliation: stigma, pointing fingers. He knows before he goes what there is to fear. If he has been previously he knows even better; though he may not fear it as much he will try to avoid it. A few homeless, hopeless old lags actually prefer to be inside, especially in winter: prisons have warmth and food. But most defendants are anxious, even desperate, not to go to prison. If they feel they have to go, they want as short a sentence as they can get.

I am not referring to a defendant who knows he cannot properly be convicted, because, for example, he was nowhere near the scene and has been wrongly identified. There should be no question of such a man pleading guilty and so plea-bargaining ought not to arise. In most cases the issue is: 'What did the defendant, who was admittedly there, intend and do?'

Take a fairly typical case which is shortly to come up at a crown court. Smith is charged with wounding Jones with intent to do him grievous bodily harm: section 18, Offences against the Person Act 1861. A less serious alternative is wounding without that intent: section 20. When section 18 is charged the jury is entitled to convict of section 20 only. And the defendant may offer a plea to it at the start. Smith and Jones argued in a pub as both held beer glasses. They scuffled and both ended on the floor, Jones' face cut by Smith's glass. Each says the other struck first. Smith told the police it was part accidental, part self-defence. He has no convictions for serious violence. Eye-witnesses' accounts divide into pro-Smith and pro-Jones; none is independent and reliable, all being tainted by their loyalties or their records.

The attitudes of the participants in the case at the crown court, before it starts, can be typified as follows:

*Smith:* I want to get out of this as cheaply as I can. I know I could get sent down, and for section 18 I am bound to be. I must keep my liberty at all costs. My lawyers know more about it than I do and I want to know:

1   What is the likely verdict if I plead not guilty to the end?
2   Will I go down if I plead guilty to section 20 now?
3   What will I get if I fight and the jury do me for section 20?

*Smith's lawyers:* We want to get you out of this as cheaply as possible,

Smith. The shorter the case lasts the less we'll be paid, but that won't affect our advice. As to your questions:

1  The likely verdict if you plead not guilty to the end? Who can tell with a jury? Twelve unknowns, chosen at random, untrained. We've advised defendants to plead guilty who've refused to and then got off. The odds look against your getting off altogether, but only you can decide what to do. Defendants usually get a lighter sentence for pleading guilty.

2  Plead guilty to section 20? We can speak to the prosecution; that's easy. They might agree: they know we have eye-witnesses and that theirs can be shot at. But the judge might not agree to section 20. And even if he does he might still jail you. He's tough on 'glassing', though he can be affected by a speech in mitigation. He may be glad if the case goes short as a plea of guilty: the sun is shining and he's a golfer. Yes, on the whole a plea of guilty to section 20 seems best, if we can be sure you won't go down. It's a bit tricky but we'll see if we can sound out the judge.

3  The sentence if you fight to the end and the jury do you for section 20? It could well mean prison. The judge will have seen the witnesses in the box, examined Jones' scars and maybe taken pity on him: Jones is smaller than you. The judge will have heard you give evidence and might not like you; he may think you pushed it much too far and bullied Jones. But if you plead guilty he'll only hear you say that one word – and you don't look a bad chap from a distance. Oh, and if you get done by the jury, even if only for section 20, bang goes most of the mitigation: you can't deny doing it and then say you're sorry you did it.

*Prosecution lawyers:*  This is a bad case and there are too many like it. Smith should go to jail. We must be realistic, though: we've had cases like this where defendants have got off everything. Our witnesses are shaky. We'd agree to section 20 if we could be sure Smith would go down, but we can't ask the judge that; we're not allowed to say anything about sentence. If the judge agrees to section 20 and indicates a non-custodial sentence we can stand up to him for a bit, but there's no point in antagonising him. We have to live with him.

*Judge:*  It gets harder to typify here. A solicitor sitting as an assistant recorder for the first time is not like a high court judge with fifteen years on the bench. Some judges are restrained; they sit back silent and let things flow, not giving their views on sentence unless the defence asks and even then giving them reluctantly, if at all. Other judges take a strong line before the case even starts and are bursting to see counsel in private to 'carve it up'. I can give only a broad, average judicial reaction. 'This case will take about four days if it remains contested. All that expense, and those other defendants waiting to be tried. If it becomes a plea of guilty it will take about an hour, and as there's no other case in the list the rest of the day will be wasted in one sense. On the other hand I shan't have to sit through all the tedious evidence or the repetitive speeches by counsel: there'll be no summing-up for me to prepare and get right. And the golf-course beckons. *But* I mustn't let my own convenience come into it. If I have to try this case as a contest, well that's why I'm here. The public has to be protected. I must not be soft with Smith just to shorten the case, though if he pleads guilty he is entitled to a more lenient sentence. If the jury are not likely to convict for section 18 we might as well face that now and consider section 20. I'll look again at the prosecution witnesses' statements and Smith's record. If there is a social inquiry report, and the probation people will let me see it, I'll read that too.

[The policy of the probation service is not to do a report in a case where a plea of not guilty is expected.]

If the judge decides that section 18 must be left to the jury there is no way of shortening the case, even if both counsel would agree to section 20. In practice, I usually let the prosecution decide whether a plea of guilty to a lesser offence should be accepted. They have more information than I have: about the quality of their witnesses, for example (I only have statements). I put my foot down sometimes, however, as where a deadly weapon like a knife is used. In one way a knife is worse than a gun. The latter can be aimed so as to limit injury, whereas when two men fight and one has a knife anything can happen.

If the judge thinks that section 20 – wounding without the intent – is appropriate, there are three main possibilities for his views on sentence. First, he may think immediate loss of liberty is unnecessary. Second, he may think that it does seem necessary on what he knows now; but defending counsel's mitigation may persuade him otherwise. Third, he may think it is too early to think about sentence.

The difficulty arises where the defendant has not yet pleaded guilty to section 20, and will not do so unless he can be sure that he will keep his liberty. Can he find out what the judge thinks? How can this be done? Is it wrong for the judge to say, even though that would immediately lead to a plea of guilty, thereby shortening the case? These questions lie at the heart of plea-bargaining.

The results of the above attitudes and other factors may be summarised in this way. In most cases the chief worry in a defendant's mind is whether he will get an immediate custodial sentence. The chief worry of a man with a bad record may be whether he will get a very long sentence. Similarly for a man charged with a very serious offence, whatever his record. In a minority of cases the main concern is about conviction rather than sentence. For an MP, lawyer or policeman, conviction for stealing a bar of chocolate is a calamity, so plea-bargaining does not arise. In most cases an accused will be advised and be ready to plead guilty if he feels that he is likely to be convicted *and* he knows he will keep his liberty – or in some cases get a prison sentence that he regards as short.

In some cases a defendant will take a gamble on his sentence because the judge is known to be lenient: plea-bargaining does not come into it. Ideally there should be one predictable, 'computered' sentence for any set of facts, but no two judges are alike. Sentencing is a lottery: much depends on which judge you happen to get.

During plea-bargaining the judge has to try to read the defendant's mind. If the defendant is told what type of sentence awaits him on a plea of guilty, and it is one he will not be able to face, it is pointless for the judge to give any indication: if he does, he will only encourage the accused to take his chance with the jury and fight doggedly on.

*The main justification for plea-bargaining is this: it is intolerable for a case to go on for days or weeks because the defendant cannot ask what sort of sentence a plea of guilty would attract – even though the judge knows the answer, and if the defendant could be told it the case would stop dead.*

What is the present law about plea-bargaining? It is in a tangle. One decision of the Court of Appeal\* (an appeal from me, as it happens) says that plea-bargaining does not even exist. Other cases say that the judge may indicate the type of sentence he is minded to impose. *But* this must be the same whether the defendant pleads guilty or pleads not guilty and is convicted. Another case says that if he pleads guilty a defendant is entitled to a lesser sentence and his counsel may tell him this (but the judge may not!). The Court of Appeal has said that counsel must have access to the judge, openly or privately, to give him new information about the case, or obtain a decision on such matters as whether a plea of guilty to a lesser charge would suffice, or what type of sentence would follow a guilty plea. Private discussions with the judge by counsel are to be regarded as exceptional. One exception is where the defendant is dying but does not and should not know, but the judge should.

Many of the difficulties surrounding plea-bargaining come from counsel going to see the judge in his room. The practices of crown court judges vary widely. Some see counsel whenever counsel ask. A few judges refuse to see them at all, or only in very rare situations. One judge told me that he only sees counsel he can trust. Surely that raises as many problems as it solves: suppose he only trusts counsel on one side. Some judges take the initiative, sending for counsel before the case starts and virtually giving directions: 'If X pleads guilty to count 1 he'll get a suspended sentence.

\*See R. v. Atkinson, 1977 67 Criminal Appeal Reports 200 (Court of Appeal).

Count 2 can lie on the file. If Y pleads guilty to section 20 on count 3, that will do and he'll get community service.' Some judges negotiate more subtly, sending and receiving messages through their clerks or court-clerks.

I do not like these private discussions in judges' chambers. Why do they go on at all? First, because they always have. Few lawyers can resist the seductive charm of such an argument: 'If it has always gone on, it *must* be right. What the wisdom and experience of generations have hallowed . . .' Second, almost all judges are ex-barristers. This is one of the strengths of our system. We judges understand counsel's problems because we had them. We all belong to one fraternity. At the bar one lives with the lively, the generous, the profound (they are not all like that). Judges miss that life as day after day they see their former colleagues only across the formal court-room. It is good to chat with the lads. How tempting to sit down and sort it all out, wigs off and feet up. Privacy brings relaxation; the tension of open court has gone. There is no one writing down what is said, though the shorthand-writer will come in and do so if asked. There are no press or public peering over one's shoulder. Even the defendant – around whose fate it all revolves – is not there and his solicitor may not be. Counsel can say things about the accused and the case that they could not say out there in court. There is no need for pretence in here; the nod need not be concealed nor the wink suppressed. In court, counsel hesitates to say to the judge, 'My client denies it, but he'd like to know what would happen to him if he admitted it.' In chambers such anomalies are easily swallowed. The judge knows what it is all about: he played the part countless times and judges understood. In this easy atmosphere the rules can be overlooked in a genuine effort to find a sensible short-cut, off the record.

In many cases these private discussions succeed and no one complains: the result is just. But in a number of cases defendants later raise grievances, and there is embarrassment for the trial judge and counsel. There is unseemly dispute about what went on in the judge's room. In more than one case counsel have had to go into the witness-box in the Court of Appeal. The two sides disagree about what was said. The judge may be asked for his written recollection, but he does a lot of cases. A transcript would settle it, yet there is not one. Some appellants get their convictions or sentences set aside, against the real merits.

It is wrong to discuss the case behind the defendant's back. His barrister, and sometimes his solicitor, is there, but that is not a complete answer. Look at it from the accused's angle. Lawyers are not his favourite people; courts are not his favourite places – he was here before and did time. When his barrister and the prosecution's disappear into the judge's room together, what is going on? They must be talking about his case. When his man emerges he is cagey about what did go on. He says he has reason to think that if the defendant pleads guilty he will not go to prison. This must have come from the judge, but why cannot the man in the wig and gown say so outright? When the court resumes no reference is made to the private meeting; they all pretend it never happened. What a charade! Later the defendant may feel and allege that a deal was done at his expense. He and his new lawyers properly seize and air any argument to quash the conviction or reduce the sentence. Look again into the defendant's mind. He may have a special reluctance to admit his guilt. The offence may have distasteful features, so how can he tell his family that he did it? Or his wife may have threatened to leave him if he committed one more crime. If he pleads not guilty to the end he can blame the jury if it goes wrong. Should he plead guilty on judge's-room advice, he can blame his counsel and the judge for forcing him.

Going back to Smith's case, his barrister says, 'If you plead guilty to section 20 I'm fairly certain you won't go to prison. But if the case goes on and you are found guilty for section 18, as you may well be, you're bound to go down. So I advise you to plead guilty to section 20.' This is probably the best advice. But Smith may later say, 'My barrister told me that if I didn't plead guilty I'd go to prison.' This type of situation has caused public concern and this will continue until everything is done openly.

For years I have usually refused to see counsel privately about criminal cases. There are rare exceptions, but I then insist on the shorthand-writer being there. I encourage counsel to raise their problems with me in open court. They can ask for my views on sentence at any stage and if I feel I can properly assist by giving my views I do. Counsel should take the initiative; only they know whether they want to ask. Sometimes I start the ball rolling by exploring the position. This may be necessary with very junior counsel, who are understandably diffident, especially because judges vary so much. If I am asked to approve a plea of guilty to a lesser offence it is done in open court — why not? I do plea-bargaining in the same open way. It is possible to exclude the press and public, but justice is done best in full public view. There are, however, cases where it is vital that jurors should not learn what has been said, in fairness to the defence. If the defence wish to tell me that the accused is dying but does not know it — it happened to me once — a statement or affidavit from a doctor can be handed to me without being read out.

My proposals, then, are these. Private discussions between judge and counsel should be forbidden in all criminal cases. The shorthand-writer should always be present and usually the defendant also. Unless there are very good reasons, everything should be done in open court. Plea-bargaining should be acknowledged to be part of English law. A plea-bargain should be defined thus: it arises on a plea of guilty after the judge has indicated the type of sentence he would pass on such a plea. The defence should be able to ask the judge, at any stage in the trial, to indicate the type of sentence he would pass for specified pleas of guilty. After such a request the judge should be able to give such indication as he thinks fit, giving credit to the defendant for pleading guilty. If, after such an indication, the defendant does not plead guilty but is found guilty, the sentence should depend on all the facts then before the judge, who should not be bound by his previous indication. (The present law assumes that if the judge says that a plea of guilty will attract a lesser sentence than a conviction by the jury, the defendant may plead guilty even if he is not. Yet a defendant does get credit for pleading guilty, and his counsel is free to tell him that. This is an unsatisfactory situation.)

# Chapter 9

# *Sentencing*

The chairman – a brainy judge who has since gone up to the House of Lords – asked the professor of criminology, 'Why has the idea that wickedness deserves punishment gone out of fashion?' The professor, who now has the top job in his field, replied, 'I don't know.' This struck me as astonishing yet somehow typical. It was 1977, I had been a judge for just over a year, and this was the annual 'residential judicial seminar' organised efficiently by the Lord Chancellor's office for experienced judges and recorders.

No week in my life has had such an effect on my views about crime and criminals. Superficially it was like going back to university; my fellow-students came from all over the country and a few from abroad, and it was good to meet and talk to them. But for me it went deeper than that: my ideas about sentencing were brought sharply into focus. As a student I learned about criminal law, and as a judge I was used to passing sentences, but I had never studied criminology or penology, which try to make the treatment of criminals a science. English barristers and judges do not take easily to theories; we are essentially practical. We go on doing things the way our predecessors did, and we instinctively react against professors and probation officers who tell us we have got it wrong. For the first time I began to think deeply about sentencing: why we do what we do and how we might do it better.

Work on the first day began at 9.15 a.m. and went on for about twelve hours with breaks for meals. We heard from a lord justice of appeal on 'the tariff system' – the accepted levels of sentence for particular types of offence. A high court judge spoke on 'miscellaneous problems in the conduct of a trial, including plea-bargaining and the award of costs'. A circuit judge dealt with 'judicial pitfalls'. In the afternoon an assistant chief probation officer addressed us on 'options in the sentencing field, with particular reference to community service, suspended sentence supervision and the deferment of sentence'. In the evening the director-general of the prison service spoke on 'the prison scene', emphasising how full penal establishments were. During the day we had been given a copy of what we called 'The Serota Report', its full title being: 'The length of prison sentences: the interim report of the advisory council on the penal system'. Lady Serota chaired the council, which had been set up by the

Home Office. The report was, in effect, a plea to the courts to avoid or shorten prison sentences.

That was the theme running through the seminar: penal establishments were full and the government was looking to the courts to reduce over-crowding, as cheaper than providing more accommodation. I had known for some time that home secretaries, lord chancellors and other politicians had been preaching this in parliament and to groups such as magistrates, but now the message was booming out clear and insistently. We heard it from the staff at the borstal and Brixton prison which I visited. At the borstal we were told that they could only cope by reducing the time served as numbers increased. The reconviction rates were high: over sixty per cent offended again within two years of their release. A colleague and I were allowed to speak in private to two detainees, and they hinted they were likely to go back to crime. It was all very depressing, despite the efforts made by the devoted staff to teach the inmates new skills and discipline.

Brixton prison was sardine-full and falling down through years of neglect: the politicians had simply refused to allot money for maintenance. There were no votes in it. I went round the section for 'category A' men, the dangerous ones who might try to escape; they certainly looked a desperate group. The prison officer who showed me round said that if he was ever sentenced he hoped he would be in category A, as the facilities were much better, including a separate area for exercise. (The sophisticated electronic equipment, including closed-circuit television, was supposed to make escape impossible, but not long afterwards prisoners did escape.) One cell had a specially strengthened door; in the next cell five prison officers sat playing cards as they waited for the next outbreak by the occupant, a strong, wild man from the north. He was like an unpredictable, mad animal. He has since died in prison.

On the fourth day we had the same message from the same professor (who was on the parole board), on 'the criminologist and the sentencer'. He produced statistics to show there is no proof that a long prison sentence deters others from similar crimes. That even applied to the sentences passed by Mr Justice Salmon in the Notting Hill race riot case. We listened in brooding silence to the professor, feeling in my case that criminologists know more about books and statistics than they do about criminals, but then he referred to 'a bifurcated dichotomy', and this was too much. A circuit judge, whose forbear was Chief Justice of the Common Pleas a long time ago, and who has a deep voice, said, 'Do you mind speaking English, sir?' The professor never recovered after that, his message having lost such impact as it had had. He had confirmed what we had suspected about theorists, although I am sure there are things they can teach us.

The chief inspector of the probation and after-care inspectorate at the Home Office spoke on 'problems of the probation service and its relationship with the courts, including the preparation of reports'. (Social inquiry reports are very helpful in criminal cases; we could not do our job properly without them. They go into a defendant's past and his problems in great detail. Probation officers are dedicated and helpful but their recommendations are sometimes unrealistic, and this not only leaves their 'client' feeling cheated when the court does not agree, but the judge tends to be sceptical about the rest of the report. Also the language used is sometimes as bad as the professor's. One report stated, 'He has failed fully to internalise his own self-control mechanisms.' 'Do you mean he can't control himself?' I asked. 'Yes, that's it,' said the probation officer, as if I had thrown fresh light on the matter. In another case I read that a probation order would be beneficial as 'in an effort to cope with unforeseen events in his young life he would need to broaden his points of view beyond those acquired within his home setting'. Perhaps we should all be put on probation as an aid to growing up.)

A forensic psychiatrist spoke on 'prognosis in personality deviance, including drugs, alcohol and sex'. Then came a forum at which some of the previous speakers and others answered our questions. I asked an assistant under-secretary from the Home Office criminal policy planning unit what would happen when crime increased further, penal institutions already being full. He shifted uneasily on his feet and said, 'We can't be sure that crime *will* continue to increase.' So that was it! The Home Office cat *was* out of the bureaucratic bag. They had no plans to increase accommodation. (There is a prison building programme now.) The civil servants were not to blame, of course; the politicians were. Both parties had refused to spend more on prisons, through the rising crime of the sixties and seventies, and that was still the attitude. A succession of well-meaning home secretaries had not only had their heads in the clouds, but also in the sand. In addition to introducing needed reforms, as on the law concerning homosexuality, they had given the impression that they had gone soft on crime and criminals. Examples are the introduction of parole in 1968, the Bail Act in 1976 and the continual pressure on the courts to reduce sentences. Parole and the Bail Act were not wrong in themselves, but they must have been seen by criminals as part of a general policy of weakness, having regard to the way they were put across by the Home Office. No one will ever prove how far all this helped to increase crime, but I think it played a part.

In private, several judges at the seminar agreed with me that it was for us to decide who should go inside and for how long and for the Home Office to make room. I do not recall much being said openly, and I can understand that. High officials from the Lord Chancellor's office were at the seminar; no one could be sure what would be noted or reported. In that situation a man who will speak against establishment policy is either rash, or lacking ambition, or both; I fear I was both because I did say what I thought.

Whilst we judges have in the past ten years or so properly moderated our sentences, we have not given way to Home Office pressure completely. Magistrates, who sit with judges in the crown court and hear us address them at training sessions, have been confused about what to do, and I do not blame them. They are ordinary folk trying to do what is right and it was hard for them to stand up to politicians of both parties, though many felt unhappy about the situation. I noticed the effect of Home Office policy on the way that magistrates operated the Bail Act. I saw case after case where magistrates had given bail to defendants who had already broken bail and not been sentenced. One man had eventually to be sentenced on five separate indictments. A great deal of unnecessary damage was being suffered by the public.

I decided to set out my views and I did so in a case at Sheffield crown court on 28 April 1978. What I said can be read in Appendix II. I had copies sent to the magistrates' clerks in the areas where I sat and the *Justice of the Peace* got hold of a copy, publishing it in full. What I had said seemed to strike a chord, and since then I have been invited to address magistrates in various parts of the country, even as far away as South Wales. My message – that the Home Office would have to provide more accommodation and that we in the courts must deal firmly with defendants – usually got a sympathetic response. For example, in November 1981 I spoke to 300 magistrates at Lancaster University and they were enthusiastic. When one JP, left-wing politically, asked about the effects of imprisonment on a man's wife and family, I replied that they were *his* responsibility, and that brought the house down so noisily that the chairman briskly ended the discussion.

Once a year there is a meeting of judges on our circuit attended by the (high court) presiding judges. I raised my views at two of those meetings, but the response I received – especially from the presiding judges – was unenthusiastic. 'Why doesn't the Lord Chief Justice [then Lord Widgery] stand up to the government?' I asked. The reply: 'We'd rather not touch this; it's too difficult; there are problems.' Soon after the bail case I went to see my then MP who was a secretary of state at the Home Office under Mr Merlyn Rees. When I gave her a copy of my remarks in the bail case her reaction was, 'Has this appeared in the press?' I said I had no idea. She promised to put my document before the Home Secretary. I met the then permanent secretary to the Lord Chancellor and when I said that more prisons would have to be built his reaction was, 'It would be very expensive.' I told him that expense was not the only consideration.

On 25 March 1981 I wrote to the Lord Chancellor, Lord Hailsham:

## Prison accommodation. Sentencing policy.

Some judges and magistrates whom I meet are becoming increasingly concerned, as I am, about the policy of the executive on the above matters. In the circumstances I am taking the liberty of sending you the enclosed, which contain some of my views. I have not been authorised to speak for others.

I enclosed copies of three speeches I had made – two to magistrates and one to a rotary club. I do not know what the Lord Chancellor's reaction was, as I had no acknowledgment.

Pressure by the Home Secretary, then Mr Whitelaw, on the courts continued. I saw no public reply from any member of the judiciary and eventually I decided that someone had to say something. On 14 October 1981 at the annual dinner of the Inner Manchester Magistrates' Association I decided to speak out. My speech is in Appendix IV. I sent it to the press. Even *The Times* reported my remarks, with a photograph. The reaction of the Lord Chancellor's office was immediate. Requests went to the clerk to the magistrates in Manchester and to me for the full text of my speech, and they got it. The Lord Chief Justice, Lord Lane, for whom I have a genuinely high regard, wrote to me in moderate and reasonable terms, as a result of which I kept my mouth shut in public for several years.

As Home Secretary, Mr Leon Brittan did not threaten the courts. His approach was more subtle. He curtailed parole in some serious cases but he extended it substantially in others. Parole may now be granted after six months or a third of the sentence, whichever is longer.

Crimes continue to increase. Judges and magistrates are confused. We feel the public tugging at our gowns, telling us to be tougher and some politicians, criminologists and probation officers telling us to be softer. We have no philosophy of sentencing; we need to think things out afresh. Here are my thoughts, which I admit I keep modifying. I certainly do not claim to have any definitive solutions.

No legal system can succeed unless it has the support of most of the public for most of the time. If the public thinks we have got it wrong, we have. Many do think that some defendants have it too easy. That does not mean that we have to revert to the treadmill or the rule of silence, and my own approach can be put in two words: enlightened firmness. I must do what I think right and fair, bearing in mind what I take to be the feelings of reasonable people. I have to pursue one or more of the four objects of punishment: reform, deterrence, punishment and containment. They cannot all apply in any one case. For example, reform and containment do not go hand in hand: the former is for those who can be and should be helped to go straight, whereas the latter is for those who have shown by their conduct that they are beyond help. When deciding which approach to adopt, a quality which a judge needs is imagination. He has to try to see what went on in the mind of the defendant when he did what he did, what is going on in it now as he awaits sentence and how he will react to the sentence.

## Reform

Another, uglier, word is rehabilitation. There are defendants who one feels should be helped up rather than struck down. This applies obviously to many young or first offenders, but there are times when it can be tried with others. About ten years ago the Home Office set up and funded four experimental day training centres, and one of them is in Sheffield. When I sat in South Yorkshire I got to know it quite well; I went there several times. It was an expensive but constructive alternative to imprisonment, aimed at helping offenders to look into their lives, to see what is wrong and how to put it right. Attendance is during normal working hours. Some of those there are so afraid of authority figures that they are too timid even to apply for state benefits. There are group discussions, which are recorded on video. By the end of the course they go into the street to interview passers-by 'cold' whilst being recorded.

I used to chat with the inmates and I found this revealing. A judge does not normally get that opportunity. A part-time prostitute – she only goes on the 'game' when she needs to pay, say, an electricity bill – told me that a certain solicitor used to advise her to plead not guilty even when she wanted to admit soliciting. He told her there was always a chance of getting off; he did not tell her that under legal aid he was paid by the hour. On another visit one of the assembled men said to me, 'You're evil!' There was silence; I did not react. Then another man asked what I would have done if that remark had been made to me in court. I said I was not in court and they could say what they wanted. At the end one of the audience came and shook me by the hand. On another occasion I was asked, 'Why did you give me three years?' 'What did you do?' 'I stole £700 from the market.' 'It was rather a lot of money.' He did not seem to hold it against me; I had my job to do. We were discussing burglary once and an old lag asked me if I had a dog, indicating that for a burglar a dog was a deterrent.

Face to face, such people do not seem like 'criminals', a race apart. Most of them are drifters who in particular circumstances are tempted to help themselves to others' property. They are not clever and if they added up their gains and the penalties they have paid for them it has probably not been worth it. The people at the day training centre were interested in capital punishment, and most of them seemed to favour it. In fact, they were surprisingly harsh in their ideas of punishment. I asked them what sentence they would give a man of twenty-five with a good character who had on one occasion burgled in the night, accidentally terrifying the woman occupant by his presence. None of them thought that less than eighteen months' imprisonment was fitting and some thought three years. I told them that most of them were on the top side.

I visited a day centre that is a converted house. There is always a probation officer on duty and people can call in at any time of the day or evening for a warm, a chat and a snack; mostly they have been in contact with the probation service previously. Almost all I talked to said that for single people, living accommodation was their most difficult problem. They find themselves in the hands of unscrupulous landlords who let rooms. Several said that but for the centre they would have gone back to crime. Day centres of various kinds – some with 'structured' programmes – have a very useful role in keeping weak drifters out of trouble.

Offenders can be required to go to a day centre for up to sixty days as a condition in a probation order. The programme in one such day centre covers such areas as awareness of oneself and others; rights and advice; offence avoidance; literacy and numeracy; parenting; values, beliefs and attitudes; use of leisure; health and safety; housing and accommodation; job search; living alone; personal communication; sex and sexuality; cooking for survival. This is a very useful alternative to the custodial approach in many cases.

When considering whether to take the 'reform' road with a defendant, what information do I have? His previous convictions, the facts about his life (in the social inquiry report) and about his present offence(s). How many chances has he had in the past? How did he respond? Does he want to be helped now, or merely to keep his freedom? If he is set free, what risk is there to the public? A skilled housebreaker may do enormous harm before he is caught; not so a petty pilferer or a man who has been violent on a single occasion.

I am prepared to take a chance with a man who has often been to prison before, has done a relatively petty crime and has not recently had leniency. For instance, a man who when in drink breaks a window and steals goods of little value. Prison will not do him much good. He will not like it, but he is used to it and he will soon settle down into the expensive, wasteful regime. It will not shock him into changing his ways. He cannot be imprisoned for a long time; after a few months he will emerge with the same old problems, only worse.

When trying to reform I prefer a positive sentence to a negative one. Attendance centres run by the police for young people and day centres are positive. So is 'intermediate treatment': for example 'outward bound' type activities in the open air. Community service is positive in one sense but the only supervision is as to the work itself. A conditional discharge or a fine are negative. A suspended sentence is negative unless coupled with a supervision order. A straight probation order is positive, although in practice it may mean less than an hour a week with the probation officer.

Can prison or youth custody achieve reform? In some cases. If I get a man in his twenties who is of previous good character but has taken to house-burglary, I almost always send him to prison as the best way of reforming him. Statistics show that such a person does not hurry back to court. We must not let men like that think that as first offenders they will be treated leniently: if treated so, many will think such crime worth while. Some offenders were taken too far along the reform road when young, and I have used the phrase 'educated into crime by repeated leniency'. Many youngsters must feel 'It's not so bad. All they ever do is talk at you.' No wonder they re-offend. A short spell in youth custody or a detention centre early in their careers may pull them up short: by the time they reach me it may be too late. They have gradually climbed the ladder of penalties and become hardened. To be sent away at thirteen or fourteen must be like a cold shower on a hot day: however bad a boy's home is to our eyes, to be removed from it and subjected to an alien, disciplined environment must have a traumatic effect. It will not deter all from crime, of course. A lad whose character has been twisted from his earliest years – by parental neglect, anti-authority attitudes, a broken home – cannot easily be made law-abiding. He may settle down in his late twenties, as many do, preferring a job and a family to repeated loss of liberty – or he may never settle down, and slither into degradation and hopelessness.

The Victorians thought that prison could bring penitence, and they put prisoners in solitary cells with the Bible to read. They gave them hard, humiliating tasks such as breaking stone or the treadmill. They were wrong. Prison can instil fear and so a reluctance to repeat the crime, but it cannot make men repent or feel more moral. Prison may make a man bitter against authority, if he was not that already.

## Deterrence

Some theorists say our sentences do not deter, and the Home Office has latched on to this theory. It cannot be proved that a sentence has turned other men from crime. I believe, though, that the known level of sentences for a particular type of offence *does* have an effect. Some burglars are careful to avoid houses, as they know that the tariff is imprisonment.

In 1969 at Leeds Quarter Sessions I sentenced a soccer fan who had assaulted the police at Leeds United football ground to a total of two and a half years' imprisonment. The case got wide publicity; it was the first item on the TV news that evening. Later the police gave me figures for arrests at that ground at matches before and after my sentence, and the sudden drop was startling. Admittedly that was not a typical situation:

the chances of detection and conviction at a football match are probably greater – in the minds of those involved – than in other circumstances. That man has had no conviction since his release.

A few years ago an ex-convict wrote me a letter which set out to criticise words of mine which had been in the press. He wrote that after a sentence served in a prison like Leeds or Dartmoor, 'you do not come back in a hurry. If you are lucky and are sent to an open or semi-open prison, you usually have it easy and soon forget things . . . If a law could be brought in that all school-leavers must go through a trial detention, there would be a seventy per cent drop in crime.'

I have expressed my views on deterrence and allied topics to the staff and students at two provincial universities, and some of the staff have been hostile. The professor I had met earlier at the seminar called my approach 'anecdotal' and stamped out in anger after hearing me address staff and senior students.

There is a gulf between those who teach law and those who practise it. I have tried to bridge this by encouraging law-teachers to send their students to my court to see how we do things. I have not had much success. Teachers and judges are on different wave-lengths. It is not like medicine where the teachers *are* practitioners. Judges concentrate on real cases; we see the harm offenders do. Lecturers do not often come to court. Some – including the professor – are neither barristers nor solicitors, and study in quiet libraries, poring over books and statistics. The practical and the academic sides should be brought together; I enjoy telling students what goes on. I was called to the bar before I had seen a brief. Can one imagine a medical student becoming a doctor without seeing a body?

The academics correctly point out that deterrent sentences have a limited effect. Criminals tend to be gamblers and if they are sure they will not be caught the likely sentence does not deter them. And if there is a sudden flare-up between two people there may not be time to think of the results of one's actions. Several years ago I had an experience bearing on that type of situation. I rebuked a young motorist who had driven fast towards me along a narrow private road. As he angrily got out of his car he began to take off his watch. He was tall and broad and I knew that if I put a foot wrong he would floor me. His young colleague in the passenger seat called out, 'Don't hit him, Bill.' When Bill said what he intended to do to me, I said, 'I can't stop you, but you'd better find out a bit more about me first.' Bill lowered his fist and I knew the danger had passed. But why didn't he hit me? Because he knew that the police would inevitably come into it and he would probably go to prison?

When are deterrent sentences needed? When a type of crime is particularly prevalent and harmful. Examples are house-burglary; robbery; attacks on police-officers, bus-conductors or at football matches; violence against children; rape; the theft of metal in Sheffield or wool in Bradford.

What types of sentence deter? Only loss of liberty, in my view. Imprisonment, detention and youth custody are unique; no other sentence bites as deep or is feared as much. Any defending lawyer will confirm that most defendants seize on any alternative to loss of liberty. A suspended sentence may be some deterrent, but not by what it does to the defendant – it is merely a form of words – but what it threatens to do. Suspended sentences are sometimes over-done. I had one case in which magistrates had imposed suspended sentences on three different occasions, and they were all running at the same time.

## Punishment

This is another controversial area. Some cry 'retribution' and condemn this approach as primitive. But the public rightly thinks that a person who has wickedly harmed another should himself suffer. Society should reward the good and cast down the wicked. What *is* wickedness? We have to look into the mind of the defendant. Wickedness involves a deliberate choice, knowing of the harmful consequences to the victim. Take two robberies. In one, an intelligent adult has been well brought up and was not in real need, but when sober planned to rob and did rob an old or infirm person, using a weapon and causing injury. Such a crime shrieks out for punishment in the form of a long prison sentence, and if the defendant does not get it the public feel aggrieved. At the other end of the scale is a young unintelligent lad from a bad home who was drunk when he robbed on a sudden impulse, using only his hands upon a victim of similar age and strength, causing no injury and taking property of trifling value. It might even be possible to take the reform road with him, especially if he has a relatively good character.

How far should drink be a mitigation? We often say that it is not one, as the defendant took it knowing what it would do to him. That certainly applies if a man takes alcohol to give himself the courage to commit an offence, which happens quite often. However, if a man has taken drink and an incident suddenly arises which he could not foresee, drink that makes him think less clearly and act more impetuously may be in his favour. We get many cases in the crown court for violence arising out of incidents at or outside pubs and clubs. Usually the violence is not premeditated. There is a sudden loss of tempers over something which may be quite trivial. A. thinks B. is staring at him and resents it. C. sees D., who had an affair with C.'s girl-friend in the past. E. knocks into F. whilst walking by, spilling F.'s beer. A judge has to go carefully into how the trouble started, who was the aggressor and what was in the defendant's mind when he did what he did. If he was holding a glass when confronted by an aggressor, his blow may have been little more than an instinctive reaction. That is not so if he breaks the glass before striking with it or goes to pick one up. Kicking a person who is lying on the ground is always wicked.

We do not usually seek to punish very young offenders. Mostly they have been twisted by parental neglect or a broken home, or both. In a sense they start out in life as innocent victims of others' actions or neglect. They are pulled by forces which they cannot easily understand or control. The time comes, however, when every sane person must be treated as being capable of making his own decisions and accepting the consequences of what he chooses to do. At what age does he reach that stage? Certainly by eighteen – the age at which the young can vote and serve on juries or be conscripted in wartime.

When punishment is the object the options are: immediate imprisonment, youth custody, community service or a fine. Nothing punishes like loss of liberty and all that it means: being denied one's pleasures; being herded and ordered about; living in squalid circumstances; pointing fingers on release. If the experience is new it need not be long in order to bite deep. A suspended sentence is not punishment at all, as it may never be served. The Court of Appeal has told courts to decide whether imprisonment is necessary and then whether it can be suspended. I have tried but failed to follow the logic of that. To decide that a defendant should suffer imprisonment and then go on to say that he will not suffer it, does not seem right. There are those who say that the pronouncement of a prison sentence shows the disapproval of the community, which is still there when the same sentence is suspended. The public does not swallow that; it wants to know what will actually happen to the man in the dock. If the judge has merely talked at him and let him go, the public feels let down in some cases. I do, however, suspend a few sentences, as where a weak defendant needs the thought of something unpleasant hanging over him to make him keep his hands off others or their property. But if he deserves to go away today, he goes.

Community service is useful from various angles. The community benefits from the work; the defendant is reminded of his wrongs; the work and the discipline are good for him. As punishment, however, it does not compare with loss of liberty: the work is done a few hours at a time. Defendants who fail to do community service properly have to be brought back to court, and the sentence must then be loss of liberty, or the scheme will fail for the lack of an effective sanction. A fine can be regarded as punishment, but it does not bite deep. Fines or other payments, as for costs or compensation, can be counter-productive in that a defendant may be tempted to steal in order to pay. What if a man is unemployed and on state benefits? This is a problem. On one view the payments are intended to cover basic necessities and a fine will cause hardship. However if the man drinks, smokes or runs a car, he can afford small payments up to about £3 a week. Some magistrates order unrealistically high payments and the crown court has to reduce them on appeal.

## Containment

This aspect of imprisonment tends to be overlooked nowadays. Some people ask, 'What good does prison do?' One answer is that it prevents those inside from harming those outside. A persistent offender may have to be put away for a long time, simply because there is no other way of protecting the public from him. He has forfeited his right to liberty. Extended sentences are available to the crown court for some persistent offenders: the court can pass a longer sentence than the normal tariff, or even than the normal maximum, having regard to previous convictions and the likelihood of further offences being committed. Extended sentences have gone out of fashion. One reason is probably the shortage of prison accommodation; another is that a three-day notice has to be served on the defendant, and this may involve an adjournment. I favour longer sentences for some persistent criminals such as house-burglars and con-men. Removing them from the community for long periods will not only protect others from them but will act as a deterrent.

## Some Real Cases

A few years ago I noted at random some cases I tried at the crown court as part of a project which came to nothing. These show how I went through the sentencing process.

1   *The Orphan*: A. (eighteen) pleaded guilty to burglary at a shop and stealing goods valued at £33-odd in August, taking cars in September and October, and assaulting the police officers who arrested him in October – he struck an officer on the eye with his fist, then lashed out with his fists and feet. He asked for six further offences to be taken into consideration. In a statement to police A. said: 'I'm sorry for smashing you and that other copper. I was just showing off a bit. That Capri I nicked: I was just walking past those gas tanks when I saw it. It looked great – wide wheels, painted black, something written on the bonnet – so I decided I was going to have it. I put a screwdriver in the door and got in. I started it with the screwdriver and then I was off. Driving about, it felt great. Anyway I saw this bird and pulled her, drove her about and decided to shag her. Anyway she didn't want it so we had this row and she fucked off. I decided to dump the car . . . I've done a lot of thieving from motors. There was one where I nicked a right load of sweets from a motor but I can't remember when; I do most of them in the daytime. Last year I

did – 's shop on – Road. I kicked the front window in and got about a thousand fags. I might as well say that all the gear I get is flogged at second-hand shops on – ; they are the only people who want it.' A. also pleaded guilty to a second indictment containing two offences, both against his foster-parents. He stole a tin-box containing £250 cash and a bracelet. He spent the cash 'on booze and fags'. On a later occasion he stole a record-player and two speakers, which he sold in a swap-shop. He said to the police, 'I've had to take these things because I'm not on the dole – they won't give me any money.'

A. is single. Strictly, he is not an orphan. When he was eighteen months his father deserted his mother, three of whose five children, including A. were taken into care and put with foster-parents. A. lost contact with his mother when he was three and now looks on his foster-parents as his only parents. The family have a large Victorian house in a city suburb, bought with the aid of Dr Barnardo's. They always have several foster-children living with them. In his first year at school A. was regarded as retarded intellectually and educationally. After that he presented no serious problems until his final year, when he truanted and was expelled. He had several jobs, usually leaving of his own accord and giving no good reason for doing so. He made three appearances in the juvenile court for burglaries, thefts and taking a car, receiving fines, a conditional discharge, probation and an attendance centre order. In the year prior to appearing before me he had twice appeared in the magistrates' court, for burglary and theft and failing to surrender to bail, receiving fines and a probation order. During the previous year the pattern of A.'s behaviour was: money missing from home, arguments with foster-parents, he left home and committed offences.

The probation officer found it difficult to get A.'s confidence. He wanted to give the appearance of a tough character, but at the remand centre where he awaited trial before the crown court 'he found the experience of being locked up almost unbearable, and it is not something he can shrug off like many young men. At the present time I do not think the probation service can do much to change the accused's behaviour, but it is my opinion that a custodial sentence would be likely to harden his attitudes. A borstal sentence would separate him from his girl-friend, and I do not think he would be able to make constructive use of such training. I have met his girl-friend and her mother, who is happy to have him live with them, and my impression is that the relationship with his girl-friend is the one factor that offers some hope for the moment. If the court is prepared to consider an alternative to a custodial sentence, the accused would be accepted to do community service.'

I sentenced A. to borstal training. His early family life probably made him what he is. If he had been sent away for a short period earlier, that might have pulled him up sharp. Borstal has now been replaced by youth custody, which is more flexible. A. would probably serve between six and eight months. The outlook for him was bleak, but he might settle down with a suitable woman eventually. Community service would not have been an adequate penalty.

2  *Pieces of Silver*: B. and C. were charged: B. with stealing silver valued at £428 from his employers over eight years; C. with trying to sell the silver on B.'s behalf knowing it to have been stolen. C. pleaded not guilty, and I do not know what happened to him. The silver was all recovered, as the police intervened before any was sold. B. worked as a silver-spinner for silversmiths. He accumulated the silver by taking small quantities, and when in financial difficulties he decided to sell it. He was such a good worker that his employers had not sacked him. He made three appearances in the juvenile court, the last one being nine years ago. B. left grammar school at fifteen without qualifications. He lived with his wife and three-year-old daughter in a semi-detached house in a residential area. He had been apprenticed to his employers and earned £165 a week. His financial difficulties stemmed from legal fees and repairs when he bought his house. A stomach ulcer caused him to lose time at work. His wife was under medical treatment because of worry about the case.

I ordered B. to do 150 hours community service and pay £75 towards his legal aid costs at £1 per week. For breaches of trust over a long period, B. deserved to go to prison. But the attitude of his employers was crucial: they were the victims and they had, in effect, forgiven him. He had no previous similar convictions and was unlikely to offend again.

3  *Any Old Iron?*: C. (fifty-two) pleaded guilty to stealing drilling rods worth £1,500 from the yard of a forge. He had seen them there for several weeks and thought they were scrap: he certainly did not know their true value. He told the police that he stole the rods with two other men who had them when he last saw them, so he got nothing out of it. C. is the thirteenth of fourteen children. He left school at fourteen and worked in a timber yard. At eighteen he did national service in the army, after which he had several jobs. For the previous year he had been self-employed dismantling crates and selling the timber. He said he made £45 profit per week, and that his wife earned £6 in a market. They had a mentally handicapped daughter. A few months ago the electricity was cut off because they owed £400. C.'s only previous conviction was ten years ago for stealing lead valued at £8.

I sentenced C. to eighty hours community service. If he had known the true value of the rods it might have been a case for imprisonment. Similarly, if he had had a bad record for dishonesty. I was happy to leave him supporting his family.

4  *A Mental Case*: D. (thirty-three) was charged with assaulting a sixty-

eight-year-old woman in the street. He grabbed her handbag, pulled her to the ground, then kicked her repeatedly. When a man intervened D. ran off empty-handed. D. had without permission left the local psychiatric hospital where he had been for five and a half years under a hospital order. He told the police that he wanted some money to get away from the hospital, which was making his mental condition worse. He wished he had killed the woman and would do it again.

Subnormality was diagnosed when D. was eight and he was at a special school until sixteen. His only confirmed employment was at a colliery for six months thirteen years ago. There was a history of violent incidents with his mother. Efforts to establish him in a community hostel for the mentally handicapped with daily attendance at an adult training centre failed: when he tired of the novelty he became disruptive and aggressive. His reminiscences and aspirations were detached from reality. He had made repeated applications to the review board for release, but his mental condition made residence in a psychiatric hospital inevitable. There was no vacancy in a special hospital like Broadmoor, so I remanded B. in custody until there was a vacancy. This was a case for hospital treatment with security. For a long time the Home Office failed to implement the Butler Report, which recommended the provision of secure sections in mental hospitals. This led to most prison hospitals housing men who should have been in special hospitals. The position is better now than it was, but there is still a long way to go.

5  *Thuggery*: Cases pass through my court in a steady stream. As soon as one is over I am on with the next, and it is impossible to remember them all. One I do remember is that of Jones in the crown court; I even followed up his case afterwards as I have done with no other. He was seventeen and appeared with several other youths, including eighteen-year-old Brown. Jones pleaded guilty to violence on three separate occasions, amounting to wounding, grievous bodily harm and actual bodily harm; he also pleaded guilty to thefts and taking vehicles. He asked for eighteen further offences – none for violence – to be taken into consideration. Brown's offences were similar but not as bad; he was in two of the violent incidents and asked for twelve offences to be taken into consideration. Neither had a significant criminal record. Jones was a labourer and Brown unemployed.

The first incident began in a telephone kiosk in which three young women were making a call one evening. The two defendants began to bully the girls by shouting and banging on the door; eventually they cut off the call. After the girls left, one of them found her purse was missing. Her boy-friend went to the kiosk, saw the defendants and asked them if they had seen the purse. They knocked him to the ground and attacked him as he lay there; he lost consciousness and at the hospital he was found to have a fractured nose and ribs and facial bruising. The next victim was an eighteen-year-old male student of excellent character who was standing at a bus-stop when youths, including Jones and Brown, asked him where he came from. The village concerned was the 'wrong' answer, because the student was promptly set upon. He fought back but he was soon surrounded by between five and ten youths, whom bystanders said were like a pack of wild animals. The student was repeatedly punched and kicked and blood poured from his face. A bus came and the conductor and passengers rescued him; the bus drove him to hospital for urgent treatment. A third victim was a young man who, intoxicated, left a public house with friends. Jones and other youths attacked him for no reason. As the victim lay on the ground unconscious Jones applied his feet to the man's head and neck causing a broken nose and bruising.

Gratuitous violence is becoming common and it has to be dealt with firmly. I took the view that the sentences must not only punish and express the public's feelings of outrage, but deter the defendants and others. At that time the sentencing options were borstal training or imprisonment for up to six months or for three years or more. I sentenced Jones to five years' imprisonment and Brown to three. The Court of Appeal reduced Jones' sentence to three and a half years and dismissed Brown's appeal. I was interested to find out how long Jones would in fact serve so I wrote to the Home Office. He was paroled slightly less than eighteen months after he appeared before me. What has happened to him since then? Did his spell inside chasten him? Has he been in trouble since his release? I do not know and probably never will.

6 *Two young burglars*: Smith and Robinson were both twenty-one. Smith burgled his parents' house after they turned him out; both defendants took a car and stole from it. They were both seen by the police and bailed. Then they really put their backs into house-burglary: they raided thirteen houses, stealing property valued at over £4,000. Smith had twice been to detention centre and once to borstal. Robinson had been to borstal twice and to prison for two years.

Smith told the police: 'I've been using my own car on the jobs we've done, and ferried the gear about in it. All the jobs I've done with Robinson, and we've always worn gloves. In all from the gear we've nicked, which must run into thousands of pounds, we've not had much. We've sold most of it to swap-shops, but all that stuff from the house at – and the tellys and a load of radios, we sold to a bloke called D. who has a swap-shop in – Road. For all the gear we've given him – and he knew we'd nicked it – in total he only gave us about forty or fifty quid.' (I was told that D. had appeared before the magistrates for receiving and been given a suspended sentence. I said that was encouraging crime, and when this appeared in the press the magistrates did not like it, and their chairman came to see me. D. had pleaded ill-health. Men like D. play a key part in house-burglary; as has often been said, if there were no receivers there would be no thieves. Immediate imprisonment is essential for men like D.)

Smith's background was fairly typical. He was the oldest of six children. In detention centre and borstal he was helpful, co-operative and amenable to discipline. After he left borstal he had several jobs, some well paid, and he enjoyed them. At the same time he appeared to be seeking a stable relationship with a girl, so that he could fulfil his ambitions to marry and settle down. The probation officer said that Smith's almost desperate search for a steady girl-friend seemed to affect his willingness to work regularly. The pattern was: losing jobs through failing to work regularly; arguments with his parents for failing to pay for board; leaving home. His parents did not like his girl-friend. When arrested he was sharing a flat with her. He felt the relationship would be lasting and talked of marriage. 'Some of the present offences were committed when the accused was already on bail and seem to indicate that he thought further custody was inevitable.' My main concern was to protect householders from the defendants, and I sentenced them both to five years' imprisonment, which the Court of Appeal reduced to three and a half. I do not know when the parole board let them go, but I assume after about eighteen months. The chances are that both have been to prison for burglary in the intervening years. There is a possibility that they may settle down by the time they are thirty.

7   *A reckless driver*: The forty-two-year-old unemployed motor mechanic pleaded guilty to recklessly driving his van at 11.30 p.m. near a city centre. He turned right at a junction without warning despite a 'no right turn' notice and collided with a car coming towards him. He failed to stop and did not stop when ordered to by the driver of a police car who had seen the accident and followed. The defendant turned off his lights; he drove through traffic-lights at red and the wrong way along a dual carriageway. Eventually police cars boxed in the van and forced the defendant to stop. He gave incoherent replies and refused a breath test; he was obviously under the influence of drink. According to his counsel he could not remember the events of the night in question. The defendant had a fair number of offences connected with driving, including with excess alcohol and without due care ten years previously, and with excess alcohol seven years previously. He had never been sent to prison, but had spent ten days inside after his arrest for breach of the Bail Act by failing to come to the crown court on the first occasion: he said he had muddled up the date.

The defendant had been unemployed for seven years. He was happily married, but preoccupied by his health: he had had head pains since a motor-cycle accident twenty-five years ago. Fifteen years previously he was seen by a psychiatrist for depression and was on valium for the next ten years. He turned to drink to relieve the pains in the head. I decided that the defendant's health problems had no bearing on my task.

I sentenced the defendant to three months' imprisonment for reckless driving plus one month for breach of bail. The driving was very dangerous and could have killed or injured others; it had a degree of wickedness which could only be punished properly by imprisonment. Defendants who fail to attend for trial cause a lot of inconvenience and extra expense, and a short prison sentence is usually appropriate. I also disqualified the defendant from holding a driving licence for three years – he was unfit to be driving and a danger to others, but he would not necessarily remain so indefinitely; and the time might come when he got a job as a motor mechanic.

8    *An inadequate young man*: The defendant (twenty-six) pleaded guilty to burgling a council flat that was unoccupied and unfurnished, as could be seen from the outside. Neighbours heard him breaking a window and rang the police; the defendant did not steal anything. Before he was twenty-one he was in trouble for dishonesty several times and went to a detention centre; then there was a gap of five years after which, for a burglary and a theft, he was sentenced to a total of twelve months' imprisonment suspended for two years. The burglary was at a school – nothing was stolen; the theft was shoplifting. Four months after that the defendant committed the offence at the council flat, so prison was on the cards. The defendant was said to be dull, weak and lazy; he liked drink too much and work too little. He had worked as a packer, grave-digger, machine operator and hotel porter, but had been unemployed for eighteen months. When he was eighteen he had married a girl from a deprived home background; there was one child aged three who was showing emotional and behavioural problems. Four years previously the couple were divorced, but they continued to spend most of their time together; she was currently five months pregnant and in hospital.

I ordered the defendant to do 180 hours community service and pay £25 for the window at £1 per week. I re-suspended the suspended sentence for a further two years. He deserved to go to prison, but I preferred a more constructive course. He was weak and inadequate rather than wicked or dangerous. He would come out of prison with the same problems; it is doubtful if the experience would chasten. In the meantime his ex-wife and child would suffer by his absence. He required work and discipline, and community service would achieve that to some extent.

9    *'You can't back down'*: The thirty-seven-year-old defendant had a long record, mainly for dishonesty but on three occasions for violence. It was three years since his last conviction. A twenty-seven-year-old male neighbour came to the door to ask about trouble there had been between their respective children. Both men had had some drink. The defendant said to

the police, 'You can't back down. Well I can't anyway . . . I didn't argue. I gave him one with the nut, hit him with my fist and put the boot in once.' The victim had a black eye, a cut nose requiring two stitches and facial bruising; there was no permanent injury. The defendant had been unemployed for eighteen months; his marriage was having difficulties. The probation officer recommended a probation order or a suspended sentence. The defendant had had suspended sentences on four previous occasions, and I sentenced the defendant to fifteen months' immediate imprisonment. I pointed out that in these days it is common for people to resort to violence over petty quarrels. Kicking a person in the face can cause serious injury. The defendant had to be punished and he and others deterred from this sort of behaviour. Probation or a suspended sentence would not achieve those aims.

# Chapter 10

# *Prisons*

Imprisonment as a punishment came into the British penal system comparatively late. For centuries, offenders were held in prison before sentence, which usually consisted of fines, branding, transportation or execution. Prisons were owned by dukes, landowners, the church and local authorities, and administered by jailers who made profits from them. Conditions were scandalous.

In 1835 prisons were brought under Home Office inspection. In 1877 ownership of all prisons passed to the Home Office, and a prison commision was set up. Prisons were built on the cell system, the (mistaken) notion being that solitude, silence and hard work would bring penitence. Cells are now usually occupied by more than one prisoner.

Since I became a judge I have through the courtesy of the Home Office, which I appreciate, been round three adult prisons, a young man's prison, two borstals and a detention centre. There are over 120 prison establishments in England and Wales. They are expensive in cost per person, but prisons take only a small part of the total law and order budget. They vary widely. The 'local' prisons such as Wormwood Scrubs in London, Winson Green in Birmingham and Armley in Leeds, are overcrowded: they hold men awaiting trial or allocation after sentence, and they keep some sentenced to shortish terms. Three to a cell is usual. Other prisons tend not to be overcrowded.

For years after the 1939 war, goverments of both parties refused to spend money on building prisons, or even repairing existing ones. There were not enough votes in it. As crime increased, the Home Office looked to the courts and the parole board to solve their accommodation problem. Parts of some prisons were literally falling down through neglect.

Soon after my appointment I went round Leeds prison. They asked me when I wanted to arrive, and I asked when things started to happen. Slopping out of the cells began at 7.30 a.m., so I got there then: no judge had done that before, they said. I saw the men carrying out their buckets, and the governor 'trying' prisoners for minor infringements. One man lost a few days' remission for refusing to change his shirt. They did not show me the workshops; presumably little work was being done, due to lack of space. Many prisoners spend twenty-three hours a day locked in their cells.

More recently I visited a semi-open prison: there is a fence, but the determined can get over it, though not many do; prisoners know they will probably then go to a secure prison – much less comfortable. The prison I saw takes men doing sentences up to eighteen months. Some of them are in for sex offences, but this is kept secret, and if fellow-prisoners find out, the man is immediately transferred to a prison where he can be segregated from other prisoners. The prison used to be an army camp, and the prisoners live in huts that are centrally heated, dry and not overcrowded. Even so, they were being replaced by modern blocks costing several millions, which would provide for only about fifty more prisoners. The staff did up to thirty hours a week overtime and were happy to. (At a county court where I sit the number of clerks has been reduced, but the overtime now being done is equivalent to the pay of four and a half clerks. This is part of the 'numbers game' being played by the government, which aims to reduce the number who work as civil servants.) There is a choice of four dishes for the main course at lunch. The gymnasium – for badminton, table-tennis and weight-lifting – could be part of a prosperous youth club. As they stood around chatting or limbering up in a relaxed way, it was hard to tell staff from prisoners. The prisoners' text- and exercise-books are envied by the staff, whose children are not treated as generously by the state. The library is well stocked and books can be ordered through an outside library. There are classes in various subjects, including painting and sculpture.

In one workshop the men were sitting waiting for materials. The prison workshops I have seen have rarely looked very busy. Workshops make a loss, despite the very cheap labour. There were probation officers at the prison, but they were engaged in welfare work – contacting prisoners' relations and so on – and they did no structured rehabilitative work with prisoners. As I strolled round the large campus with its playing-fields, that prison could have been a residential college for adults. The atmosphere was relaxed; nothing seemed to be done even briskly. Nothing I saw there amounted to punishment, except loss of liberty. The Home Office considers that people go to prison *as* punishment, not *for* punishment, but this needs re-examining. When I asked the staff what they were trying to do with the prisoners the reply, in effect, was, 'We keep them in until it's time to let them out.' Is that good enough?

Things have got out of balance in the way defendants are sentenced and dealt with in prison. Some people say I am too tough on some defendants, and the Court of Appeal (Criminal Division) has said so: I have a drawer full of transcripts from it. I try to keep in step with that court but this is not easy, as the decisions vary with its composition: as with sentencing generally, much hangs on who the judges are. No two judges think exactly alike, any more than two laymen do. When I attend sentencing conferences at which we say what sentences we would pass in theoretical cases, I end by feeling what a lottery it all is.

When I receive a transcript from the Court of Appeal I can usually tell the result by looking at the names of the judges on the front. There are 'wets' and 'non-wets'. The theory that high court judges are so clever that they can tackle anything leads to civil lawyers, who have not often been in a criminal court and never met a criminal, sitting in the Court of Appeal as soon as they go on the bench. Their previous appearance as recorders and their attendance at sentencing conferences give them some help, but I would be happier to see the system altered. Circuit judges who have spent their lives grappling with criminals should sit in the Court of Appeal, presided over by a high court judge. Sittings should not all be in London as they are now, but also in provincial cities like Manchester, Birmingham and Leeds. The more important cases would still go to London, before the Lord Chief Justice. Dispersal of other cases would speed up hearings and reduce time and travelling for lawyers and others.

Some sentences by recorders, assistant recorders and magistrates horrify me. Some recorders think that a lot of appeals will ruin their prospects of a judgeship, so they play safe. They are wrong: the Lord Chancellor's men expect a good strong judge to be appealed against. Naturally a vast number of successful appeals, especially against conviction, is another matter. Magistrates have been so brainwashed by the Home Office and politicians that understandably they shrink from incarcerating.

I am sceptical about parole. So are prisoners, for different reasons. The parole board was set up in 1968 to reduce the numbers in prison. Members of the board include a few judges, through none sits on the local review committees which look at parole cases first and make recommendations to the Home Office and the parole board.

How many prisoners get parole? In 1985 the percentages for whom it was recommended by the board to the Home Office on the first application by a prisoner were: for those in for violence, 66; robbery, 53; burglary, 66; theft, 72; fraud, 77; handling, 77.

In one case I had at a crown court I noticed that the defendant had on his last appearance, before the same court, been sentenced to four and a half years' imprisonment for a nasty robbery and a separate assault that stopped short of robbery. He had been paroled after eighteen months and was still on licence. I wrote to the parole board, which passed me on to the Home Office. An official from there wrote that he could not tell me (a judge of the sentencing court!) why parole had been granted: the reports they got were confidential. I suspect the truth was that they needed the cell. Parole, operated in secrecy, undermines judges' decisions given openly. I sometimes feel – unfairly – that as soon as the defendant descends from the dock out of public view the bureaucrats do all they can to let him slip out of the back door unnoticed. It is fair to say that the board has eminent people with various occupations and backgrounds who go into great detail before recommending release. But what is the result in practice?

I decide that six years' imprisonment is the proper sentence. I am not allowed to take parole into account – the man may never get it. When I sit with magistrates in the crown court they usually ask, 'How long will he actually serve if we give him x months?' and I have to tell them that that will be for others to decide. The man with six years goes to the Court of Appeal, which says, 'Oh, what a very long sentence,' and reduces it. Yet everyone in both courts knows that there is more than a fifty-fifty prospect that six years will mean two, and probably not more than three. With sentences up to two years, parole is almost automatic after six months or a third. Thus any sentence from nine to eighteen months leads to release after six. We are in the realms of 'double-think' (see R. *v* K. & C. in Appendix VI).

I have come across Home Office officials when addressing magistrates and at the Roehampton seminar. At one meeting of magistrates I met an official from the prison department and the then governor of a London prison. As I expected, I found them to be educated and dedicated, trying hard in difficult circumstances which they did not create. After talking to them I thought judges and Home Office people work in separate though related worlds. We do not understand each others' problems. Some judges rarely, if ever go round prisons or meet Home Office representatives. In court we see the victims and what the defendants have done to them; the Home Office see the defendants as numbers in overstretched prisons and the need to let them out as soon as they dare.

I wrote to the Home Office suggesting they send someone to sit with me in court, so that I might explain afterwards why I do what I do. I got a polite if curt flea in my ear: 'There would be objections if individual officials of the Home Office were to discuss sentencing policy with individual judges.' The objections were not listed. I received a similar though more sympathetically worded response from my judicial superior.

It is time for a deep inquiry into imprisonment and how it should be used. Let me make a start, hoping that others more qualified will follow.

What are the features of imprisonment? Near total loss of liberty; humiliation: being in the hands of prison officers and at the mercy of fellow-prisoners (both groups may contain sadists). It is hard to get grievances listened to outside whilst one is inside. The conditions in some prisons are degrading: the overcrowding, slopping out and so on. If one had a job outside, it is likely to be lost. Personal relationships are disrupted: a wife or girl-friend may be unfaithful or even abandon a prisoner, alienating his children. The effect of all this on a sensitive person may be breakdown.

Most defendants fear imprisonment, and leap at any alternative offered to them. Prison has some deterrent effect on some people. It prevents all those imprisoned from offending against the community whilst they are inside. The effect of a sentence on the man differs enormously, however, from one to another. A bank manager or police officer – or judge! – must be devastated by the experience, however short it is. A man or woman who has had previous sentences will find it irksome to be sent back, but will soon settle into the regime again.

Which defendants need to suffer imprisonment as we know it today? The dangerous ones, for example those addicted to rape, house-burglary or obtaining by deception, and so likely to repeat their crimes when released or given partial liberty. Second, those who are guilty of great wickedness, having chosen to do much harm to others, as by murder or attempted murder, nasty robbery, violence or stealing from old people in their homes by posing as officials. Third, those who may be deterred from further crime by a spell behind prison walls.

For others sentenced to loss of liberty, a modified form of imprisonment is appropriate. There is no need to lock up night and day a petty thief or one who has failed to pay a fine, or committed motoring offences, except in very serious cases. For such defendants, imprisonment should be more flexible. Community service should be extended, so that a sentence could be served, say, for five days a week from 9 a.m. to 5 p.m., doing hard, useful, unpaid work, but going home at night. Some of those who have a job could serve their sentences from Friday evening to Sunday evening.

More use should be made of the curfew – a requirement that a defendant stays at home between the hours of, say, 8 p.m. and 8 a.m. At present this is quite often imposed as a condition of bail, but never as part of a sentence or, so far as I know, a condition of parole. Former defendants have told me that the police usually do not check that a curfew is kept, and this would have to be tightened.

Another condition could be that a defendant who is allowed partial freedom shall not go outside a defined area or to specified places. In certain American states they attach a homing device to a man's leg, so that his movements can be monitored. If he goes where he should not, he is returned to jail. It is fair to say, however, that when I mentioned this to young men and women at Liverpool day training centre, they reacted strongly against it; they would go to prison rather than suffer such a humiliating restraint.

Productive work should be available at all prisons for those who are fit, and prisons made as self-supporting as possible. Those who have no trade should be taught one, as some are now. Trade unions are naturally opposed to competition from prison labour, but work is already done for the government – and not only on mailbags – and I have seen items such as electrical equipment for outside industry.

The need for facilities for those with personality problems, including addiction to alcohol and other drugs, is obvious. There should be group therapy, not run by prison officers but by probation officers, psychologists and other skilled people. Little work of this kind seems to be done at present in prisons, but the need for it is considerable. Such work is no doubt best done in conditions of liberty, but I am thinking of those who have had to lose it.

We need more alternatives to custody. It has to be accepted that prison has an embittering effect and before it is resorted to efforts should be made to reform a man by gentler methods. I have referred to the day training centre approach elsewhere in this book,* and I know the centres at Sheffield and Liverpool. When I went to the latter place recently, several of the clients there told me of the good the place was doing. I remember two of them, who came from deprived areas and had no educational qualifications; they had drifted into crime and served sentences, but both hoped to go on study courses. A girl in her early twenties, unmarried but with two children, who had been to prison for shoplifting, was intelligent and articulate, and I foresaw a bright future for her. 'Why couldn't I have come here *before* I was sent to prison?' she asked rightly.

The UK could lead the world with a new system based on enlightenment and firmness. We could protect the public by locking away the hopelessly wicked who prey on them, yet give a helping hand to those who want and deserve it. The unsatisfactory system of parole could be dismantled – except for a very few – and the good members of the parole board and the local committees released for other public work. I doubt, however, whether I shall ever see the sort of changes I envisage. The Home Office works from day to day, from hand to mouth, from crisis to crisis. There is insufficient vision. Without vision, someone said, the people perish. That is one reason why the British people are perishing and languishing in so many areas, including this one.

*See pp. 139–40.

# Chapter 11

# *Capital Punishment*

It was dark as K., my client, climbed into the warehouse holding his sawn-off shotgun. The night-watchman came up and K. shot him, sending him to the floor. As K. said later, 'I knew I'd get no more for murder than for attempted murder, so I shot him again and killed him.' Dead men tell no tales. A police inspector arrived and he too got a fatal blast. The death penalty had been abolished and many years later K. is still in prison. If it had not been abolished would these two men still be alive? Should K. have paid with his own life? My views about the death penalty have wavered.

There are two strong arguments for hanging people. The first is that it saves innocent lives by deterring men who would otherwise kill, and my client's remark seems to confirm that. But he was not a man on whose word anyone would normally rely, so how can we be sure that he was telling the truth about why he killed? Most murders do not involve a careful decision about consequences: they take place within the family, using that word broadly. A man kills his wife or girl-friend during a violent, frenzied argument, or goes mad and decides to kill himself and take his family with him. This happened to a friend of mine at school: he was the only one left when his father did that. Men who kill in such circumstances are not thinking calmly and logically about consequences or anything else. Nor is the psychopathic killer who rapes and stabs to death a woman he has never met, but who attracts him as he sees her in the street.

The bank-robber who takes a loaded gun intending to use it if he has to is thinking calmly, but he does not expect to be caught or he would not be there, so even if there were the death penalty he might say to himself, 'They won't hang me, because they won't catch me.' Criminals who go for big money are optimists, like all gamblers. Since parliament abolished hanging, murders have increased but so have other crimes, and criminologists tell us that statistics do not point to the death penalty as a deterrent. Even so I have a feeling that K. may well have been right in what he told the police, and that some criminals would leave their gun behind or keep their finger off the trigger if we still had the gallows. Take an extreme case. Suppose a convicted murderer, who knows that he will be kept in prison for the rest of his life or most of it, takes a prison officer hostage. He knows that if he kills the officer there is little more that the

— 159 —

authorities can lawfully do to him. They cannot even put him on bread and water. The death penalty might save the victim's life.

The other big argument for the return of the rope is that a majority of the public favours it. It is important for the law to keep in step with public opinion. The public is right to feel very strongly about some of the things that happen: men who torture and kill children or terrify an area for months by killing women for no reason, except a terrible, twisted urge they have. Those who, while burgling a house, stab or shoot the occupants to death; and the cold criminal who kills a policeman while robbing a bank. Few shed tears if such men are shot by the police who are trying to arrest them, so why not kill them afterwards by court order? I understand such feelings and share them to a substantial extent. But feelings – emotions – are not enough. We must think calmly and logically about this.

People say that murderers, or some of them, *deserve* to die. This is retribution, and I agree with it as a principle of punishment when dealing with the wicked. A person who wickedly harms another deserves to suffer. But the only sensible definition of suffering is harm inflicted on a living person. We do not know what happens to people after they die. If we could be sure that a murderer would go to some sort of everlasting hell, that would be retribution, but we cannot be sure. So the suffering a condemned man goes through is limited to the few weeks of waiting. The extent to which he suffers will depend on the man: for some, every minute will be mental agony, but others will accept their coming death as a release or even look forward to it. Interestingly, the act of putting a person to death is made as painless as possible. Why, if the object is retribution? Why not torture him and draw out the process for as long as possible? Some people might favour that, but only a minority, even of the keen hangers. If suffering is an object, twenty years in prison is surely as bad as a few weeks under the shadow of the rope or electric chair. Gary Gilmore thought so and chose death.

Another argument for ending a murderer's life is that otherwise he may do it again. Straffen escaped and killed another child. Young was released and killed by poison again. But both men were mad and madmen were not hanged. The most shocking murders are often the work of those whose mind is diseased. Some people point to the cost of keeping murderers alive for years, but this is of small weight as an argument. Heavier is the fact that we are collecting in prisons many dangerous and desperate men who would formerly have been hanged. They know they have little to lose as their release is so far off, if it is ever likely. They must be difficult to deal with, but if the prison authorities are given enough resources they should be able to cope.

What are the arguments against restoring death as a penalty? The strongest is that human life is sacred. One does not have to be religious to think that. Indeed, many people have been put to death in the name of religion, but none in the name of humanism, rationalism or agnosticism. Our first duty is to preserve and enhance human life, and to kill a person in any circumstances (except the defence of oneself or another), goes against that. By killing a murderer the state does what he did, stooping to his sordid level. If a condemned man tries to cut his throat the state does not stand by and let him die, but does all it can to preserve his life. This is not because it wants the pleasure of taking his life in its own time and way, it is because man's normal instinct is to preserve life and go to the help of one who is suffering. It is contrary to our normal feelings to stand by and let a man die, whoever he is and whatever he has done; similarly as to taking another's life in a cold and calculated way.

Putting a person to death by court order arouses morbid feelings. Twisted men used to go to the police and confess to murders they had not done, apparently to obtain notoriety, to become someone important instead of being one of life's ignored and trampled on nobodies. Presumably it was easy to eliminate them for not knowing enough about the facts, and how many of them would have gone through with it to the point of being hanged is hard to say. Some people are probably twisted enough even for that. There were morbid feelings in a prison as the time for an execution approached; unhealthy feelings in the inmates and the staff. On the morning when Ruth Ellis was hanged in 1955 the children in a school nearby were in a feverish babble of excitement, which cannot have been good for them. Can it be good for the prison officers who have to chat with the condemned man as the minutes tick by, trying to keep him cheerful and knowing that they will soon take him to be killed?

When a man is sent to prison it is always hard on those close to him, such as his wife and children; they suffer too. Of course he should have thought of them before he did his crime; his family are his responsibility, not the court's. We say that to defendants when we send them to prison. Logically it applies to a man who is sentenced to death. But most men who are sent to prison will come out one day. Think what it must be like for a wife, child, girl-friend or parent, to visit their beloved for the last time. The anguish and the tears, the final lingering look and embrace, the forcible tearing away as time is up, followed next day by the agony of waiting for the final moment. Then the years of shame. Ruth Ellis' daughter surfaced recently and became the object of attention by the media. Her mother's death has blighted her life, yet the daughter was entirely innocent.

Death leaves no scope for repentance or reform. There is some good in all criminals, whatever their crimes. The 'birdman' of Alcatraz became a changed man after many years in prison. Toughened by his early life, years in jail brought out the softer side.

Mistakes cannot be put right. One of the main influences leading to abolition was Ludovic Kennedy's brilliant book *Ten Rillington Place*. If it had been known that Christie was a mass murderer, Evans would not have been hanged. We cannot now be sure that Evans murdered at all. There is a real possibility that an innocent man was hanged. In recent years several men found guilty of murder have later been cleared.

We never hanged all murderers; some were reprieved, even in darkest Dickensian days. Latterly some murders were made 'capital' – subject to hanging – and others 'non-capital'. There are bound to be injustices where such distinctions are made. A man who poisoned a woman for sexual reasons – such as his love for another – could not be hanged, but he could be if he shot her, or killed her in the course of stealing from her. Whatever the system, someone has to have the final say as to life or death. Some home secretaries made blunders. In 1923, Mrs Thompson was hanged for the murder of her husband. Her lover Bywaters used the knife, and the extent of her complicity will always be doubtful; letters she wrote to Bywaters turned the scale against her. The scene at her execution was horrific; she was in a collapsed state and had to be tied to a chair. Lord Chief Justice Goddard tried Craig and Bentley in 1952. Craig fired the gun which killed the policeman, but he was too young to be hanged and he has long been at liberty. Even Goddard – no soft-liner – expected the nineteen-year-old, backward Bentley to be reprieved, but the victim was a policeman so Bentley went to the gallows. So did Ruth Ellis for shooting one of her lovers. By hanging people like those three, home secretaries weakened the case for hanging anybody.

The ritual of hanging is not only spine-breaking for the condemned, but spine-chilling for those who watch it or think about it. By the time executions were abolished they were done quickly and 'humanely', but the process was awful even so. The hangman had to observe the prisoner through the spyhole in the cell door to gauge the precise length of drop: too little would not kill, too much would pull the head off. Then the final words from the parson, the entry of the hangman, the pinioning of the arms, the short walk, the placing of the cap on the head, the rope around the neck and the pulling of the lever. No degree of efficiency can make this 'humane' in any sensible use of the word. There are other methods but none that is without objection, even to those who believe in the process. Any method requiring the participation of a doctor is 'out'. Electrocution seems just as ghastly as hanging, but it may not bring death as quickly. Whatever method is chosen does not alter the grisly nature of what men are doing to a fellow-human being.

No country in western Europe now uses the death penalty. If we in Britain were to bring it back we would be out of step and regarded by our fellow-Europeans as barbaric. We would be grouped with the Iranians, Turks, Pakistanis, Saudi-Arabians and some states in the USA. When I was young Mrs Van der Elst, dressed in black, used to appear outside a prison at the time of an execution in solitary, silent protest. If executions were brought back there would be more than one protester each time and they would not be silent. There would be scenes like those at Grunwick and Greenham Common. If there were overwhelming reasons for hanging murderers, civil commotion would have to be endured. But if the case is marginal the commotion has to be taken into account. The state should try to reduce those situations which lead the well-intentioned and others to get together in large numbers, put people in fear, do damage and injury and strain the police.

If the rope did come back I would not protest, were I a judge or not. I would shed no tear for men like the Yorkshire Ripper. One side of me might rejoice a little at their passing. But, on balance, I am not in favour of restoring the supreme penalty. There is some evidence that the death penalty might deter in a few cases, but the evidence is tenuous. The arguments against outweigh the arguments for. I would, however, lock up some murderers for the rest of their lives: those who have shown themselves unfit to be in uncontrolled contact with innocents. If this means that some murderers would sink into mindless senility over the years, I still would not release the worst of them.

When the House of Commons debated this subject in 1983 the Home Secretary, Mr Leon Brittan, spoke in favour of the death penalty for 'terrorist' murderers. This is disturbing because the case for that is thin. At Easter 1916 the IRA of those days staged a hopeless uprising by seizing the Dublin post-office, proclaiming a republic and holding out for a few days. There was little Irish support for such a venture. But then the British began to shoot the leaders. Irish public opinion turned and its intensity led to the British withdrawal from the twenty-six counties in 1921. Today the leaders who were shot in 1916 are national heroes, an inspiration to the modern IRA. Where a large number of people have a strong sense of national grievance based on oppression – as held by the nationalists in Northern Ireland and by some Palestinians who claim to have been driven out by Israel – the situation is not a normal 'law and order' one. Killing the dissidents only makes things worse. The conflict becomes self-generating. Feelings intensify as colleagues are killed; the cry for revenge is heard. Those who feel oppressed and incapable of getting justice through democratic or legal processes resort to violence, which has in the past succeeded – as in Palestine and Cyprus. I do not condone violence. I do say that the only effective way of dealing with 'terrorists' in such situations is to remove the underlying grievance. The gallows have no place in that process.

# Chapter 12

# *A Police State?*

What do we mean by the expression 'a police state'? A dictatorship certainly comes within it: the executive is free to arrest, torture or even kill those who do not conform with the regime. The police have a free hand against them. There is no independent legal profession. Individuals have no rights which can be enforced. The courts are tools of the government. Some of these wrongs exist in states which claim to be democratic, such as some of the new independent African countries. There are police-state tendencies in every modern state, including the UK and the United States. We all remember Watergate. Modern technology has made it easy for those who control the state to control individuals: telephones can be tapped; conversations overheard in other ways; bugging devices planted; mail intercepted.

We are here dealing with power, the effect it has on those who have it, and how its use can be controlled. By power I mean the making of decisions which control or influence the actions of others. Almost every group which acts *as* a group gives power over the others to one or more of its members. Lord Acton wrote, 'All power tends to corrupt, and absolute power corrupts absolutely.' He was right. By corruption he meant misuse of power. All power tends to be misused; it is a natural human tendency. We all like power over others, and we use it selfishly at times, if we are allowed to. We need to be watched and corrected – as judges are, by the Court of Appeal and the media.

How can corruption by power be prevented? First, by spreading power between various people or groups. The US Constitution does that. The President chooses members of the Supreme Court, but the Senate has to confirm his appointments. A candidate can be cross-examined in public about his opinions and his record, which is healthy.

The next safeguard is the media. The public should be able to know what is going on and being done in their name. There is a case for having more newspapers and radio and television stations. It is wrong to have the media in too few hands. Every town should have a television station, social groups having access to the camera. Investigative journalism, satirical magazines and radio and television programmes have been useful in curbing and deflating the powerful and the pompous, including judges. Some countries, including the United States and Australia, have Freedom of Information Act and there is a strong case for having one in the UK.

All the actions of public representatives and officials should be open to the public, unless a real need for secrecy can be shown. Who remembers Crichel Down now? A man had had land taken by the government in wartime, and civil servants, acting in secrecy, tried to prevent him getting it back. Happily it all came out and a ministerial head rolled, but how many such injustices go undetected because officials are still allowed to work in secrecy?

There have been promises by political parties when in opposition to repeal section 2 of the Official Secrets Act 1911, which enables the government to threaten individuals and shut their mouths even when there can be no harm to state security. But no party in power has got round to repeal. ('They wouldn't, would they?' a cynic might say.) Recently Peter Wright, who left MI5 twelve years ago, intended to publish a book in Australia alleging that things had gone wrong in MI5, and even that its former head had been a Soviet spy. The UK government went to great lengths to try to stop its publication in Australia and here. The English court of appeal even, at one time, forbade publication in the UK of what was said in the Australian courts. Yet no one suggested that the book held anything of interest to the Soviet authorities. All governments want to suppress anything that embarrasses them, or puts them in a poor light, but they should not be allowed to get away with it. If there were misdeeds in MI5, we should know about them. A bill of rights, incorporating a section about the freedom of information, is needed. The public cannot look to the courts for protection as things are.

The law of libel is too strict. In the United States they differentiate between private individuals and people in public life. It is harder for the latter to get libel damages: the public have a right to know about them. Private individuals are in a different position, or should be: our law makes no distinction. It is too easy for journalists to be muzzled by the issue of a writ and the threat of heavy damages. Who can imagine our politicians proposing a law that would curtail their power to stifle criticism? Yet public persons should not be able to have it both ways: the media should be free to comment widely on what we do, even if they hurt us – subject to a duty to correct false statements.

In recent years our courts have developed the judicial review as a curb on the activities of officialdom, and I welcome it. Those who make decisions now have lawyers looking over their shoulders in some situations. Another bulwark against the misuse of power is a strong and independent legal profession, and I include the judiciary. We need judges who can stand up for what they think right, stand up even to the man who at present feeds them. But I have dealt with that elsewhere in this book.

The cry 'police state' can be overdone. Take identity cards. In some European countries everyone has to carry one, bearing his photograph. In the 1939 war and for a few years after it we in the UK had to carry one; the civilians' cards did not have photographs. Identity cards can also act as passports, as in Germany. A majority of our population would probably cry 'police state!' at the suggestion that we should have to carry cards. Those fears are groundless. There would be no oppression. There would be some inconvenience, as there is with passports, but the advantages would be substantial to all except criminals – and why should they be protected? It would be easier to convince the police or other officials who we are, and this would avoid the need for arrest in some cases. There is a big criminal trade in stolen cheques and banker's cards. Millions of pounds in money and goods are obtained by them every year. If I go to a shop or bank with a cheque with 'John Smith' printed on and a card signed in that name, it is possible to copy the signature on to the cheque. If I had to produce an identity card in the name John Smith bearing a photograph of myself, deception would be much more difficult. This has nothing to do with a police state.

I would not go all the way along this road. The compulsory finger-printing of the whole population would aid crime detection. The innocent would have nothing to fear, but they would rightly resent the incon-venience and the imputation. They would feel like cattle, being herded about and branded. They would not feel that about identity cards; most people go abroad and have to apply for passports. Under my system everyone would have to carry what would also be used as a passport, and the state would pay the cost involved.

Another area in which the cry 'police state!' goes up is the right of silence. Under the Judges' Rules a suspect who is being interviewed by the police has to be cautioned – told that he is not obliged to answer any questions. If he does refuse to answer, this must not be held against him. I think it is time to modify this right. In these days of deluging crime it is a luxury we can no longer afford. It irks me to see plainly guilty men being shielded by the right of silence. 'Do not hold his silence against him, members of the jury,' I have to say. 'He was entitled to keep his mouth shut.' One sees question after question to which an accused has replied, 'No comment,' or, 'No reply,' has been recorded – especially where the defendant's solicitor has been present. Rightly we bend over backwards in favour of an accused, but sometimes our posture makes the system look foolish. We must protect a suspect against unfairness, but it is possible to be unfair to accusers too. The present system favours those with something to hide. Why should it?

What would the new rule be? That a person against whom there is substantial ground for suspicion that he has taken part in a crime should be obliged to answer questions about his activities and knowledge. He should be told that any refusal to answer may become evidence against him when a decision is being made whether to prosecute him, and at any later court hearing at which he is an accused. The extent to which a refusal is self-incriminating should depend on all the circumstances, including the facts that are put to the suspect. No one ought to be convicted on his silence alone. There should be other reasons for being sure – taken with his silence – that he is guilty.

There is an unfortunate by-product of the right of silence: malpractice by police officers. Knowing that a suspect is entitled to keep his mouth shut they try to get him to open it. Without admissions the police often do not have enough evidence and they are understandably reluctant to let go a man whom they believe is guilty. They are in order in putting searching questions. They may try to convince the suspect that it is in his interest to speak, for example by saying, 'Your pal has admitted it, and he says it was your idea.' If the pal *has* said that, there is nothing wrong. If the pal has not, there is no breach of the Judges' Rules but it is getting near the border. The next ploy may cross the border, for example, 'We can keep you locked up for weeks if you don't admit it.' Or – the same thing in different words – 'Give us a statement and you'll get bail.' Or, 'We'll put a good word in for you with the judge.' (As criminals know, if the police say in court that a defendant was frank from the start, co-operated with the police, has given valuable information or tried hard to go straight, this can reduce a sentence or even purchase liberty.) Other improper pressure includes threats that a friend or relative of the suspect will be arrested or will not be released; violence or the threat of it; such prolonged and bullying questioning that the defendant would have signed anything; insufficient food; no bed or blankets; a cold cell. We also get allegations that the police invented or 'improved' questions and answers; or did not let the defendant read his statement before he signed it and that they put words in that he did not say.

It is impossible to know how often the police resort to the tactics I have referred to. I feel sure they do in some cases. When they do they usually believe that the defendant is guilty – they are not trying to get a man convicted whom they think is innocent. In my early years at the bar I used to do criminal cases at Sheffield. Violence by the police was often alleged, but judges usually brushed that aside. In one case I was prosecuting, an accused said the police had beaten him up. I asked his barrister – who later became a judge – why he had not raised this with the police officers when they were giving evidence. He said he had not thought it would help his client's case. Then, about twenty years ago, it came out that for years it had been police policy in Sheffield to use violence, including blows with a 'rhinoceros whip'. After a public inquiry, heads rolled.

I feel that most police officers are honest and obey the rules. But when they feel that a suspect is guilty there is an obvious temptation for them to break the rules. Sometimes they do so where the offence is fairly trivial. I tried a case in London where an Indian was found with plastic cards he should not have had. I was sceptical when he said the police had used violence to obtain a confession. But then he called a doctor who had noted the injuries, and there was no doubt in my mind. The officers had probably misused their power. We in the courts must always be vigilant for such cases.

There are three ways in which police officers can make notes of an interview with a suspect. The first is for the officer or officers to wait until the interview is over before writing anything. The second is to record the questions and answers as they are spoken, in a 'contemporaneous note', to read them to the suspect at the end and ask him to sign them as accurate. The third method is for the questions to be written beforehand and the answers recorded as they are given. The third method is used by inland revenue investigators; it has the obvious disadvantage that it is not flexible enough – it is impossible to foresee precisely how the questioning will go. For years after I began at the bar the usual method was to take notes afterwards. Recently some forces have introduced the contemporaneous note system where this is practicable – not, for example, where things are said in a moving car or shouted during a chase in the street. In some forces this method seems to be optional, at the discretion of the officers; others stick to the old notes-afterwards system.

The latter system is thoroughly unsatisfactory. I have thought so for over thirty years and said so openly for several years, as I did in my evidence to the Royal Commission on Criminal Procedure. Sometimes several hours pass before a note is made. On occasions the typed notes run to several pages, and I do not believe that the interviewers could have remembered it all accurately. Sometimes I suspect they had a hidden tape-recorder; that would be some guarantee of accuracy though not of honesty, as the police always deny using such devices. In the old days the police used to claim word-perfection; presumably they thought that to admit the possibility of even one error would devalue the whole. Now they tend to concede that there may be small errors but to insist that they have got the meaning right. One means of checking accuracy would be to require officers to make their notes independently of each other. Cross-examiners would have a field-day, unless the police felt obliged to break that rule too. As it is they are allowed to make a joint note.

Officers sometimes say when being cross-examined that to take notes during an interview interrupts the flow of the questions and answers. It may do to some extent, but contemporaneous notes *are* taken in many cases. One reason for not writing notes during an interview is that once a notebook comes out some suspects shut up. Some defendants say that they thought they were having an informal, off-the-record chat.

One of the worst features of taking notes afterwards is that the suspect does not take notes himself, and he does not know what is in the police notes until weeks or months later when the prosecution statements are served on him prior to the hearing in the magistrates' court (I am referring to cases which come to a crown court). Above all, the system is wide open to abuse. It is far too easy for policemen to insert things that an accused has not said or to alter what he has said. A friend of mine was stopped for speeding; she has an excellent memory and is certain that the police account of what she said contained things she never said at all. If there is the possibility that they get things wrong in trivial cases it is even more likely that the police will do that in serious cases. This is an area in which all chief constables could do a lot *now* to improve the system by requiring a contemporaneous note whenever that is practicable. This would improve public confidence in the police and ensure fairer trials of defendants.

In the end we will probably adopt a system of video-recording police interviews. This would be less open to abuse, though some defendants would allege malpractice – for example, allege that the police threatened them *before* the recording, and told them to act naturally. There would be allegations that the recordings had been edited. We are, however, too reluctant to use modern devices as they become available. We are too conservative and complacent. We should welcome any innovation that makes it less likely that the cry 'police state!' has credibility.

# Chapter 13

## *Prostitution*

I will call her Miss A. She was about twenty-two when she came before me at a crown court. Her coloured father, who was almost certainly a seaman, had left her and her white mother years ago. She had a pretty, dusky face and a slim body and her clients must have found her attractive, though several teeth were missing from the top centre. So on the rare occasions when she smiled she went down a few notches in the scale of attraction – at any rate in my eyes, which viewed her, I hope, with a certain detachment.

I first knew of the defendant when I heard hysterical wailing from the cells downstairs. The building is old, so the waiting prisoners are not kept miles down in the earth as they seem to be in modern courts. 'I want to see Dr—' she cried, referring to a local psychiatrist. She cried out so often and so loudly that I sent for her in court and lectured her about the noise, and then I sent for Dr—. He came and said he could do nothing for this despairing young woman. She then began to shout hysterically that she wanted to see the judge, me. That she soon did, in court.

On the face of things, Miss A.'s position was serious. She had many convictions for dock trespass, which in her case indicated loitering or soliciting for prostitution on private land. She was at the crown court for four offences of stealing from clients, crimes which prostitutes tend to drift into as an adjunct to their main trade. Two of the four were suspended sentences and the other two involved breaches of those. She had not yet graduated to robbery, which can be the next step for such women: luring a man to a house where a big, strong male companion suddenly appears and says he is the husband and he wants money and valuables – or else. Many such clients are too afraid or too proud to go to the police and risk publicity and derision.

In the worst case, Miss A. had met a foreign sea captain in a club and accepted his invitation to go back to his cabin. She asked him for the fee in advance, as any prudent prostitute does, and it was about £25. He took his keys, opened a cupboard and peeled off the notes. Foolishly he let Miss A. see that the rest of the ship's money, about £900 in English notes, was also available at the twist of a key. Miss A. duly earned the £25, the captain showing his appreciation by slipping into slumber. She then took the key and helped herself to the £900.

I had more sympathy for Miss A. than for the sea captain or his fellow-complainants. Broadly, the defendants I sentence are villains or victims. A villain knows what is right, but coldly chooses what is wrong at the expense of others when he need not. A victim is pulled by forces which he did not make and cannot easily understand or control. Miss A. came from a deprived family and the only earning asset that she had was her body. She was trained in nothing else and honest work would be hard to get. She never made a cold decision. She never sat down and thought about her life and where it was going; that was beyond her. She was an hysteric; life was too much for her to fathom; she lived from one day to the next – or rather one night to the next. If she had been asked, 'But isn't it immoral and dangerous and short-sighted to degrade yourself like this?' she would have stared silently, then burst into tears.

But I saw no point in imprisoning Miss A. Men like the sea captain 'ask for it'. If I were to go with a prostitute – which I never could or would – I would leave my watch and other valuables at home, apart from the fee. If she tricked me in any way I would blame myself, not her. To expect decency or morality in such an area is to expect the sea always to be calm. The probation service said they had tried hard but could do no more for Miss A. Those dedicated officers, optimists by nature, do not give up easily and are reluctant to say, 'Prison is the only answer,' but they had reached that this time.

I decided that the day training centre at Sheffield should be approached and they agreed to take the defendant. So I made a fresh probation order with the necessary condition. This meant her going to live in a hostel in Sheffield, far from home and friends. An inadequate, bewildered girl was bound to find it hard. When she got to the centre Miss A. was something of a sensation with the other attenders, all men, and she became the centre of interest. I do not think she carried on her trade there, but she did upset such concentration as her colleagues had for the work in hand. After a few weeks Miss A. absconded and returned home, and she was brought back to me for breaching the condition. I still did not send her to prison; she had not committed any further offence, and so the constructive approach had not failed entirely. I last saw her leaving court subject to yet another suspended sentence and a final warning. What happened to her after that? I shall probably never know. A happy future seemed unlikely. A slide down the sleazy slope is often the fate of such women. Drink, drugs, beatings and imprisonment push them further and further into the marshland of misery. Their prematurely ageing bodies can no longer earn as much; the clientele becomes further 'down market'. Most prostitutes who stay on the game must die squalid and fairly early deaths, and if not, then live increasingly miserable lives. Yet how can they be reclaimed from such a life and saved from such a death? Their business is so easy for them, and pays more than the state does.

Miss B. appeared earlier in my professional life: I defended her when I was at the bar. She was different from Miss A. She was about twenty-nine, white, strong, confident, articulate; tall, dark, hard in manner, coarse in features. She would never call out hysterically from her cell, though she was worried about the outcome of the case, which was certain imprisonment if it went the wrong way. She was charged with keeping a brothel and she had a suspended sentence for a like offence at her house where the present offence was also alleged to have taken place.

Miss B. had several previous convictions involving the game. Prostitution is not an offence in itself. It becomes so if a woman loiters or solicits for that purpose in public; or if two or more women act as prostitutes in one house. One woman in one house or flat does not add up to a brothel, whatever she does there. Miss B.'s case turned on that. The prosecution had to prove that at least one other woman was on the game at Miss B.'s house, where she freely admitted she was. She was frank and direct about her past and I admired her for it. In a long conference she told me that when she was sixteen her father left her mother, her and the other children and she had to support the family. She was buying a modern 'semi' in a good-class suburb – there lay the problem, as we shall see – and ran a new car. When I asked her why she could not get off the game, she said, 'How could I possibly? The only other paid work I've ever done was as a stable-girl for a few weeks.' There is no way in which a social worker or judge could persuade Miss B. to abandon prostitution. Marriage to a man of means could do it, but that seemed unlikely. Otherwise only time will achieve it, if it does happen.

Miss B.'s attitude to her way of life was interesting. 'When you are young, men give you a good time. But later come the bad times and the beatings. It's a hard life, and I know there's no future, no happy future, in it. I've done all I can to keep my young sister off the game. She's studying for her A levels, and I'm determined she'll have a better life than I've had. If she ever becomes like me, I'll beat the daylight out of her.'

Miss B. charged £6 a time and earned £10,000 a year tax-free: this was over ten years ago. It worked out at about five men a day. There was a complication though: £6 was for a short-time – about twenty minutes from a man entering her house to leaving, according to the police evidence. An all-night session was a matter for negotiation.

One man who negotiated one regretted it. He was a Pakistani: most of Miss B.'s clients were coloured men, many of whom had left their wives behind in their home country. Miss B. went to this man's house and he paid her in advance. In the morning he showed his satisfaction and virility by asking for another 'go', and took the money for the further fee from his briefcase on top of a wardrobe. Soon afterwards Miss B. said that a cup of tea would be nice and her happily exhausted client went downstairs to oblige. After he had said goodbye to Miss B. he found his briefcase was empty.

It was this side of Miss B.'s work that made me and my instructing solicitor's clerk — a retired police inspector — go off her. We had been sympathetic towards her until she told us about a visit to Scotland. She used to spend some weekends in Glasgow, where the police were tolerant: a prostitute could give any name and they did not bother to find out her real identity. Also they let a brothel operate. By going to that house and paying 'madame' a percentage Miss B. could service clients and earn £150 in a weekend.

On one visit to Glasgow Miss B. met a man who asked to go to England with her and spend a few days at her home. She agreed and they set off in her car, his wallet bulging with notes and his heart with expectations. On the way Miss B. said that she felt hungry and could eat some fish and chips. Her companion, hungry in more than one sense, had a hasty clinch in the car and went to a shop. When he got there his wallet containing £200 was missing and so was Miss B. and her car. 'He was going to spend the money on me anyway,' she remarked, when the solicitor's clerk and I naïvely said what a dirty trick she had played. 'But suppose he'd traced you.' Apparently he had not. She even had information the moment he left town for Scotland. He did not go to the police as the Pakistani did. If the Scotsman had traced her she would presumably have relied on her lover, a large coloured man, to protect her.

Miss B. told me that when submitting to sexual intercourse with a client, she felt nothing. She provided him with a sheath, removed such clothing as was necessary and lay back. It was as exciting for her as washing her hands. Yet she was presumably able to feel something as she lay with her own man. What did *he* think of her life? He was not my client and I never spoke to him. He only came into the dock at the end of the case, when he and Miss B. pleaded guilty to possessing cannabis. He probably thought her prostitution was a convenient way of making money for them both, and felt no jealousy. He was not a pimp in the accepted sense: Miss B. found her own clients. And he did not live at her house. I cannot understand his attitude.

Miss B. had built up a flourishing connection with (mainly coloured) men, and there lay the reason for her being prosecuted. Her neighbours were understandably concerned about the way men came and went, day and night. Their cars blocked drives. Sometimes there was trouble, as when Miss B. had to chase away a drunken or difficult client. All this lowered the tone of the area. Children might be molested by frustrated men. And, worst of all, the value of a house would go down once a prospective buyer knew what was going on. So neighbours complained to councillors and the police. Something had to be done to stop her. Instead of going to the county court for damages and an injunction for nuisance — which might have worked — a further prosecution for brothel-keeping was brought.

The trial was before the late Judge Henry Scott QC (Uppingham and Cambridge), who was one of the most admirable men I have known. He feared nobody. (When at the bar he once wrote to a high court judge that if he did not withdraw, in court, an aspersion he had made against a young member of the bar, he – Scott – would get up in court and demand it. The high court judge did as Scott had asked, and cancelled his next planned visit to our circuit. That incident was the basis of an early radio play of mine, *The Circuit*.) Scott tried the Miss B. case in a relaxed, quizzical manner, pulling faces from time to time but never interfering. The police had done a lot of work in assembling evidence. Simultaneously they had men in the house on the opposite side of the road and in the adjoining semi. As a man entered or left, his description was noted and he was timed. The officers across the way had a telescopic camera, but a tree cut off the faces of most of the men. Visitors to the house were mostly male clients; Miss B. was open about it. A few women prostitutes did call, but as she said to me, 'You're a barrister, so some of your friends are barristers and they visit your house. Well, I'm a prostitute.' There was a policeman with his ear against the wall on the first floor next door, noting what he heard and when. Another man lay on his back under the floorboards on the ground floor, listening through a stethoscope with the end stuck to the boards with chewing-gum.

There was ample evidence that as a client came to the house Miss B.'s mother or sister called out that someone had come 'for business', and that she duly went upstairs to serve him. There was a suggestion that her sister had been in a room with a man, but the sister said he was only her boyfriend. In the end Miss B. got off the brothel charge. For stealing from the Pakistani and having cannabis, she was fined and given a suspended sentence. We appealed against the latter, successfully. When I told the Court of Appeal that they would appreciate how likely it was that a woman like Miss B. might get convicted of some further offence, having regard to her way of life, one lord justice said that I must not assume that their lordships knew much about that sort of thing.

What lessons are to be drawn from these two cases and what is there to say about prostitution generally? It has always existed and always will. Prostitutes do necessary work: a quick release of sexual tension for the man, with no emotional strings or comeback, in return for money which the woman needs. If two adults wish to enter into such an arrangement the law should not interfere. The criminal law is mainly there to protect people from harm which they have not chosen to accept. If prostitution harms either party – and it might bring disease to either or feelings of guilt or shame to the client – that is their affair. The law should not punish what is merely thought to be undesirable. That is the trap that the well-intentioned Mrs Whitehouse falls into.

Prostitution *is* undesirable. It degrades both parties. I would never commend it to a son (or daughter) or to anyone. I cannot imagine myself resorting to it – or rather, I can imagine it and I find the idea repulsive. Sex should be a joyous and unselfish giving by a man and a woman who have genuine feelings for each other, not a mechanical, animal-like exercise. (But how often does it become the latter in marriage?) There should be love, whatever that is – and it has different meanings – or at least affection and respect. But many men can do it and enjoy it and some women can do it and suffer it in the absence of such emotions.

The only persons who can complain of harm by prostitution are innocent third parties. These can – as in Miss B.'s case – be neighbours; or women or girls who get accosted by kerb-crawlers or foot-crawlers in areas where prostitutes operate. I am driven to conclude that areas of large towns should be set aside for brothels and that the brothels and those working there should be licensed and inspected. This worked in France for British and other troops in the 1914 war. It has worked in other places at other times. It involves looking at the problem in the face and accepting that it will always exist. So it ought to be controlled, thereby avoiding harm for innocents. Run-down houses or warehouses in inner city areas could be found, or large converted barges moored on rivers or canals.

There would be opposition from the churches, Mrs Whitehouse and others. They would say that by accepting prostitution the state was encouraging it. That is not so. The state accepts the smoking of cigarettes – far more harmful than prostitution – but does not encourage it and indeed, by forbidding television advertising and requiring warnings on cigarette packets, discourages it timidly.

Efforts would still be made by social workers and courts to deter young girls from going on the game, before their standards of life became geared to it. Licensed brothels would not solve all problems. Some amateurs would solicit or loiter outside the new red-light areas. But courts could then hit at them with a clearer conscience. The women would have a lawful alternative, which they had refused. Not all male clients would go to red-light areas. The married lawyer or bank manager might fear embarrassment or blackmail if seen there.

Years ago early one morning in Dortmund, West Germany, I went to the Linienstrasse; it is similar to the Reeperbahn in Hamburg, in that prostitutes' houses line the street. I was there to observe only, as most of those milling about seemed to be doing. I did not see any man go inside, although some were going to the windows and asking prices – more as a joke than a genuine inquiry, it seemed. In one room were three beautiful young women; they looked refined but I had no means of checking that. Perhaps they had made a cool decision to make a few thousand and then retire into marriage and children. That would be better than slowly sliding down the sleazy scale which seemed to be the fate of Misses A. and B.

# Afterword

Those who have read this book have been able to see me at work as a judge. I have tried to explain, with examples, why I do what I do, and what changes I wish to see. Many things are wrong with our present system. Above all there is too much complacency, conservatism and conformity, from the top down, in those who run it. (We all have shortcomings, and I have not tried to hide my own.)

I hope that what I have written may not only interest the general reader, as one of the public whom I serve, but also some of those whose duty it is to make changes. If so, I shall be amply rewarded for the effort I have put into this, my first book.

# Postscript 1988

Various things have happened since I finished writing the hardback version of this book in September 1986. The book was published in April 1987. I had no reaction from Lord Hailsham, although I had at times thought there might be one. After all, he had threatened to dismiss me for writing a newspaper article which is reproduced in the book together with stronger material. I sent him a copy, but I do not know whether he read it, and if so what he thought about it. He must have disapproved, as he thought that only senior judges should be seen or heard outside their courtrooms. I had many letters from the public, most of them complimentary. For example 'A couple of weeks ago I read your book. As a consequence I made my husband read it too. We have vivid discussions about the death penalty; he is for it, me against. He has not quite changed his mind yet, but understands arguments better now. Thanks for a great (and the only) inside view into the English legal system. We wish for more judges like yourself. Has the retirement of Lord Hailsham made any difference yet?'

As I wrote in reply, his (enforced) retirement *has* made a difference. How far this book contributed to his going, is impossible to say. It may have added to the growing rumble of discontent with Lord Hailsham which had gone on for years. The Prime Minister may have thought a younger person, less rooted in the past, was needed. When he was finally separated from the Woolsack, it was to the (muted) relief of many judges and lawyers, including me. This is not the place fully to assess Lord Hailsham's stewardship of the Great Seal, but I cannot let his departure go without comment. Embodying as he did the conservatism, complacency and conformity that I write about in this book, he left many things undone. I may be thought prejudiced, but he did me a lot of good, unwittingly. But for him I would not have written my article *Kilmuir Rules – OK?* which *The Guardian* published on 14 February 1986. That piece changed my life. It swept me from the obscure judicial cellar on to the public balcony. It led to the publication of this book. I am now recognised on distant railway stations and invited to appear in the media and to address students and others all over the country. None of this would have happened if Lord Hailsham had dealt with me in a restrained and temperate way.

Lord Havers only reigned for four months, and then he was led from the Woolsack because of his poor health. This was somewhat mysterious, as his health was known about when he was appointed. The chief result of his short stint was to earn him, I understand, a pension of about £40,000 a year for life. In framing legislation, politicians do not neglect themselves or their own. Civil servants have usually to work for forty years to earn a full pension, and judges for fifteen years (I have only three years to go). The September 1987 issue of *Counsel*, the journal of the bar of England and Wales, carried an interview with Lord Havers, given whilst he was still in office. 'So we asked about the so-called Kilmuir rules. Did the Lord Chancellor think some relaxation might now be appropriate? "I do not feel inclined to change the Kilmuir rules. 99.9% of the judges are happy with them. We do not have many problems." We did not need to ask who might be the 0.1%.' Presumably the last comment referred to me, though I was not the only judge who opposed the tight control kept over junior judges by the Lord Chancellor's department.

To the surprise of many, Lord Mackay of Clashfern then came riding down from Scotland to become Lord Chancellor. I found his appointment refreshing. The son of a railwayman, he rose in the law by brilliance and effort. He is not part of the English old-boy network, or even a member of the English bar. I know little more about him, but many such Scots are like us in the north of England: forthright, down-to-earth, spurning affectation. A few days after he was sworn-in, our new Lord Chancellor gave a press conference which was reported on 4 November 1987. He thought 'the so-called Kilmuir rules governing judicial comments in the media were ripe for reform. Times had changed. He would not lay down rigid or detailed rules. Judges should be given more discretion when there were approaches from the media. It should be left to them to decide what to do about interviews by the press or broadcasting media, as long as they do not prejudice their judicial work.' I do not know whether Lord Mackay had read in this book my views on the Kilmuir rules, but I feel he may have done. He would surely want to know what was happening in the judiciary of this 'foreign' land where he had suddenly been given so much power. Without the public attention that Lord Hailsham and I focused on the rules, it is doubtful whether Lord Mackay would even have mentioned them. I find irony in the outcome. All that effort by Hailsham and his civil servants to uphold Kilmuir; the curt threats; the repeated advice 'Don't do it, judge'; Hailsham's strenuous insistence that judicial independence itself rested on the rules. Then the new Scot sweeps them away in a few cool sentences, bringing a healthy Scottish breeze into the fusty air of Westminster. As one who seeks no favour from him, I say to Lord Mackay 'Welcome. A good start. Give us more. Bring reform into our musty mansions, our cobwebbed corridors.'

What is new about Manus Nunan (see page 29–41)? He has taken well the treatment Hailsham gave him. He knows he can never clear his name or have his conduct looked at by an independent tribunal, but he is cheerfully getting on with his life (unlike the people who write to me about their grievances against the judicial system which they have kept alive for years: of course I cannot help them). Nunan has built a house in France near to Andorra, and my wife and I hope to visit him and his new wife there soon. He lectures impressively on Oscar Wilde (another Irishman who was used ill by the English legal system, and who was probably the most brilliant conversation-alist of all time) and on Dr Samuel Johnson and his circle. Nunan has inherited a histrionic streak from his actress mother, and this is one of the things that has drawn me to him. Perhaps he finds the life of the artist superior to that of the lawyer, and if he does I agree with him. The artist strives to find truth and to express it. The lawyer does not strive for truth, and often strives to conceal it. I worry about Nunan's case more than he appears to. It shows Hailsham at his worst and indicts the system of judicial appointments which he operated and tried to justify. It could be looked on as yet another wrong done by the British to the long-suffering Irish, and some influential people in the Republic think that. The transcript of the 'hearing' of 26 September 1986 shows how Hailsham acted in this area, and it is disturbing. It is fair to note that he followed the system his predecessors had adopted, but he could have changed it. The hearing was a shambles. There was no procedure. The prosecutor was also the judge, but presented no evidence. He acted on reports – most of them containing hearsay – which Nunan never saw. There was no right of appeal. The position is now known to have been even worse than when this book went to press. Soon after the Nunan hearing I sent to Sir Derek Oulton, the permanent secretary to the Lord Chancellor, the Nunan material that is in this book, so that Lord Hailsham could consider it before reaching his decision. On 13 January 1987 Oulton wrote 'The Lord Chancellor has asked me to tell you that he has not read the memorandum nor does he intend to do so.' This is astonishing. Hailsham read and acted on the views of judges and others who were against Nunan, but he refused to read the views of a judge known to support him! What sort of justice is that? Events like these would be impossible if we had a properly instituted judicial appointments board, with rules and procedure and a right to appeal to another body. Oulton's letter ended 'You may like to consider whether . . . the Lord Chancellor's modern judicial appointments system has worked efficiently and well in the public interest.' I realise that he has to do as he is told, but he could surely have worded that differently. Lord Mackay has said that he will consider suggestions for altering the appointments system. There is plenty to con-sider. I suggest he starts with the Nunan case, which I know he is aware of. But there is more.

On 5 November 1986 *Hailsham's Law* was televised by BBC2. The programme was to have quoted words I had used on radio 'The fact is that most of us do come from a narrow, privileged class. It would be better if the bench could be drawn from all sections of society, but this tends not to be so.' Before transmission the producer showed the script to the Lord Chancellor's department, and at their request my words were cut out, though a still photograph of me was shown together with a press cutting of my reference to Hailsham as 'a brooding quixotic dictator'. I had a contract to take part in a live discussion about the programme on the following day at BBC Manchester, but this was cancelled. The producer had decided that 'something lighter was needed'. That may have been genuine, though the BBC has been known to yield to government pressure or the fear of it? In contrast, Yorkshire Television refused to undertake that I would not appear in a programme on judges in 1986, and so all official co-operation was withdrawn. In the end I decided not to appear, so Yorkshire suffered for their principles and are to be commended. It is fair to say that the efforts to suppress my views were in line with the tendency shown by all governments everywhere. Lord Hailsham's defence, in the BBC2 programme, of the appointments system, was weak. He rejected an appointments board, which would be too narrow: he always consulted – on high court appointments – the Lord Chief Justice, Master of the Rolls and President of the Family Division. There is a simple answer to that: those judges could be on the board, which in any event could easily be told of their views and those of others who are consulted now. Civil servants would have much less influence. The final decision ought to be that of the board as a whole. Appointments to the bench should be taken out of the political arena altogether, and the board should be housed and staffed separately. As Lord Acton pointed out, those who have power are corrupted by it. That is why it should be spread between different groups, as the US Constitution provides. Over there, presidential nominees for federal judgeships can be questioned in public by senators, who may reject nominations. This goes against the British tradition of secrecy, but it would be healthy to have it here. Openness is better than whispered words between old pals. The need to spread power can be seen in the way Hailsham dealt with Nunan and me. He threatened to sack me for writing a newspaper article, yet failed to carry out his threat when I wrote further articles, took part in radio and television programmes and published this book. As I suspected all along – gambling on it, if you like – he was bluffing. Threats to other judges must have worked; they had been brought smartly back into line. Hailsham's reaction to my 'going public' gave me a real insight into the way such people work. There was no reaction save inaction; not one word of rebuke.

There are moves to change the appointments system, and some of us look to Lord Mackay to crown these with action, even though he will be limiting his power: politicians rarely do that, but he is not a party politician in the accepted sense. On 7 April 1986 *The Times* reported mounting pressure from the English bar for a radical change to the system of appointing judges. The Bar Council was expected to set up a working party to recommend alternatives. In July 1986 *Counsel* published an interview with Sir John Donaldson, Master of the Rolls, in which he said that judges should have a more formal and structured part to play in advising on appointments. David Pannick, a barrister and fellow of All Souls' College, Oxford, published his book *Judges* (OUP) in 1987. Much of it is a collection of lawyers' sayings, but the author also has his own comments. On page 69 'However a judicial appointments committee were to approach the task of helping the Lord Chancellor, it could hardly fail to improve on the unarticulated criteria, acts of God and secret processes of nature which currently govern judicial appointments.' *The Times* of 8 October 1987 reported remarks of Lord Scarman 'We have got to revamp the judicial selection process. It is just not good enough to rely on what the Lord Chancellor, Lord Chief Justice and Master of the Rolls told someone privately. Terrible mistakes have been made between those people because of the failure of one to attend a meeting. It is all too haphazard: an old-boy network when we have grown out of school. The system worked well when the profession was smaller and the senior judges knew the able candidates. However, there is a need to open up the selection process.'

In *Hailsham's Law* his lordship said that he 'would like to be remembered, not as a great reforming Chancellor but as an honourable man who tried to do his duty'. To put it slightly differently, he loved the power and pageantry, the trappings and tradition. He was there to conserve, and content to leave things in much the same state as he found them. The result today, to any impartial observer (which I do not claim to be) must be dismal. The legal system has suffered from years of neglect. The very office of Lord Chancellor is hopelessly antiquated and unfit to do the job it should do. Civil and criminal cases gather dust through delays. Many cannot exercise their rights in civil cases because the costs are so heavy and failure so ruinous. Now that the reform train is, as I hope, back on the rails and moving forward, what have I to say to Lord Mackay? First, that he could go down in history as a great reforming Chancellor. He is better fitted to fill that role than most holders of the Great Seal, because there is bound to be opposition from judges, barristers and solicitors in England and Wales. Large institutions tend to be run in the interest of those who run them, who view all change in the light of the effect on themselves. Lord Mackay comes from no group in England, presumably does not identify with any of them and should be able to stand up to them. I do not know much about legal interests in Scotland or what they would say about reform. They may be as conservative as their English counterparts, but their system being separate from ours, reform can for the most part be tackled separately. The first task for a truly reforming Chancellor is to consider the setting up of a Ministry of Justice. The office of Lord Chancellor could be retained, but he would be similar to the Speaker of the Commons and have no departmental duties. The minister – sitting in the Commons – and his junior minister would be able to plan law reform. A judicial appointments board would be at the top of the list. The board would have some *ex-officio* members such as the Lord Chief Justice, Master of the

Rolls, chairman of the Bar Council and president of the Law Society. Other judges and retired judges would sit on the board, together with lay persons. Civil servants would gather and compile information about candidates, but have no other role. The minister or junior minister would preside, but have only one vote and a casting vote. There would be no possibility of a person's career being blighted through displeasing one or two people. There would be no suspicion of nepotism. Eyebrows were raised in 1979 when Lord Hailsham appointed to the high court a woman registrar of the Family Division. No-one had ever leapt over circuit judge level in this way before. The judge was the sister of a government minister. She has turned out to be a good judge. If she had been appointed by a board, there could have been no talk of nepotism, which was bound to arise, whether justified or not.

There should be a thorough inquiry into whether the two professions – barristers and solicitors – should remain divided as they are now. In 1979 the Royal Commission on Legal Services, presided over by Sir Henry Benson (now Lord Benson) reported against fusion:

> We consider it likely that in a fused profession there would be an unacceptable reduction in the number and spread of the smaller firms of solicitors and an increase in the proportion of larger city firms. This would accentuate the present uneven distribution of solicitors and reduce the choice and availability of legal services. We are satisfied that in the future there will be a greater need for specialisation. Fusion would disperse the specialist service now provided by the bar and we consider that this would operate against the public interest.

I confess that in evidence I sent to the Commission I was against fusion, but I am not so sure now. I have read an excellent book *Are Two Legal Professions Necessary?* (Waterlow 1986) by Peter Reeves, a solicitor. He kindly sent me a copy and other documents on the subject, after he had read this book. Fusion exists in the United States, Canada, New Zealand and two of the six states in Australia: all those countries originally based their legal systems on ours. The main argument for fusion is that it is unnecessary and unduly expensive to have to employ both a barrister and a solicitor. In a fused profession there would still be those who specialised in advocacy or giving advice on difficult points of law, and those who did the preparatory work. Another wasteful feature of our system arises from the rule against barristers being partners. Whilst this makes for competition and keenness, at the bar I often thought it anomalous that I and my colleagues in chambers – about fifteen of us when I left – had all to try to cover the same wide field, instead of being able to divide it up into crime, accident claims, divorce and so on. The first step towards drawing the two professions together is to devise a common system of legal education and require all law students to spend time in counsel's chambers and a solicitor's office. Those who hope to do judicial work later should study for, say, an extra six months such subjects as criminology, sociology and psychology.

I know of nothing further on delays since I wrote Chapter 5; the situation remains bad in civil and criminal cases. Coming from Scotland, Lord Mackay knows how to tackle this. Not so easy to tackle is the expense of litigation and the injustice in giving legal aid to one party and letting the other party – not necessarily affluent – pay his own costs and, if he loses, his opponent's also. This introduces injustice before the case starts. A legally aided party with a nil contribution is virtually 'bullet-proof': even if he loses, he will have no costs to pay. A friend of mine recently had a civil action against a neighbour with a nil contribution, and my friend was affronted when the neighbour – who had given up his job to obtain legal aid – flew abroad on holiday! Should we have the American system whereby a plaintiff can agree to pay no fee to his lawyer, who takes a percentage of any damages? It is worth considering.

There are a few law centres, publicly funded and staffed by salaried lawyers. They advise and represent the poor in certain non-criminal types of case. Litigants who cannot obtain legal aid are helped by these centres, as I know: there happens to be one in Bradford, where I sit, and I have directed litigants there. In *Hailsham's Law* his lordship was reluctant to discuss law centres, telling the interviewer 'I don't know why you are so preoccupied with this; it is not a matter which preoccupies me very much'. He refused to meet the Federation of Law Centres. When the Lords debated the subject in February 1986, he did not even enter the chamber. Law centres have never been more than a frail patchwork, depending mainly on local councils. Many were closed down during Lord Hailsham's Chancellorship, especially by rate-capped authorities. The seven funded by his department suffered large cuts, and he only kept those going because he inherited them. Law centres cannot make long term plans, being under perpetual sentence of death. Most private solicitors are opposed to them as competitors, and the suspicion is that Hailsham preferred the interests of lawyers to those of poor litigants. I hope that Lord Mackay will look into this – I do not know whether they have law centres in Scotland – and facilitate the setting up of a full network.

There is so much that needs doing to improve the English legal and judicial systems. How ironical, yet acceptable to me, that a Scot should take on the job. He will have the support of many non-lawyers, but not so many within this conservative profession. There are some, however, and I am proud to be one.

# Appendix I

## *My Daily Telegraph article: 22 March 1985*

### A Place for Punishment

The scales fell from my eyes at a sentencing conference run by the Lord Chancellor's office in 1977 when I asked a man from the Home Office: 'Penal institutions being full, how will you cope with further increases in crime?' He said, 'We can't be sure that crime will continue to increase.' So the Home Office was looking to the courts to solve its accommodation problem.

Politicians such as the Lord Chancellor and the Home Secretary were imploring magistrates to avoid or shorten prison sentences. The Bail Act 1976 – sound in its terms – was put across by the Home Office in such a way that some magistrates lavished bail on defendants despite repeated breaches of bail. They wanted to do their duty to the public, but how could they resist all the pressure from ministers? Eventually in 1978 I sent guidelines on bail to my local magistrates and addressed magistrates in various parts of the country.

Government pressure continued. The then Home Secretary, William Whitelaw, threatened courts with legislation limiting our powers if we did not comply. I expressed my views privately to the Lord Chancellor, Lord Hailsham, senior judges and my own MP.

On 15 October 1981 the national press reported what I had said to magistrates, protesting about Lord Whitelaw's attitude. I received a polite request to keep quiet, and I have. But increasing frustration has been too much. There is too much secrecy in public life and the public is entitled to know what is going on.

There is a case for reducing the prison population, but it is not being done in the right way. Tailoring sentences to the room that happens to be available is unprincipled. Reducing most sentences across the board, by parole, is illogical. We need a philosophy of sentencing and radical reform of our prison system.

I am not for blind severity: I believe in enlightened firmness. The weakness being shown in some quarters horrifies me.

The use of suspended sentences and parole show what is happening. The Court of Appeal has told courts to decide whether a prison sentence is necessary, and then whether to suspend it. But surely, if a man deserves to go to prison, normally he should go. In my view a suspended sentence is merely a form of words. Defendants think they have 'got away with it'.

Parole was begun in 1968 to reduce the prison population. In 1983 the percentages of prisoners recommended for parole on their first application was: for those in for violence, 53; robbery, 53; burglary, 57; theft, 64; fraud, 67; handling, 72.

The Home Secretary, Mr Leon Brittan, has restricted parole for some serving long sentences but he has extended parole substantially in other cases. Parole may now be granted after six months or one-third of a sentence, whichever is longer. Whatever sentence a man gets, between nine and eighteen months, he is likely to be freed after six.

The parole system is also unpopular with prisoners. They can only apply once a year; no reasons for refusal are given; and hearings are in private, in the applicant's absence.

Increasingly, judges' sentences are being cut. The next move will be to take sentencing out of judges' hands altogether. Some probation officers advocate this and if that is what the public wants, I will gladly step down. With some other judges, I increasingly feel that my efforts to protect the public have little effect. The forces of weakness are too strong.

Parole should be abolished except in a few cases. There would be no need for it if we had a properly thought out sentencing policy. To get the balance right, some who go to prison now should be dealt with differently. Others should spend much longer behind bars.

My over-riding consideration in passing sentence is to satisfy the broad mass of the public, but there are four other possible objects in a sentence: reform, punishment, deterrence of the defendant and others, and containment.

Reform usually involves a non-custodial approach, but not always. A man in his mid-twenties, of previous good character, who decides that house-breaking pays, should go to prison for a short period. Leniency would only confirm his attitude.

There is controversy about punishment: some call it retribution, and say it is primitive. But the public feels, as I do, that a defendant who has wickedly harmed another should himself suffer.

There is also controversy about the deterrent effect of sentences. Criminals tend to be gamblers, and a man who feels sure he will not be caught is not deterred by the likely sentence. But experience tells me that some can be deterred from crime.

Containment involves locking up a man for a long time, because he has shown that when free he habitually harms others.

Certainly imprisonment is expensive. But it is the only sentence that bites deep as punishment. So when should courts use immediate custody? First, as a punishment when other penalties are inadequate. Second, where custody seems likely to deter the defendant from further serious crime, and third, where there has been a deliberate defiance of a court order.

Lastly, the incorrigibly wicked should be locked away for longer than is now usual. 'Extended sentences' – giving a persistent offender an above-tariff sentence – have gone out of fashion, as could be expected.

However, many defendants who come before me are weak, inadequate drifters for whom prison will never be the answer.

Sadly, there are not enough alternatives to prison for such men. The Home Office mistakenly abandoned the day training centre experiment where defendants could be sent for intensive training for up to sixty days to give them an insight into coping with their problems. The centres are expensive, but cheaper than prison. We need more non-residential places where drunks and the mentally unbalanced can get shelter and a crutch.

Why not introduce an order that for a period the weak drifter must be subject to a curfew, and only go within a defined distance of his address and to specified places? Or we could try the American system by which some miscreants are freed on condition that they wear a homing device. Only if a condition is broken should they be sent to prison.

One reason why prisons are out of favour is that they are not run correctly. There are about 120 widely varying custodial establishments in England and Wales. Only the so-called 'local' prisons – such as Leeds and Birmingham – are overcrowded.

There is too much idleness in prison, inmates have things too easy and no attempt at reform is made. At one prison the food, library and gym facilities were superb. Nothing but the loss of liberty itself could be construed as punishment. Taxpayers are not getting value at places like that.

The prison system needs sorting out. There should be three main kinds of prison where productive work is compulsory so that they are as self-supporting as possible.

First, there must be prisons for punishment, in the cases of prisoners who merit it, where the experience should be unpleasant without being sadistic. Sentences could be shorter, if they were more intensive. Second, there should be prisons for training. Third, containment prisons for the incorrigible. Prisoners could be transferred from one category to another as their merit deserved.

# Appendix II

## My Judgment in a Bail Application at Sheffield Crown Court on 28 April 1978

I wish to make some general observations before I deal with this application for bail. During this week I have had several applications in chambers under the Bail Act 1976, which came into force recently. This is the first application in open court. It is in open court because another judge on a previous occasion so ordered. Many people obviously misunderstand this statute, including some magistrates, police officers and lawyers. What I say now may clear the air in places where I sit: South Yorkshire and Humberside. I would not presume to address those elsewhere.

For some time bail has been granted too freely. This is partly due to the barrage of government statements about prison overcrowding. I have in the past year or so come across a fair number of cases where an accused has repeatedly committed offences on bail yet has repeatedly got bail. One man eventually appeared before me on five indictments. He got a much longer sentence than he would have done if bail had been refused, thus making the overcrowding in his prison worse. The silent public suffered. And many criminals like that man are coming to think that we have gone soft. To some extent they are right. Section 4 of the Act has of course to be read with paragraphs 2 and 9 of part 1 of schedule 1. These provisions when read carefully and applied properly do not justify the wide granting of bail which is now taking place in some areas.

I make the following general points about the Bail Act:

1   We must interpret it strictly according to its terms. In any event I agree with it. It has tidied up the law and removed anomalies. Its terms are common sense. It is we who have gone wrong in applying them.

2   It is wrong and dangerous to suppose that an accused is entitled to bail pending his trial in almost all circumstances. Yet this is what some people are saying.

3   'Substantial grounds for believing' in paragraph 2 does not mean 'satisfied beyond reasonable doubt': the standard is less than that.

4.   An assertion by the accused that he will plead not guilty is by no means conclusive, especially where he has signed admissions. The court is entitled to assess the apparent strength of the prosecution evidence and act on it when considering bail.

5   The more serious the alleged offence or offences, the heavier the

likely punishment if the accused is convicted and so the greater his temptation to abscond meanwhile.

6    Some accused, especially the young, think that they 'might as well be hanged for a sheep as for a lamb'. If allowed liberty pending trial they are tempted to go on the rampage feeling, for example, 'all they can do is send me to borstal' (they are often wrong). Certainly a borstal sentence will be no longer for 200 offences than for two. Similarly some defendants of all ages think that taking offences into consideration merely wipes them off without additional punishment (they are not far out in this sometimes).

7    Experience has shown that burglars often repeat such crimes if bailed, more so than with, say, crimes of violence.

8    An accused who is already alleged on strong *prima facie* evidence to have committed offences on bail or absconded, during the present proceedings, should not normally be given a second bite unless the offence on bail was trivial or the absconding was technical. The position is stronger still if the accused has acted similarly in the past.

In this present application of W. what are the relevant facts? He is thirty-two. He has a bad criminal record for burglary and other offences. He has been to prison several times. He has one conviction for the unlawful possession of drugs – on 17 April 1978 at Manchester Crown Court. He now faces two serious charges of burglary, both at chemists' shops, in which substantial quantities of drugs were stolen. He is also charged with possessing such drugs for his own purposes and with the intent to supply others. This type of offence is prevalent. Its danger to the public needs no elaboration. W. has committed offences on bail in the past. He recently broke a condition of residence attached to his bail. It is alleged that attempts have been made to interfere with prosecution witnesses in these proceedings. The first burglary was at Penistone at the end of May 1977. When interviewed the accused denied it, but there is substantial prosecution evidence against him. He was bailed. The second burglary was in Bury on 7/8 February 1978. The accused was on bail then. If he did this burglary – and again there is substantial evidence – he did it on bail.

Of course the defendant has yet to be convicted. We have not reached that stage. But there are substantial grounds for believing that if released on bail, whether subject to conditions or not, he will commit offences and will interfere with potential witnesses. Paragraph 9, subparas. (a) (b) (c) and (d) have been considered by me: they all apply. If I granted bail to this man I would deserve to have the public battering on my door – chemists especially – crying 'What's happening? What's going on? Have you all gone mad?' Of course they would not do that. The public suffer in silence on these occasions, usually without voice and always without remedy. But I do not forget them.

Finally a diffident word to the Home Office: 'You will have to make room for Mr W. pending his trial. The public interest requires it. I know about your accommodation difficulties. I know about your government's financial problems and their commendable efforts to deal with them. I also know what priority successive administrations have felt obliged to give to expenditure on prisons. I do what I can to help. It is sometimes possible to pass shorter sentences. But there is a limit to this. Crime is increasing and will continue to increase: You will have to provide more accommodation (and I hear that to some extent you are doing so already). In the end there is no sensible alternative which accords with the public interest.'

Bail is refused. The case will be tried within four weeks if possible. I will try to take it myself.

[A Home Office official later wrote to me saying that he had quoted my remarks about the Home Office to a parliamentary committee which was considering overcrowding. The committee had asked whether judges knew about the overcrowding.]

# Appendix III

# My Judgment in a Jury-Vetting Case
## on 31 March 1980

## The background to the present application by the prosecution to revoke my order

The two accused police officers are indicted for assaulting a member of the public on 23 September 1978, causing bodily harm. The committal for trial was as long ago as 26 March 1979. On 4 October 1979 the defence applied to me for what for brevity I will call 'a jury-vetting order'.

The attitude of each accused was broadly this: 'My reputation, liberty and livelihood are at stake. Jurors with criminal convictions are bound to have come into the hostile hands of police officers. They may be biased against all policemen, including me. If I knew that a juror had convictions I would challenge him or her. The only way to find out is through police records. The Attorney-General lets the prosecution look at them in certain cases where jurors may be biased. Why can't I?'

That seemed reasonable. But did the law permit it? Without reserving judgment I said yes. But it was a new point, so far as I knew then, and I said I would welcome a review by superior judges.

On 10 December 1979 the Divisional Court of the Queen's Bench Division rejected an application by the Director of Public Prosecutions to quash my order. Section 10 of the Courts Act 1971 prevented it. In giving judgment the Lord Chief Justice said that the possibility that jurors with criminal convictions might prevent a fair trial was obvious. I respectfully agree.

On 3 March 1980 the Court of Appeal by a majority dismissed an appeal by the DPP against the decision of the Divisional Court: section 10 again. All three members of the Court spoke disapprovingly of jury vetting. It was suggested that I might revoke my order, and that is why we are here.

The dicta of the Court of Appeal are obiter: they do not bind me. They are of course strongly persuasive and I have thought long and hard about them. They shed light which helps me to pick my steps. But I must not let that light blind me, or I may lose my way. The responsibility remains with me.

I am in no sense purporting to change the law; I could not possibly do that. I am settling a point in the case before me, applying existing law as I find it to be. An unreported decision of a High Court Judge is before me which was not before the Court of Appeal. In the end it has weighed with me decisively.

As I am unfortunately unable to act on all their Lordships' dicta I shall give my reasons in some detail. I do not want them to think that I have misunderstood the issues, or that I am just being stubborn.

## The Problem

The term 'jury-vetting' has become emotive. This is partly because the purpose and implications of vetting have been misunderstood by some. They say it helps one side – usually the prosecution – to pack the jury. They say it is unfair to jurors.

It is vital to think about jurors. Ordinary folk, they come into what would otherwise be the cloistered preserve of lawyers. They bring the human touch into the cold, hard world of logic and law book. They do a stalwart job. We need them.

So if we do anything to make jurors resent the way we treat them we may harm the system. Some resentment is inevitable. A juror may resent being summoned for service at all. If jurors are vetted and get to know, they may resent that too. So it should only be done when it is necessary for achieving justice between the parties. The impact on the jurors themselves should be kept to a minimum. But in the end the interests of the parties, and especially the defence, must prevail. Jurors surely realise this. Any one of them may be back some day, sitting in the dock instead of the jury-box.

What need is there to vet at all? The jury is an institution which if it were not so ancient we would think odd. Lay members of other tribunals of fact such as the magistracy are carefully selected for their proven qualities. They are trained in how to be unbiased, impartial. Jurors, however, are taken blindly from lists of electors. They get no training at all.

Realising the need for impartiality the common law from earliest times gave to both prosecution and defence certain rights to object to jurors. But if you only have a name and address, and later a face, how can you decide whether to object? I am told that in Blackstone's* day a defendant had thirty-five challenges. Two days before the trial he was given the

*Sir William Blackstone, an eighteenth-century jurist whose *Commentaries on the Laws of England* became an indispensable text book for lawyers for nearly a century, and was a model on which the body of English law was built up in America and the British colonies.

names and addresses of the jurors *and also their antecedents*. Rights to object have been reduced over the centuries, but they still exist.

The Master of the Rolls says that at the Bar and as a judge of first instance he never had an objection to a juror by either side. In my thirty-five years in the criminal courts I have known a fair number. I have challenged peremptorily. I have seen a juror stood by for the Crown. I have never seen a challenge for cause, though the right is still there.

The issue we are considering in the instant matter is 'How far may the prosecution and the defence elicit, or have elicited for them, information about jurors, for deciding whether to object to them?' Or, more pertinently to this case, 'How far may they elicit, or have elicited, information *from official sources?*'

## Law and Practice

There have to be limits. I am not advocating the system they have in the United States. Where do we in England and Wales draw the line?

If a policeman at the Crown Court sees in the building a juror whom he recognises as having a record, the officer has a duty to tell his superiors so that the juror may perhaps be asked to stand by. Suppose the officer is not sure if he has got the right man. May a check be made with police records? Surely yes.

If the defence had enough resources they could make wide inquiries about jurors on the panel, to find out what sort of people they are and if they have convictions. Perhaps they could approach the jurors informally and question them. This would be so easy to confuse with an attempt to pervert justice that I do not recommend it. Certainly a juror would not be obliged to answer.

Suppose the facts of a case are likely to arouse strong emotions in some class or classes or persons – emotions which may imperil impartiality. For example, the victim is a licensee or bus-conductor who has been savagely attacked, and his colleagues in the area are or may be up in arms about the case. May the defendant have the jurors vetted to discover if any are licensees or bus-conductors? Yes. I have done it whilst sitting as a judge. That is, I have approved it. In such a case it is usually agreed to by both sides. But if it can be done by consent, surely it can be done on a contested application. Consent of the parties cannot confer a power on the court or a right on the parties which would not otherwise exist.

In *Price and Others* in September 1973, at Winchester Crown Court, Sebag Shaw J., as he then was, agreed that no juror with close relatives in the Army should sit on the jury trying the Price sisters. (See a footnote on page 287 of 1979 *Criminal Law Review*.) That was vetting. We must remember that vetting is not confined to a scrutiny of police records.

The unreported case not referred to in the Court of Appeal was *Bumstead and Others*. It began at York Crown Court on 15 January 1979 before Boreham J. The defendants were all prison officers, charged with assaulting prisoners during or after the Hull prison riot. The transcript shows that the learned judge agreed to a defence application that no one who had served a prison sentence at any prison – not just Hull – should be on the jury. The jurors were even obliged to give their dates of birth, so that the police computer could get to its precise task. Mr Peter Taylor QC prosecuted, instructed by the DPP. It is fair to say that the DPP did not come into the vetting decision personally.

Mr Taylor said of the application, 'I have no objection. I am happy it is being done. I am entirely, as far as the Crown is concerned, content to leave it to your Lordship.' The learned judge then said, 'Of course in almost every case a judge would refuse such an application but of course the circumstances here are such that it is a very particular case.'

Was the danger of partiality in the Hull prison case so different from that in this case? Different in degree perhaps. Not different in principle. They both fall on the same side of the line, in my view. I feel bound to follow Boreham J.'s decision and the line of reasoning I have already explored.

## The Attorney-General's guidelines

These were issued in 1975. They apply to cases involving terrorists, official secrets and gangs of professional criminals. They authorise the police to check jurors' names with the Criminal Records Office, the Special Branch and local CID officers. This is wider vetting than under my order. I make the following points on the guidelines:

1  The last and the present Attorneys-General consider that jury-vetting is lawful. That is strong persuasive authority.
2  I agree with the principles behind the guidelines. But vetting as a means of eliciting information in cases where bias is known to be likely, is either right or wrong. There will be argument about the precise cases in which it should be done. But if it is sometimes right for the prosecution to vet, it cannot be always wrong for the defence. Brandon L. J. expresses misgivings on this aspect in his judgment at page 22 of the transcript.
3  At B on page 13 of the transcript the Master of the Rolls says, 'To my mind it is unconstitutional for the police authorities to engage in jury-vetting.' At C on page 14 he says, 'I will assume, for the present purposes, that the Attorney-General's guidelines are legitimate.' With profound respect, I am puzzled. My own view is that the Attorney-General and the DPP have put themselves in an impossible position by

supporting the guidelines and opposing vetting for the defence. They are trying to have it both ways. I say that they cannot. The public will not like it and neither do I. If jury bias one way has to be dealt with, so has jury bias the other way. Of course I am not imputing bad faith to anybody. We are all struggling with a difficult problem, doing our best to reconcile conflicting interests.

4   In my personal opinion, and it is no more than that, all jury-vetting should be under the control of the court. We should hear both sides in the presence of each other, and the judge should decide whether it is fair to order vetting. The prosecution should not use police records to vet a panel without a court order. We could, if necessary, sit in court-in-chambers for such applications.

## Conclusions

1 For the reasons I have indicated I have decided not to revoke my order. Regretfully I have not found it right to act on the dicta of the Court of Appeal, save in one respect. The Master of the Rolls infers that it would be unfair for jurors' spent convictions to be disclosed. I respectfully agree, on the facts of this case. My order is therefore amended by inserting in brackets after the word 'convictions' the words 'save for spent convictions'.

2 Presumably the whole law on jury-vetting will in due course be authoritatively clarified and codified by parliament or by, say, the new Lord Chief Justice and the judges of the Queen's Bench Division (there being no effective appeal against decisions such as mine). Meanwhile the floodgates will not be open. Few defendants will qualify for a vetting order. Applications to me will be closely scrutinised. I will hear them in court-in-chambers. I do not want to worry jurors unnecessarily.

# Appendix IV

## *My address to the Inner Manchester Branch of the Magistrates Association on 14 October 1981*

The explosion of crime in the last twenty-five years was bound to require more prison accommodation. Yet the Home Office has refused to provide enough, or even to maintain existing buildings adequately. Its remedy is shorter sentences. When school children increase in numbers do the politicians lower the leaving age? They build more schools; but there are no votes in building prisons.

To the Home Office, prison accommodation is a matter of logistics, but to us judges and magistrates it is a matter of morality. Wicked people who harm others deserve to suffer and the only way of doing that in some cases is to lock them up. We have to deter the wavering, and nothing does that like the shadow of prison. We have to contain the incorrigible in a place where they cannot do harm.

Some crime lies at the door of the Home Office itself. It put across the Bail Act in such a way that many magistrates give defendants bail repeatedly despite repeated crimes: I see case after case. If the public knew the full facts there would be a scandal. As for parole, a man who got four years for a wicked robbery and a further six months for a separate assault was released after eighteen months. The Home Office refused to tell me why. There are many such cases: the men's cells are needed. I am not against parole, but it has been pushed too far.

Wide bail and parole and shorter sentences mean freedom for more criminals and so more crime. Criminals have the impression, correctly, that some courts have gone soft. We are in the most vicious of circles. Prisons are full, so we shorten sentences, causing more crime and worse overcrowding, so we shorten sentences further. Where is this to end?

The Home Secretary, [then] Mr Whitelaw, has threatened courts with legislation if we go on imprisoning non-violent offenders at present levels. Such threats should not be made. The judiciary is not a minor branch of the executive but an independent arm of government. It is unconstitutional for the Home Secretary to come into our territory waving the big stick. It is for us to decide who goes inside and for him to make room. Mr Whitelaw is a kind, well-meaning, busy man, but this does not affect the principles involved.

Some politicians are out of step with the public. If all the victims of crime for say the past year marched together to Whitehall hoisting placards, shouting slogans and threatening to vote for the opposition, there would be swift action. The Prime Minister would come into it, an inquiry would be held and money voted. But such demonstrations will not happen (and I would not want them).

The couple whose house has been pillaged of its precious possessions will not take to the streets. The woman tricked out of her savings grieves quietly alone. Yet these are the sort of people whom you and I have to protect. When Mr Whitelaw says, 'I will bring in a bill if you send people to prison for non-violent crimes,' we are entitled to reply respectfully, 'Then do so and see if you can get it through.'

My advice to the many magistrates who are perplexed by government policy is: 'Do your duty to the public. If you feel a defendant should be denied bail or go to prison, be firm about it.' We must obey statutes and superior courts, but we do not have to obey ministers as such.

We would all like to see fewer people in prison, but reducing sentences across the board is not the answer. Where are the day training centres, the mental hospitals which the Butler Committee recommended, the detoxification centres and the hostels for inadequates? Why does the Home Office refuse to spend money on those too?

Prisons have a bad name with some MPs, who rightly condemn three-in-a-cell, idleness and lack of lavatories. They should tell the Home Office to reorganise the whole prison system. No prisoner ought to sit in his cell for long hours. There should be hard, productive work for all who are fit, and intensive training for all who might be reformed. We should experiment with new ideas. Day-time attendance for some and night-time attendance for others is one. Camps with prefabricated buildings should be built by prisoners. There is so much that the Home Office could do to improve things. We could lead the world with a new system based on firmness and enlightenment. But drive, will and flair will be needed.

# Appendix V

## *Part of my evidence to the Royal Commission on Legal Services in April 1977*

### The Chambers System

1   Getting into chambers as a tenant is the most important step a barrister ever takes. If the chambers are busy and he fits in, his future is secure. Setting up his own chambers is out of the question. Unfortunately, the number of practising barristers has in recent years increased faster than the number of sets of chambers. Existing chambers have not increased sufficiently in size. It is therefore difficult for beginners to obtain pupillage and more difficult to obtain a tenancy. Many young barristers drift off to other jobs, never having been given a chance to show what they can do.

2   The state of affairs on the NE Circuit can be summarised in this way. All the sets of chambers are regarded by their members as full. The notion of fullness is apparently based on these considerations:

*Lack of accommodation.* Leeds is the main centre. The chambers there (and in some other places) are physically overcrowded and this is used as a reason for not expanding. Extra accommodation could, however, be obtained if the will were there. Further, there are two sets of London chambers most of whose members live and practise on the NE Circuit: effectively they enjoy no chambers accommodation or chambers life at all (not a desirable situation, incidentally). Lack of accommodation is not a real obstacle to expansion.

*Conventional size.* This varies but about 12/15 is a fair average. But experience in London shows that 20/25 are viable.

*Clerk's remuneration.* Until recently the NE barristers' clerks had a united front. It was usual to pay them ten per cent of gross fees. One clerk probably earned as much as the Lord Chancellor! About five years ago I broke the united front by paying five per cent to my new clerk (in the teeth of bitter opposition from the other clerks: at first they refused even to speak to my five per-cent clerk). The ten-per-cent barrier has been broken by other chambers since then. At least two sets, however, still pay ten per cent to the sole clerk. If chambers go above about fifteen in number, a junior clerk becomes necessary. The clerk refuses to pay a junior out of his ten per cent. Chambers refuse to pay more than ten per cent for clerking. Result: no junior clerk and no increase in the size of chambers. (The position of a barrister's clerk is unique. He is unqualified except by experience but can earn more than most of his employers. He commonly has more say in the running of chambers than the head of chambers. He can make or break a young barrister.)

*Resistance by existing members.* Those who do not have a lot of work tend to object to new entrants. Having climbed into the loft with difficulty they want to haul up the ladder. It *is* desirable to allow a bottom-ender to get on to his feet before another tenant arrives. Bottom-enders sometimes forget though that they are not all competing in the same chambers' pool of work. They are not all equally acceptable to a particular solicitor. The pools overlap. Existing members tend to be too afraid of new competitors. It is in the interest of all members to build up a strong team and provide for future wastage.

3 In London it is still common to be thrown out of chambers after pupillage. Ex-pupils are usually allowed to hold over for a time, 'squatting' and getting any surplus scraps whilst they desperately try to find a tenancy elsewhere. It is usual on the NE only to take a pupil if there will be a tenancy for him at the end of the twelve months. If he is thrown out he will have little prospect elsewhere. I prefer our attitude to London's.

4 Practice concerning pupil-admission varies from chambers to chambers. It may help to describe the system I adopted when head of chambers. All applications for pupillage were referred to me. I normally offered to see applicants. Those who came were introduced to as many members of chambers as were available. Sometimes an applicant spent all day with us. We then decided by vote whether to offer pupillage. Undoubtedly some members – especially the junior ones – were influenced by what they thought would be the effect on their practices of a new entrant. We told pupils that there would be a tenancy at the end of their pupillage unless we had found some real personal objection, of which he or she would be told. In fact we never had to reject anyone at the end of pupillage. I gradually increased the number of tenants whilst I was head of chambers, but I could only go at the speed of the majority. (Not all chambers have a 'one man one vote' system.)

5 Several years ago statistics showed that the NE Circuit had a smaller proportion of counsel to judge-days than any other circuit except one. Certainly we are still thinner on the ground than industrial areas like Manchester and Liverpool. The mass emigration from bar to bench in recent years has left a lack of experienced juniors. Young counsel tend to get big cases too soon. Some incompetents make a living: a sure sign that there is insufficient competition. The bar on the NE and elsewhere should open its doors wider to new entrants. It is in the public interest that this

should happen. There should be free competition and a wide choice of counsel. The present situation undoubtedly strengthens solicitors' demands for wider rights of audience.

6   Every qualified barrister has the right to try his luck (but not the right to make a living) at the bar. The profession as a whole should see that he can exercise that right. The newly called man has studied for and passed examinations, spent money, bought his robes. He may already have had pupillage. It is intolerable if he cannot practise. The argument 'We do not need more practitioners, there are enough' is not one that barristers can raise, as they have the strongest material interest. In any case it is untrue. There may be a case for raising academic standards on enrolment at the Inn (though I do not know much about this). Certainly any restrictions after that, such as exist now, interfere with liberty. It is true that an increase in practitioners will not increase the work available (except perhaps marginally: a solicitor might entrust a magistrates' or county court case to counsel if a suitable one were available, instead of doing it himself, but there is not much in this point). Some existing practitioners will be forced out. Some deserve to be. This is what competition involves. Too many barristers have had it too easy in the last fifteen years.

7   What, then, is the way ahead? All that I have to say on this topic I said to the NE Circuit in July 1974. It has not made much difference. Basically, I consider that each Circuit should assume the responsibility for obtaining pupillage and tenancies for barristers domiciled in their areas. Intending pupils should register with a special Circuit officer well in advance of qualifying. They should be introduced to their future chambers and spend as much time there as possible in vacations. This will not prevent 'outsiders' from coming to the Circuit if they can make their own arrangements.

8   New places in chambers are urgently required. Existing chambers must be enlarged and new ones started. Note:

(a) Members of existing chambers can be persuaded but cannot be compelled to take in new members. There has been an increase in average size on the NE Circuit in the last five years. Further pressure and persuasion should help matters further.

(b) Since the last war new chambers have been opened on the NE Circuit. In particular by Willis (Leeds), Waller (London), Walker and Hutchinson (Hull), Davey (Teesside) and recently by Bentley and Barber in Sheffield. It is not easy though. The successful have no incentive; the unsuccessful have no prospect. When chambers split, who keeps the clerk and the chambers' address? To whom will the clients adhere? How long will it take? The Leader of the Circuit, presiding judges and others should decide where new chambers are needed, after inquiry. Selected counsel should then be encouraged to take the plunge. The presiding judges have ample patronage at their disposal and there can be rewards for the brave. If one or two established barristers are ready to form a nucleus, the other places in a new set of chambers will soon be filled.

9    Will the winds of competition blow too hard, driving out or keeping out those without private means? There is a case for giving grants to beginners for, say, two or three years. A small levy could be made on established practitioners. There would be merit and means tests.

10    Women barristers need special consideration. They have in the past been treated unfairly by their male colleagues, barristers' clerks and solicitors. Clerks are reluctant to build up a woman who may leave through marriage. Some solicitors will not brief women. Some chambers in the country have never had a woman member; most will take the 'statutory woman' only. (There were three women in my chambers when I left.) Women should have equal opportunity. They need more help than men and must receive it.

*Note:*    There have been some changes since the above was written in 1977, but the position is basically the same.

# APPENDIX VI

# R. v K. & C.: Sentencing Remarks and subsequent judgment of the Court of Appeal

In order to illustrate the 'double-think' involved in the arguments over parole (see pp. 155–6), it is worth reprinting my sentencing remarks in a recent case and the Court of Appeal's decision upon it.

## 1 Sentencing Remarks, 1 August 1985

Judge Pickles: C., you are twenty-eight years of age. You have pleaded guilty on Count One to a house burglary, on Count Two to taking without consent a motor car belonging to the owners of that house, and on Count Three to an attempted house burglary. The first two offences were committed on 17 April of this year and the other offence in Count Three on 23 April, some six days later.

The house burglary was a very serious one. During the day you and your younger brother, who has a different name to you and whose character was not as bad as yours, he being younger than you, entered a house at – and ransacked it, taking away in the owner's car all that was valuable and easily portable. The owner puts the value of the stolen items at £6,591.00 and he values the recovered items at £1,270.00. You say that not all the items alleged to have been taken were taken and I must assume that to be correct. Nevertheless, the value of the items which one can fairly take to have gone was substantial. The car was recovered. It had not been badly damaged and had not been in an accident.

Breaking into a house, sorting through the owner's belongings and taking what can be taken is both common and grave. A house, of all places, should be free from intrusion and its precious and sometimes irreplaceable contents free from loss. House burglary causes shock and fear which can linger for a long time and it is, therefore, much worse than burglary at other types of premises where loss can largely be dealt with by way of insurance claims. It is said that you only received £140.00 as your share of the proceeds of sale of the stolen items. That may be so, but it is no satisfaction to the owners of the house.

Six days later you and your brother went to – . Whatever your original purpose in going there, you decided when there to burgle another house. You broke a window and, but for the vigilance of a neighbour and others which caused you to be caught, you would have done to that house and its contents what you had done at − . Of that there can be no doubt.

What are your previous convictions? I have them all before me. We have gone into them with care. This morning we had, through the industry and assistance of the sergeant who has given evidence, obtained details of some of those offences. The word 'burglary' appears time and again. It first appears in the Crown Court, and I am ignoring Juvenile Court appearances in all fairness − the first appearance in the Crown Court in 1973, when you were sent to Borstal, nobody now knows what type of premises you entered on that occasion. It may be that, I should say, almost certainly you yourself have by this time forgotten, so often have you broken into other people's premises of one kind or another. There is no need for me to go through it all, except to say that in the following year burglary appears; 1976 again and in 1977 and in 1978 and 1979. We are now approaching the time when we have some details of the types of burglaries involved. In 1979 the offence on the Indictment was apparently at a golf club when a colour television and other such items were taken. Of the sixteen offences that were taken into consideration, unfortunately we do not know except three were burglary and three were attempted burglary.

In 1980, in October, at − Crown Court, you received a sentence of four years' imprisonment in total. There was certainly the burglary of a dwelling on that occasion because it is so listed. It would be more helpful, if it were possible, in all cases of burglary for the Court to know what type it is, house burglary being so much worse than other types, as I have already said.

But, finally, in July 1983, at − Crown Court, for two house burglaries, you were sentenced to two years' imprisonment. There were thirteen additional offences taken into consideration. One was at a dwellinghouse where property taken came to £470.00. Another was − no, I am sorry, I may be wrong about this − I must get it right. The two offences of burglary were both at dwellinghouses. One was the one where I said £470.00 worth of property was taken. The other, we do not have any further details about. It is fair to say, and I have noted that of the thirteen offences that were taken into consideration, none consisted of burglary, and so we find your last sentence was in July 1983.

You were paroled in July 1984, and it is fair to say that the next offence was not until Count One, 17 April of this year. In the meantime, again I have carefully noted, you worked as a countryside warden on a Job Creation Scheme, and then in a store and snack bar run by your wife. You say you were under pressures arising out of that business. That may be so. Businesses and those who run them are afflicted with problems of all kinds in these days. Most people do not choose what you chose to do, however.

How do I assess you now as a man and what is the likely pattern of your offending in the future? The very helpful Social Enquiry Report assists me a great deal on that. I do not want to quote from it all, it is not necessary, but I think I must refer to parts because I must give full reasons for what I do this day. Unhappily you first got into trouble which cannot have been of a criminal kind because you were only seven, when you were referred to a Child Guidance Clinic. Not your fault; you were very young. You were, of course, suffering from factors which you did not yourself cause and you cannot be blamed in that regard at all. We then find you completed your education at – Comprehensive School. You had average ability, but you truanted frequently and schooling ended when you went to a Detention Centre in 1972. Unhappily – again, this was no fault of yours – while at the Detention Centre your parents separated. After you were discharged you went for a short time to a Community School and then to Borstal. You were discharged in March 1974, and it was said this – and this has, I am bound to say, a ring of prescience about it (in other words, there was an accurate forecast about what would happen to you) – it was eleven years ago and it was then said, 'It was felt overall his sentence has not really changed his attitude towards offending.' Then in 1974, later, we find that you commit offences which led to a further Borstal sentence. You were discharged in January 1976, with another youth and significantly, but not surprising, you two committed offences whilst you were actually on your way back to—on the day of your discharge from Borstal. This, of course, is some time ago, but it is all part, I am afraid, of a pattern. Everything seems to point in one direction.

It then deals in the Report with your release on Parole Licence last year and then it goes on to refer to you and – again, I find this most helpful, as I always do with the Social Enquiry Reports – you are competent and articulate and you are aware of what you are doing and the risks that you run, and then comes a part which is most significant. It is said, and nobody can deny, you have a truly appalling record and the custodial sentences have not had the slightest long-term effect upon your reoffending, and I quote, 'It is difficult, in view of his history, to see what will stop his offending. He is well able, in that he has the capacity to avoid offending, but seems to be set in a pattern, although on this occasion he appears to have stayed in the clear for a long time by his standards. A realistic man, he is expecting a prison sentence which may well have a negative effect upon his personal relationship and home circumstances.' There it is.

I repeat, 'It is difficult to see what will stop his offending.' Well, one way of stopping you offending is to put you where you cannot offend against people. I agree with what is said in that Report, in other words. I have no doubt that within months of your release you will offend again. You are likely to do what you know how to do best. You are a skilled burglar. The facts on Count One show that. How can I protect people from you except by putting you away for a long time?

Well now, how long should it be? Mr Levine concedes that the tariff sentence in your case would be about two years' imprisonment. One is bound to ask, if I am considering protecting the public, 'For how long would such a sentence protect them?' Courts do not normally consider the effects of Parole and Remission because there is no certainty that the Defendant will get it, certainly so far as parole is concerned. Remission, one gathers, is automatic, except in the case of bad conduct. It used to be the case that Parole was not certain in any case, in any one case, but the position appears now to have changed – at any rate with regard to some sentences. As I understand it – and I have made what effort I can to obtain authoritative guidance – a man who receives a sentence of two years' imprisonment is virtually certain to be released after eight months – that is to say, after one-third of his sentence, which is the earliest time at which he can be paroled, assuming he does not behave badly, and the Home Office will doubtless be able further to confirm to anyone who asks whether I am right or not.

I ask myself, 'Would eight months be long enough in your case?' I do not think it would. Even ignoring Parole altogether, a sentence of two years would not be long enough to protect the public from your likely re-offending. The time has come when you have to be put away for a long time, as the only means of doing what I have said must be my main object. If I am right about this and others receive such sentences, word will surely get about and so have a deterrent effect as well as containment. At the present time people like you see authority – by which I mean the Courts and the Home Office – as growing weaker as you grow stronger.

What are the requirements set out by Parliament as to Extended Sentences? 'The Court may pass such a sentence if satisfied that by reason of a Defendant's previous conduct and of the likelihood of his committing further offences that it is expedient to protect the public from him for a substantial time.' I am so satisfied.

The sentences, therefore, are as follows: On Count One, five years as an Extended Sentence, which is certified to be that; Count Two, concurrently twenty-one months, which I certify again to be an Extended Sentence and, of course, one cannot serve at the same time a normal sentence and an Extended Sentence. You will be disqualified on Count Two from holding or obtaining a driving licence for three years. On Count Three, there will be a concurrent sentence of five years as an Extended Sentence, so certified.

Finally, it is to be hoped that before long the Court of Appeal will give guidance as to the present policy on Extended Sentences. At the moment such sentences seem hardly ever to be passed. If it is policy that they are being phased out, we sitting in Courts of first instance ought to know so that we can act accordingly. In the special circumstances – and I have never done this before – I give leave to appeal against these sentences for two reasons: first, because leave would almost certainly be given by the single judge, understandably because of the area, which is of some controversy, that we are in and, in that event, there is no point in all the trouble and expense being gone to which resort to a single judge would entail. Secondly, and more importantly, this is a point which should be argued before my superiors so that we can all be guided authoritatively. Let the Accused go down.

## 2 Judgment of The Court of Appeal, 19 December 1985

Mr Justice Taylor: On 25 July 1985 at the Crown Court at – before his honour Judge Pickles these appellants pleaded guilty to an indictment containing three counts. Those three counts consisted of burglary, taking without the owner's consent and attempted burglary. The appellant C. was remanded so that the notice required if an extended sentence was to be considered could be served upon him. The matter came back before the same judge on 1 August 1985 when sentence was passed as follows. An extended sentence on the first count of five years' imprisonment; a sentence of twenty-one months' imprisonment and disqualification for three years on the second count; and a sentence of five years' imprisonment on the third count, the attempted burglary; all those sentences to be concurrent but to be served as an extended sentence.

Each of the two appellants appeals with leave of the single judge against those sentences.

The facts of the matter can be stated quite shortly. On 17 April 1985 these two appellants (who are in fact brothers, although bearing different names because one was adopted by an aunt) broke into a house at – . The occupier was out at work at the time. They effected entry by smashing a rear window and then taking possession of a key hanging inside so that they could open the patio door. They went through the house ransacking every room. They removed property to the value of over £6,500. Of that only some £1,270 worth was recovered. There was also the cost of damage done to the window.

When they had removed the property from the house they went to the garage where they found a Porsche motor car, which happened to have the keys on its front seat. They drove away in that car, which was later found abandoned in – , taking the opportunity of removing from it a cassette holder and some cassettes installed in the vehicle. That was on 17 April.

On 23 April the appellants were in – . They broke a window of a house clearly intending to go in and ransack it. They were, however, disturbed by someone in the neighbourhood and did not gain entry to the house. They did some damage to it. That was the extent of their achievement.

They were interviewed the same day by the police and they admitted the attempted burglary. At first they denied both of the first two matters charged in counts one and two of the indictment but finally they admitted those as well.

The appellant C. who received the extended sentence is now twenty-eight years old. He has a very bad record. There are five findings of guilt and eleven previous convictions mainly for dishonesty. However, it has to be said that although a number of burglaries are included in his previous convictions, on the evidence before the learned judge only in three instances were the burglaries shown to have been of dwelling houses. He had been sentenced variously by supervision order, by order that he be detained in a detention centre, by conditional discharge, by a period of borstal training, by community service and also by imprisonment. He had been released on parole in July 1984 and the evidence was that he had managed to keep himself out of trouble from then until April of the following year. He had also made efforts to lead an industrious life and had had a job until shortly before these offences. He was living with a woman and her ten-year-old son and had been working long hours in a snack bar that they ran together and he was serving in it at the time of the arrest. Those matters are material as will appear later in relation to the extended sentence which was passed on him.

The social enquiry report was a somewhat gloomy document in his case and it contained the phrase upon which I think it right to say the learned judge latched: 'It is difficult to see what will stop his offending.'

Dealing with his case the learned judge at an early stage of the proceedings raised the question of a possible extended sentence. Mr Levine, who has appeared on behalf of both appellants, makes two complaints against the learned judge's approach to the sentence upon C. First of all he says the learned judge wrongly took into account the effect of parole. Secondly, he says the judge wrongly refused or declined to take into account or give adequate weight to the attempt that C. had made to lead an industrious life.

It is necessary to look at the transcript of the proceedings before the learned judge in some little detail to find out what his approach was. He clearly took the view that the recent change in the Home Office's approach to parole was something which militated against the public interest. On page 10 at C Mr Levine pointed out to the judge that the appellant C. had been released on parole and had abided by its terms. The learned judge broke in and said: 'You see, that is interesting. He gets two years and he is inside for one year. That is the way things go. The Home Office let them out as soon as they dare, albeit sometimes – and we do not know what the precise grounds were – we do not know how long he had been in custody before, that is right.'

The learned judge at the end of the same page lamented what he foresaw as being the role of judges being reduced to court administration officers or something before long.

At page 28 of the transcript the learned judge raised the question of what would happen if he imposed what he called a 'tariff sentence' and he said to Mr Levine: 'If this man gets a tariff sentence for this he will be out within a very short time and there is no doubt at all in my mind that before long he would burgle again because there is a pattern of burglary . . . Well now, what would a tariff sentence be? You see, there is this dilemma for judges. The Court of Appeal, although they seem to waver, have said on many occasions, "You sentence a man for what he has done and not for what he has done in the past, but for what he has done now before the court on the indictment." ' After a few more lines he said: 'I realise that we are not supposed to take parole into account in that until recently one could never be sure whether a man would get it or not, but we know now because it has been authoritatively stated that a man who gets eighteen months can be sure of being out after six. Now, six months, is not going to protect the public, is it? That is my dilemma, Mr Levine, and I put it to you quite frankly. I do not want to trespass on the executive any more than I have to, but they will release this man on an eighteen-month sentence after six, and I am not prepared that he should only be kept out of harm's way for six months.'

A little later on he invited Mr Levine to indicate what he thought the appropriate tariff sentence would be and proceeded further to indicate that on such a sentence of two years the appellant would only serve eight months. When he finally got to passing sentence the learned judge said this: 'How can I protect people from you except by putting you away for a long time? Well now, how long should it be? Mr Levine concedes that the tariff sentence in your case would be about two years' imprisonment. One is bound to ask, if I am considering protecting the public, "For how long would such a sentence protect them?" Courts do not normally consider the effects of parole and remission because there is no certainty that the defendant will get it, certainly so far as parole is concerned.' That is at page 35. He then went on to say: 'As I understand it – and I have made what effort I can to obtain authoritative guidance – a man who receives a sentence of two years' imprisonment is virtually certain to be released after eight months . . . I ask myself, "Would eight months be long enough in your case?" I do not think it would. Even ignoring parole altogether, a sentence of two years would not be long enough to protect the public from your likely re-offending. The time has come when you have to be put away for a long time . . .' He then went on to pass the extended sentence of five years.

Mr Levine complains that it is trite law so far as sentencing is concerned that the learned judge who has to sentence must pass what sentence he thinks is appropriate without regard to the effect of parole. Whether the rationale of that is solely that parole or no is an incalculable factor, or whether it is more basically that the learned judge is simply required to pass what he thinks is the appropriate sentence and administrative consequences ought to be left to later, is perhaps irrelevant. The fact of the matter is that it is well established that to take account of parole when passing sentence is improper. (See *Gisbourne*, 1977 Crim. L.R. 490.) It is quite clear to us that the learned judge did take that prohibited factor into account. Indeed it was the *raison d'être* of his passing the extended sentence, and for that reason alone Mr Levine in our judgment rightly submits that this sentence cannot stand.

There is a second basis for attacking it. Mr Levine sought to draw to the learned judge's attention the decision of the Court of Appeal in the case of *Kenworthy* reported in (1969) 53 Cr. App. R. page 311. That indicated that the defendant's conduct, especially any recent efforts that he may have made to lead an honest and industrious life, are matters which the court ought to bear in mind when considering whether or not to pass an extended sentence.

The learned judge in fact brushed counsel's submissions based upon that case aside. The exchange is on page 30 of the transcript. Mr Levine had just indicated that the court must consider not only the nature of the present offences and the man's past record, but particularly the offender's recent efforts to lead an honest and industrious life. Judge Pickles then said: 'That used to be particularly so under the old sentence of preventive detention.' Counsel then said: 'No, your honour, I am referring to the Court of Appeal's decision and reasoning in *Kenworthy* in 1969.' The learned judge then went on to say: 'That is 1969, Mr Levine. Oh, there has been a whole world that has passed through these courts since then. I mean, sentencing ideas change over months and this is years.' Counsel then pointed out that it still figured in the current edition of *Archbold*, and the learned judge said: 'Maybe the latest one, but it does not follow that it is in line with current thought.'

Counsel then asked the learned judge whether he was saying that the efforts to lead an honest life are not to be taken into consideration, and the learned judge said this: 'I am not saying they are of no relevance at all, but all I am saying is that *Kenworthy* may not be the last word on the subject. I do not know what is the last word.' There the matter rested. In this case the evidence as I indicated is that this appellant, for all his bad record and for all the gravity of the offences before the court, had for some substantial period made serious efforts to work and to stay out of trouble. It appears that the learned judge did not give weight, or at any rate adequate weight, to these considerations. One cannot help coming to the conclusion on reading the transcript that the learned judge formed the view at a very early stage that he wished to impose an extended sentence and anything that stood in the way of his doing so was brushed aside.

The learned judge fully realised that what he was doing was out of line with normal sentencing practice because at the end of the case, having taken some four pages to sentence the appellant C., he indicated that it was to be hoped that before long the Court of Appeal would give guidance as to the present policy on extended sentences. Then, although he had not been asked to do so, he indicated that he would give leave to appeal against the sentences. He put it in this way: ' . . . for two reasons: first, because leave would almost certainly be given by the single judge, understandably because of the area, which is of some controversy, that we are in and, in that event, there is no point in all the trouble and expense being gone to which resort to a single judge would entail. Secondly, and more importantly, this is a point which should be argued again before my superiors so that we can all be guided authoritatively.'

This court has no intention on this occasion of laying down any general guidelines. All that is necessary is to say that as far as C. is concerned we are satisfied that on the two grounds advanced by Mr Levine, the learned judge's decision to pass an extended sentence was inappropriate, and in our judgment the right approach here was to pass sentences in respect of the particular offences committed. In our judgment those sentences ought to be as follows. In respect of the first count, a sentence of two years' imprisonment; so far as the second count is concerned, taking the Porsche car from the same establishment was part and parcel of the events and there ought to be a concurrent sentence in respect of that of nine months' imprisonment; so far as the third offence was concerned, that was a separate matter and we think it appropriate that there should be a sentence of twelve months' imprisonment in respect of that, which will be consecutive. Accordingly, we quash the extended sentence of five years and substitute for it the sentences that I have already indicated which in all amount to a sentence of three years' imprisonment.

# Appendix VII

## *My letter to the Lord Chief Justice, Lord Lane*

5 February 1986

Dear Lord Chief Justice

1   This is a difficult letter for me to write, but it has to be written. I have decided, after much thought, to withdraw the undertaking I gave you on 18/9/85. I shall write frankly. You may find yet another letter from me to be tedious, but I assure you that I have no present intention to write further letters to you.

Please accept that I write respectfully and with a genuinely high regard for you. You have treated me with courtesy and restraint. Though you and I differ in our approaches to certain matters, we both act in good faith. I hope that we can remain on friendly terms.

I do not claim I am always right about things I say or do. I have made mistakes over the years.

2   I have always been a radical, in politics and generally: anxious to get to the root of problems by analysis, and to improve matters by exposition to colleagues, superiors or indeed the public generally – in whose name we do all we do. I cannot explain why I am a radical; we are all made as we are made. My attitude has of course grated with many of my contemporaries in the law, including some judges. Most judges are conservative, in politics and generally.

3   I hope I have been consistent in my radicalism.

(a)   In about 1960 I proposed at a meeting of the NE Circuit Bar Mess, that we admit women barristers as members. No one had asked me to do that. The few women counsel had not, though some of them agreed with me. I felt that to exclude women was wrong and unjust; contrary to correct principles. Needless to say, my motion failed, though a few years later women were admitted to every circuit mess. Even the Bar, entrenched in its attitudes as it is, cannot hold back the tide of public opinion on all fronts all of the time. The same applies to the judiciary.

(b)   In about 1970* I circulated memoranda on the NE Circuit, agitating against the injustice done to some young barristers, who get pupillage but

---

*In fact it was July 1974, see appendix V (p. 199)

are then – especially in London – thrown out of the chambers; some never have an opportunity to have a go at the Bar. The door is firmly shut against them by their potential competitors. They have to drift off and do something else, despite all their studies, expenditure on robes and so on. This injustice still goes on. I sent written evidence on it to the Royal Commission on Legal Services in 1977. The conservatism, complacency and conformity in the legal profession resist changes in this and other areas.

Whilst I was head of the chambers in Bradford I introduced a system whereby all applicants for pupillage were interviewed. Some spent a day with us. Those we took were told that there would be a seat for them, unless there was some real objection, of which they would be told. When I left to become a judge in 1976, we had three women members – not just 'the statutory woman'.

(c) In 1978–9 I sent evidence to the Royal Commission on Criminal Procedure. It dealt with the Judges' Rules; the right of silence; police interviews with suspects and how they should be recorded; the 'prosecution machine' – stopping and starting it; the need for a national prosecution service; and plea-bargaining. How far what I wrote influenced the Commission is impossible to gauge. (No one had asked me to send evidence to either Commission; I felt I had things to say which I knew about and should write about.)

4   I have found that ideas and suggestions I make are often rejected out of hand at first – rightly, in some instances. But some are later accepted, wholly or in part. For example, on 3 November 1980 I spoke at the Sheffield Rotary Club and suggested the setting-up of what are now known as 'neighbourhood watch' schemes. The then Chief Constable for South Yorkshire – who was at the meeting – was asked by the press for his reaction. He was against it; he had Special Constables. I do not say I was the first person to suggest such schemes; I do not know. But I point to the initial reaction against what has come to be looked on as a useful way of combating crime.

Similarly I sent to NE circuit judges a document 'Delays in Crown Court Cases' dated 25/6/85 (you have read it). When this was discussed at a NE judges' meeting on 26/7/85, the reaction was tepid, negative. But I applied further pressure. I obtained from Inner London Crown Court details of their judges' 'Ginger Committee', which I was told about when I sat there in October 1985. Inner London have drastically reduced delays by applying constant pressure to police, solicitors, the Bar and their clerks, and defendants. By bringing this to the attention of my fellow-NE judges at a further meeting on 31/1/86, I caused a similar Ginger Committee to be set up at Leeds Crown Court. I believe it will be emulated in other NE Crown Courts. My agitation and arguments may have done some good.

5   There is no point in going at length into matters which are fully documented in your files, but you will recall that on 14/10/81 I made a speech to Inner Manchester magistrates about Mr William Whitelaw and Home Office pressure on the courts to shorten or avoid prison sentences, with threats against us if we did not comply. You wrote to me on 2/11/81 and 24/11/81. I wrote to you on 20/11/81, giving the history of my interest in penal policy, with special reference to Home Office attitudes to bail and parole.

Although my speech embarrassed you – regrettably – looking back, I doubt if it did any real harm and it may have done some good. There have been no further threats to introduce legislation to curb our powers; Home Office ministers are deferential about the status and independence of the judiciary. (Parole has insidiously undermined our powers, of course, and introduced unreality into sentencing. You dealt with this in your speech at the Mansion House dinner to the Judges on 9/7/85.)

6   Out of respect for you, I kept quiet in public after 1981, despite my increasing worry that judges were unable to protect the public adequately because of Home Office policies. Eventually, however, frustration led me to write my article 'A Place for Punishment' which the *Daily Telegraph* published on 22/3/85. Lord Hailsham and Oulton then wrote threatening letters to me; you have copies. I decided to stand up to those powerful men, and I wrote 'Justice Delayed is Justice Denied', published by the *Telegraph* on 7/8/85. In effect that was a shortened version of my 25/6/85 memorandum. I only wrote, in those articles, what I had often said before, publicly and in private. I cannot see what harm they did. Certainly many people told me I was correct in my views. Although Lord Hailsham and Oulton keep referring to the need to safeguard the independence of judges (necessary in itself, of course), my analysis of their attitudes leads me to believe that the real objection by them to my articles was different. Their attitudes are those which have made our society so secretive and held back our country in various fields. 'Don't let the side down. Keep in line. Don't let the public know more than is strictly necessary. Don't do anything that hasn't a precedent.'

On 23/1/86 there was an interesting programme on BBC Radio 4 about the Bar, written and presented by Hugo Young. In the programme and in an article in the *Guardian* on the same day, 'The Voices you can't hear under the Woolsack', Young referred to the efforts made by Lord Hailsham to prevent judges from appearing on the programme. One or two did appear, thereby no doubt abandoning any hope of promotion, honour or favour for ever. (I renounced any such ambition years ago. I want nothing from the Lord Chancellor – except justice.) What possible harm was done to anybody, except Lord Hailsham and his out-dated attitude, by those judges appearing in the programme?

The power and influence exercised for generations by lord chancellors and their top civil servants need looking at. Every barrister knows about their power and how they use it, yet few dare say anything, for obvious reasons. An increasing number of judges are 'champing at the bit', as I know because they have told me or I have heard about them.

7   At your request I went to see you at the Law Courts on 18/9/85. Lord Justice Watkins was present. You said that the controversy between Lord Hailsham and me might harm the judiciary by getting into the press. (Though I did not say so at our meeting, I am against the 'secretive society' which grips our country. I prefer truth to come out whenever possible. Real harm is done by the Lord Chancellor's suppression of opinions and by his blindly shoring up a legal system – including the judiciary – which has many faults, and fails to serve the public as it should.) I said I was sorry I had embarrassed you. I volunteered an undertaking not to write further newspaper articles until I retired. I was content to channel further points through you. You urged me to do so, by writing, telephoning or going to see you. *I took it that you would actively take up those matters I raised which needed action.*

8   Since our 18/9/85 meeting I have written to you on the following:

(a) *Delays.* I sent you the transcript in R. v F., together with my 25/6/85 memorandum and a document 'Delays in criminal and Civil Cases' (September 1984 revised 6/1/86). You kindly read the documents and replied on 22/1/86. Your conclusion: 'It is one thing to point out the difficulties and deficiencies, and it is quite another, as you will appreciate, to put them right.' You added that time limits under section 22 the Prosecution of Offences Act 1985 would not have assisted in F. I respectfully and profoundly disagree with your approach. There *are* things we can do about delays. I have referred to some of them above. Time limits *would* have prevented the appalling delay in F. A lead from you could transform the whole situation within months.
(b) *Bail.* I sent you a document 'Bail Application in the Crown Court' dated 30/11/84. It dealt with the large growth in bail applications to Circuit Judges since 24/5/83 when section 60 of the Criminal Justice Act 1982 came into force. I suggested remedies. You replied on 11/12/84: 'Everyone up and down the country is suffering from the increase in bail applications. Things may settle down in due course, but in the meantime I am afraid we must simply grin and bear it.' I found your reaction very disappointing and negative. Why *should* it settle down?

There is no logical reason why it should. Things will get worse if we do nothing.

In July '85 I sent 'Successive Bail Applications' to NE Presiding Judges, Taylor and Kennedy, JJ. with a request that you be asked to consider it. You did so at two meetings of Presiding Judges, the second being on 13/1/86. On 23/1/86 Taylor, J., wrote to me: 'Inquiries since I first raised the question show that in the London area the effect is to occupy on average half an hour a day of Crown Court judges' time. However, the Chief maintains that this simply has to be accepted. The only method of controlling and one hopes reducing, the volume is through costs. If an application is utterly hopeless and there is a Legal Aid certificate, costs should be refused to the solicitor. If it is privately paid, costs should be awarded against the applicant.' Respectfully, even when this decision is published – I do not know when that will be – it will be most inadequate. Solicitors need and are entitled to have guidelines indicating what are to be regarded as hopeless applications. Judges need guidelines in order to be consistent with each other and with applicants for bail. I made detailed suggestions in both memoranda – though I accept that the decision has to be yours, and it would be impertinent of me to assume that you are under any sort of obligation to act on my recommendations.

(c) *Drugs in prisons*. On 11/11/83 I wrote to you about this. In response to your request for more details I sent you 'Drugs and Related Matters' dated 18/11/83. When I wrote to you recently, asking if anything had come of it, you replied on 29/1/86: 'As you imagined, I forwarded your letter on Drugs in Prison and related matters. I have heard no more.' But I wanted to hear more. What did the Home Office have to say and do about it? Were my efforts ignored, or what? What effect have any measures had in dealing with a serious problem?

(d) *Sentencing and parole*. Recently I sent you the transcript of the judgment of the Court of Appeal (Criminal Division) in K. and C., and asked if you cared to comment on it. The case concerned a subject touched on in your Mansion House speech of 9/7/85. It is a subject about which many people, including me, feel strongly. I did not expect you to criticise the judgment in any way, of course. But I would have liked to have known your latest views and how far the Government has responded to their expression. You did write in your letter to me of 22/1/86 (on delays): 'Please do not hesitate to write to me if you feel strongly about anything. It may be that there is very little I can do to help, but you never know, an occasion may arise when something I do produces a result.' Your reply about K. and C. consisted of one line. (I do appreciate, of course, that you are extremely busy with other matters and people far more important than my matters and me.)

9   You are bound to resent what I have written, asking, 'Why is that Circuit Judge trying to tell me how to do my job, when he doesn't do his own all that well?' I have written at length however for two reasons:

(a) to explain why I have decided to withdraw my undertaking of 18/9/85 and myself deal with matters which arise;
(b) to explain why – to your relief – I shall not write any more letters to you. Please do not take it that my silence means I am happy with everything.

10   Believe that I shall be very careful what I say in public on the occasions when I feel it in the public interest to express myself. I shall be alert to do no real harm to the real interests of my colleagues or the system in which I am proud to play a humble role. Some will resent my speaking out. There is too much secrecy and suppression of opinions in our public life. We in the judiciary need, in my respectful opinion, to modernise our attitudes if we are to retain or gain the confidence of the public which is so essential.

11   I shall not send this letter to the Lord Chancellor or Oulton. I have had no contact with them since their threatening letters. You are however free to send the letter to them or to anyone else you consider an appropriate recipient.

     Believe me to be, Lord Chief Justice
Yours sincerely

*James Pickles*

# Index

**DAVID HOOPER**

PUBLIC SCANDAL, ODIUM AND CONTEMPT

LIBEL – Everyone knows what it stands for, but very few can actually define it. Here is a witty, informative and entertaining account of the libel laws plus an analysis of over forty recent famous libel cases. Colourful characters emerge, gladiatorial conflicts between barrister and witness abound.

Aneurin Bevan, Jack Profumo, Sir James Goldsmith, Shirley Temple and Liberace are just a few of the famous people neatly trapped in these provocative and enthralling pages. A timely account of one of the most infamous but ignored areas of jurisdiction.

'A penetrating examination and a witty account provides admirable bedside reading'
SUNDAY TELEGRAPH

'An informative and amusing introduction'
TIMES LITERARY SUPPLEMENT

'A superb parody'

PUNCH

POST A LITTLE HAPPINESS

# Post·A·Book

A Royal Mail service in association with the Book Marketing Council & The Booksellers Association.

Post-A-Book is a Post Office trademark

**DAVID HOOPER**

OFFICIAL SECRETS:
THE USE AND ABUSE OF THE ACT

When out of office politicians of all parties agree that the Official Secrets Act is a discredited mess and must be replaced.

When *in* office though, they tend to change their minds. Busily they use the Act to try to save themselves political or personal embarrassment. Almost all leaks reveal official incompetence, lying or covering-up. Almost none involve national security.

By now the public generally regards the Act as an unfair lottery where junior clerks are prosecuted while Cabinet Ministers get away unscathed. Juries are more and more reluctant to bring in Guilty verdicts, yet the use of the Act continues. With renewed discussions to reform the law this book could not be more timely.

David Hooper, a lawyer who acted for Wright and Heinemann in the *Spycatcher* affair, traces the use, the non-use and the abuse of the Act in cases that range from the outrageous to the farcical: Compton Mackenzie, Duncan Campbell and the ABC Treason Trial, Clive Ponting, Jonathan Aitken MP, Cecil Parkinson, Richard Crossman and many others.

**HODDER AND STOUGHTON PAPERBACKS**

**ANTHONY SUMMERS AND STEPHEN DORRIL**

HONEYTRAP

The Profumo Affair: the scandal of the century.

A Conservative Minister for War and a Russian spy share the same mistress. There are daily revelations of bondage parties and of girls' cavorting at stately homes, of drugs and clubs, titled men and call girls. Some names are named. More are hinted at. Overnight, Christine Keeler and Mandy Rice-Davies are famous; the public fascinated.

The Minister, John Profumo, resigns. But the Establishment closes ranks and Dr Stephen Ward, the society doctor and artist who had made the introductions, is hounded to suicide.

Only a fraction of the truth was told at the time. Now *Honeytrap* reveals that the real story was even more sensational, that the British scandal even threatened to bring down President Kennedy in the United States.

'Bulging with new material ... This is a book which our rulers must loathe'

*Tribune*

**HODDER AND STOUGHTON PAPERBACKS**

**CHAPMAN PINCHER**

## TOO SECRET TOO LONG

Shocks, scandals, defections have followed over the years as it has become clear that British Intelligence has been not just penetrated but riddled with Soviet agents and double agents.

Time and again the British public has been assured that the last spy, the last traitor, the last cover-up has been dealt with. Then, a matter of a few months later, there is another appalling revelation.

Now Chapman Pincher, with more than thirty dedicated years of investigation into the murky world of secret intelligence, is able to document the most astonishing accusation of all: that the former Director-General of MI5 was himself a Communist agent and was 'run' by a Moscow-trained woman agent living undetected in this country.

'Remarkable'

*Newsweek*

**HODDER AND STOUGHTON PAPERBACKS**

**CHAPMAN PINCHER**

## THE SPYCATCHER AFFAIR: A WEB OF DECEPTION

'At one stage the Detective Chief Superintendent said to me: "You hold the reins in this affair." He was right. I could have blown the whole thing sky high by going public on television, which I was repeatedly invited to do. I could, in fact, have made £20,000 at any time simply by lifting the telephone and telling a national newspaper the inside story of the clearance of *Their Trade is Treachery*.'

*Chapman Pincher*

Chapman Pincher and his books have been central to the court cases in Australia concerning *Spycatcher* and Peter Wright. It was with his meeting with Wright back in 1980 that the whole saga started. He was the first person to whom Wright leaked his secrets.

Since then MPs have called for his prosecution, he has been investigated by the police – and completely exonerated – his private correspondence has been seized and accusations hurled at him from the safety of the courts and parliament.

Now Chapman Pincher answers his critics – with the truth. And the truth, the real truth, is devastating. *Web of Deception* is an astonishing tale of deception, fake conspiracy and real conspiracy.

**HODDER AND STOUGHTON PAPERBACKS**

## MORE TITLES AVAILABLE FROM
## HODDER AND STOUGHTON PAPERBACKS

| 39648 2 | DAVID HOOPER<br>Public Scandal, Odium and<br>Contempt | £2.95 |
| 42650 0 | Official Secrets: The Use and<br>Abuse of the Act | £3.95 |
| | | |
| 43005 7 | CHAPMAN PINCHER<br>The Spycatcher Affair:<br>A Web of Deception | £2.95 |
| 05881 6 | Too Secret Too Long | £3.95 |
| 98847 8 | Their Trade is Treachery | £2.95 |
| | | |
| 42973 9 | ANTHONY SUMMERS AND<br>STEPHEN DORRIL<br>Honeytrap | £3.50 |

*All these books are available at your local bookshop or newsagent,
or can be ordered direct from the publisher. Just tick the titles you
want and fill in the form below.*

Prices and availability subject to change without notice.

HODDER AND STOUGHTON PAPERBACKS, P.O. Box 11, Falmouth,
Cornwall.

Please send cheque or postal order, and allow the following for
postage and packing:

U.K. – 55p for one book, plus 22p for the second book, and 14p for
each additional book ordered up to a £1.75 maximum.

B.F.P.O. and EIRE – 55p for the first book, plus 22p for the second
book, and 14p per copy for the next 7 books, 8p per book thereafter.

OTHER OVERSEAS CUSTOMERS – £1.00 for the first book, plus 25p
per copy for each additional book.

NAME .................................................................................................

ADDRESS .............................................................................................

.................................................................................................